K9 SUPERVISOR'S MANUAL

K9 Professional Training Series

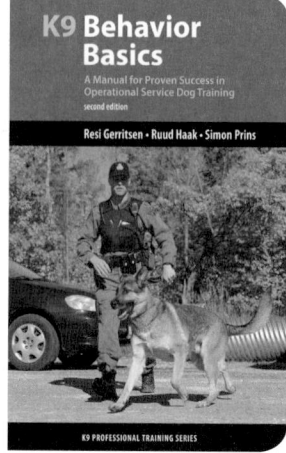

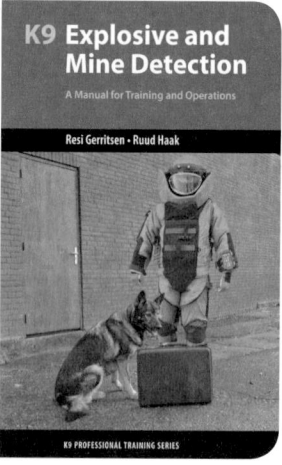

See the complete list at
dogtrainingpress.com

K9 SUPERVISOR'S MANUAL

Dynamics in Developing and Managing Police K9 Units

R.S. EDEN

K9 PROFESSIONAL TRAINING SERIES

An imprint of
Brush Education Inc.

Copyright © 2021 R.S. Eden

21 22 23 24 25 5 4 3 2 1

Printed and manufactured in Canada

Thank you for buying this book and for not copying, scanning, or distributing any part of it without permission. By respecting the spirit as well as the letter of copyright, you support authors and publishers, allowing them to continue to create and distribute the books you value.

Excerpts from this publication may be reproduced under license from Access Copyright, or with the express written permission of Brush Education Inc., or under license from a collective management organization in your territory. All rights are otherwise reserved, and no part of this publication may be reproduced, stored in a retrieval system, or transmitted in any form or by any means, electronic, mechanical, photocopying, digital copying, scanning, recording, or otherwise, except as specifically authorized.

Brush Education Inc.
www.brusheducation.ca
contact@brusheducation.ca

Cover design: John Luckhurst; Cover image: R.S. Eden
Interior design: Carol Dragich, Dragich Design
Editorial: Kay Rollans

Library and Archives Canada Cataloguing in Publication
Title: K9 supervisor's manual : dynamics in developing and managing police K9 units / R.S. Eden.
Names: Eden, R. S. (Robert S.), author.
Identifiers: Canadiana (print) 2021024951X | Canadiana (ebook) 20210249552 | ISBN 9781550598889 (softcover) | ISBN 9781550598896 (PDF) | ISBN 9781550598919 (EPUB)
Subjects: LCSH: Police dogs—Handbooks, manuals, etc. | LCSH: Police—Supervision of—Handbooks, manuals, etc. | LCSH: Police administration—Handbooks, manuals, etc. | LCGFT: Handbooks and manuals.
Classification: LCC HV8025 .E35 2021 | DDC 363.2/32—dc23

To Dr. Stephen Mackenzie, PhD

Stephen Mackenzie and Bob Eden at the North American Police Work Dog Association working dog seminar (Titusville, Florida, December 2019).

Doc, you were a close friend and mentor for me for almost 40 years. Your jovial ways mixed with K9 wisdom made the world of K9 policing, and the world in general, a better place. You were a man ahead of your time. Your exit from this life has been a tough one to digest. You had so much more to do, so much more to offer. Until we meet again on the other side…

Contents

    Foreword x
    Chief Ken Wallentine, West Jordan Police Department
    Acknowledgments xii
    Introduction xv

1 Police Dogs Are a Fundamental Asset 1
    The Lansing Study on the Efficiency of Police Dogs 4
    Police Dog Deployments as Alternatives to Deadly Force 8
    Tracking Dogs 13
    Detection Dogs 16
    Single-Purpose versus Dual-Purpose Dogs 20
    Community Relations 24
    A Swiss Army Knife on Four Legs 32

2 Ensuring K9 Unit Success 34
    Five Fundamental Factors for Success 34

3 Understanding Liability 49
    K9 Deployment and Training Standards in Case Law 50
    Reducing Deployment Liability 55
    Supervisor Approval for K9 Deployments 61
    Reducing After-Action Liability 64
    Reducing Supervisor Liability 66

4   Modern Development of Police Dogs in North America 74
    Standard Police Dog Operations Before 1970 75
    The Introduction of K9 Vendors 76
    The Good and Bad of Vendor-Based Training 86
    Selecting the Right Vendor 94
    Making a Case for Expanded Basic K9 Training 98

5   K9 Unit Culture and Training Trends 100
    Bite Culture, Litigation, and Conflict 101
    Trainer Philosophies and Agency Expectations 103
    The Influence and Impact of Social Media 106
    Addressing Public Perception 111
    Shiny Object Syndrome 115

6   Apprehension Methods: Bark or Bite? 122
    Guard-and-Bark versus Bite-and-Hold: The American Saga 123
    To Switch or Not to Switch? 126

7   Creating the Right Team 129
    Selecting the Right K9 Handler 129
    Selecting Potential Police Dogs 133
    Teaming Dog and Handler 141

8   Equipment 154
    Vehicle Design and Build 155
    Home Kennels 162
    Training Equipment 163

9   Fair Labor Standards and K9 Handler Compensation 165
    FLSA in Case Law 165
    Understanding Compensation 167

10 Certification Standards 169
    Certification Is No Substitute for Training Records 170
    Selecting K9 Certification Standards 171
    A Closer Look at Vendors and Certification 174
    Police Dog Competitions: Training to Excel 178

11	Records Management	180
	From Paper Trails to the Computer Age	180
	Records Management and the Courts	185
	Selecting a K9 RMS	193
	Best Practices in Records Management	204
	Common Requests for K9 Records	208
12	K9 Policy	212
	The Importance of K9-Specific Policy	212
	Handler, Dog, and Supervisor Policies	215
	Resources	225
	Image Credits	235
	About the Author	237

Foreword

The police K9 unit is often the black sheep of a police department. We know that we need K9, but we're just not sure where they fit in. Many, if not most, departments don't have the luxury of staffing K9 unit supervision with former (or current) handlers who understand the abilities and limitations of the service dogs, and who see management's perspective on balancing limited resources. The patrol supervisor may not have any handler experience or sense of the abilities of a K9 team. They may, therefore, have unrealistic expectations that set them up for frequent disappointments. Meanwhile, the lieutenant wonders why the K9 unit needs this piece of equipment or that training school, and the department number cruncher shakes their head at overtime for training hours and home care for the dogs.

If any of that sounds familiar, this book is for you! From selecting the right handler and the right dog, to selecting and dealing with dog vendors, to efficient and effective records management, novice and veteran K9 handlers and supervisors alike will benefit from Bob Eden's comprehensive discussion of issues critical to the success of the unit. I encourage those who want to be the best to carefully study this book. (It might just help in the promotion track!)

What's more, *K9 Supervisor's Manual* is a valuable tool in your department's risk management strategy. I recommend this book to any chief unfamiliar with K9 operations, midlevel supervisors, and government risk managers with responsibility for a K9 unit. Understanding why K9 units fail or don't meet their potential is the first step to avoiding common pitfalls.

When I first met Bob Eden over a quarter-century ago, I was just learning basic detection dog handler skills. Today, I've spent countless hours learning from and teaching alongside him. His dedication to continuous improvement shines through in this book. Keep it close at hand, refer to it often, and achieve continuous improvement in your own K9 operations.

Chief Ken Wallentine
West Jordan Police Department, Utah

Acknowledgments

As I look back over the years and my journey to where I am at today, I have a deep appreciation for all those who have worked with me, mentored me, and challenged me. I feel blessed to have spent a significant portion of my life in the service of others as a police officer, and to have that special connection with others who were there with me. There is often suffering in service, and while many do not see it, each one of us who has served has felt it at some point in their careers. Through it all, we are always there for each other. The bonds that are built with those who serve on that thin blue line are unbreakable, and I will always be grateful.

The responsibility of training and working police dogs added a unique and fulfilling dimension to that service for me. Locating dangerous suspects, finding missing persons, and taking contraband that was destined to poison our youth off the streets are challenges that have brought me significant satisfaction.

There are many who have influenced and mentored me as a K9 handler and instructor, and it is important for me to acknowledge their influence. I learned from each of you and will be forever grateful. Some are no longer with us, but for me they are still alive in my teaching.

Jack McDonald, my first hands-on instructor, and Tom Haworth of the RCMP were both instrumental in giving me my training foundation and helping me to develop as a handler in my early years.

ACKNOWLEDGMENTS

They say to always surround yourself with people better than you. I was able to do just that when I developed the International Police K9 Conference in 1991, carefully selecting the best instructors I could find. I learned from every member of my team, and the police K9 world in North America has reaped the rewards as a result. Bob Wright, Ken Wallentine, Mark Ficcadenti, Brian Hewlett, Ron Cloward, Jimmie Davenport, Steve White, Dave Stambaugh, Bruce Clark, Ed Jany, Doug Hartman, Mo Parry, Pam Carter, Sterling Johnson, Dr. John Anderson, Dr. Steve Mackenzie, Ken Green, Vince Bingaman, Marty Mahon, Mark Rispoli, Les Gray, Ken Greenleaf, Scott Fitzgerald, Brian Amm and Bruce Clark: in our 20 years of instruction together, we've helped well over 3500 K9 teams. It was you who made the conference what it became. Thank you!

Terry Fleck, you are no longer with us, but you moved this industry forward in ways that it desperately needed and were a significant part of my team. Thank you.

Dr. Stephen Mackenzie — Doc — we lost you this year and it hit hard. You have been a friend and mentor for me since 1981. I will miss your incredible insight and knowledge. Your teachings will continue to be passed on and your torch will continue to burn bright and influence the police K9 world for decades to come. Thank you for always being there when we needed you.

Thank you, also, to those who took the time to read the manuscript and provide feedback to me as I worked through it: Cameron Ford, Steve White, Mark Ficcadenti, Troy Land, Mike Kmiecik, Howard Young, Jimmie Davenport, Doug Roller, and Ken Wallentine.

Special thanks to Marie Wolfe for speaking with me regarding her experience with building search studies and to Bruce Praet who advised me and contributed wisdom and input on K9 legal aspects and policy.

I have always had a strong work ethic. I was raised by parents who always stood by me, taught me strong moral and ethical standards, and helped me to become who I am today. My mom, Elleen Eden, has passed, but her example of faith and enduring love has helped me to overcome many challenges over the years. I am blessed to still have my father, Frank Eden, in my life. His example and teachings helped to fashion the moral and ethical standards I try to live by, and I will always be grateful. I owe them so much that I will never be able to repay.

Finally, but most importantly, thank you to my lovely bride, Natasha, for her incredible, unwavering support. She has always encouraged me to continue teaching, writing, and sharing my experience and knowledge, including during the year it took to finish this manuscript. To her and to my son Jared: I am so grateful to have you in my life.

To my brothers and sisters in blue who are still out there holding the line: Stay strong. Never falter. Know that you are appreciated. Remember that the decisions you make today will affect those who follow tomorrow. Keep your standards high!

I owe much to all of you. Thank you.

Introduction

The primary objective of the police service dog is to search for suspects or evidence linked to a specific crime scene. Beyond this primary objective, police dogs provide additional support by searching for missing persons or detecting illicit drugs or explosives. A K9 team is also effective in covering patrol officers on calls where the dog's presence can have a psychological effect and where its physical abilities may prevent violent confrontation. The presence of a police dog at potentially violent situations has proven to be a powerful de-escalation technique.

Once established, your unit will be on the front line for every dangerous and in-progress call. K9 officers are involved in more gunfights per capita than any other member of law enforcement as a direct result of their unique skill set and assignment.

At the same time, your K9 teams are also important ambassadors for your agency, performing public and private demonstrations of their skills and allowing your officers to connect with the community.

It is up to you as a unit manager to ensure your officers have the best possible dogs, equipment, and training for them to do their job and to help mitigate the related risks.

When I first began my career in the early 1980s, I was a member of the Washington State Police K9 Association. To this day, they are one of the most forward-thinking K9 associations in the United States. My career was significantly impacted by what I learned during my membership with the association. During that time, I had the opportunity to attend a class on the ethical deployment of police dogs presented by Deputy Bruce Jackson of the Pierce County Sheriff's Department, Washington. A statement he gave during a segment of his lecture held profound meaning for me and became a message I have followed throughout my career, not only as a handler and trainer of police dogs but also as a police officer. Deputy Jackson's words hold as much truth today as they did back in the 1980s, and that truth will never expire. They are words of wisdom that I pass on to every officer I encounter who works in the field of police K9:

> Your mission is clear cut and well-defined. The set of philosophies you develop in order to achieve that mission will determine whether you make a beneficial contribution to the role police dogs play in modern law enforcement or whether you become a liability which undermines the good work of many men and women before you.

When it comes to the use of police service dogs in law enforcement, we need to ensure our training and performance is up to standard and maintain the highest possible level of professionalism for the community we serve. Our ethical standards need to be beyond reproach. As a supervisor of a police dog program, you will play an integral role in this process — one that makes the difference between success and failure.

A Note on Canadian and American Contexts

In my nearly four decades of working with police dogs in both the United States and Canada, I have witnessed how law enforcement has diversified its training and deployments in both countries. Police agencies in Canada and the United States have continued to develop training methodology that meets the cutting-edge needs of North American policing, implementing new technology and new ideas into both training and deployment techniques. There are, however, some important differences.

The major difference I have observed revolves around training. Canadian police agencies have maintained relatively stable and consistent training methods for the last 40 years. Canadian training programs today are still controlled and conducted by law enforcement. While there may be subtle differences from region to region, standards and expectations nationwide are relatively high and proactively managed by agency supervisors and trainers. In the United States, on the other hand, there has been a decline in the amount of training provided to law enforcement K9 teams in some areas, as well as a divergence away from training programs managed by current or former law enforcement. They have become increasingly dependent on programs operated by civilian operators with limited, unstandardized courses that cannot meet the professional expectations that were once standard in the United States.

Another difference revolves around case law. Case law in Canada has remained relatively stable, and the Canadian courts have consistently accepted evidence related to police dog operations. Unlike the United States, Canada does not see as much civil litigation. This is perhaps, and in part, why K9 policing in Canada has remained consistent. This consistency has, in turn, likely contributed to the continued support of K9 law enforcement seen in Canadian courts.

In the United States, however, the diverse training methods and the increasing influence of civilian operators on law enforcement training throughout the country has contributed to an increase in court challenges related to K9 policing. The subsequent maze of cases is a growing and ongoing challenge.

Because of the complexity of American case law around police service dogs, the court cases examined in this book are all drawn from the American context. This does not mean, however, that this information is irrelevant to Canadian policing. It should be noted that much of what we do in the industry is from shared knowledge and experiences. Issues observed in one country may lead to innovations and solutions in the other. Moreover, while case law in the United States has no force in Canadian courts, parallel challenges and decisions are often made in both countries.

Supervising a K9 unit will be different from any other position you may have had in the past. It is a learning curve. For American and Canadian K9 supervisors alike, this book will provide you with relevant and fundamental knowledge aimed at helping you accelerate the learning process so you can understand, oversee, and develop a police dog program that excels.

DISCLAIMER

While the contents of this book are based on substantial experience and expertise, working with dogs involves inherent risks, especially in dangerous settings and situations. Anyone using approaches described in this book does so entirely at their own risk and both the author and publisher disclaim any liability for any injuries or other damage that may be sustained.

1

Police Dogs Are a Fundamental Asset

The most valuable asset a dog provides to law enforcement is its incredible olfactory capabilities. Its primary purpose is to search for and locate evidence, contraband, dangerous devices, suspects, and lost persons. The canine species has a living forensic ability that can be harnessed by law enforcement in a way that cannot be matched by any other known scientific means. Fundamentally, a dog is a multifaceted search tool.

A well-managed police dog program will increase the success of patrol teams on the street in locating and apprehending suspects. It can also significantly reduce the time needed for detectives to investigate and clear a crime by locating and apprehending criminal actors during an in-progress crime or immediately after a crime has been committed. In fact, many investigations are left unsolved due to lack of evidence in cases where a well-trained police dog, had one been available, would have resolved the issue quickly and efficiently.

A well-trained K9 team can clear burglarized buildings and alarm calls on insecure buildings exponentially faster and with more accuracy than a team of multiple patrol officers searching the same space. Every minute saved by the efficient application of the dog on a case allows officers who would otherwise be engaged in clearing these cases to be proactively patrolling and available for other calls.

Figure 1.1. Tracking teams are one of the most effective tools law enforcement has available. They can locate and apprehend suspects shortly after a crime has been committed, saving valuable investigative time. In most cases, evidence located along a track is recovered and submitted for forensic analysis and the results submitted to the court as evidence. Ultimately, the deployment of a good tracking team in some situations can even mean the difference between life and death.

In lost persons cases, the rapid deployment of a tracking team can mean the difference between life and death. In my own department back in the early 1980s — before we had any police dogs — we had an incident where an officer attempted to stop a suspected impaired driver. After a short pursuit, the suspect dumped his car at the edge of an area that was known to be dangerous: a peat bog and thickly forested area covering many square miles, which included sink holes and a form of quicksand. The suspect ran into the bog area and disappeared. Pursuing officers entered the area a short distance but quickly gave up looking for the suspect, knowing that the area was high risk and that they had little hope of apprehending the suspect in the dense bush and the darkness of night.

The vehicle was towed and secured. Within days, the suspected driver was reported missing, and it was apparent that he had not been seen since the pursuit. A search was conducted in the bog and surrounding area where he was last seen. Well into the search, he was located caught in the mire of the bog, deceased. He was deep enough into the forest that he would not have been heard or seen by passersby in the days following his disappearance.

This is one of numerous examples I eventually included in my proposal to develop a K9 program for my agency. Had a police dog been available that night, it would have been an easy track to conduct and would have saved the life of this man.

Figure 1.2. A dog's ability to indicate where potentially armed suspects may be hiding while officers maintain cover also provides a tactical advantage that cannot be matched by any other means.

Near the end of my career, a similar situation took place in a forested area not far from where the previous incident had occurred over 20 years prior. Our dispatch center received a call from a distraught woman who explained that, after a heated discussion on the roadside, her husband, threatening suicide, had exited their car with lengths of rope and ran into a thickly forested area. We did not have a dog team on shift at the time. As the shift supervisor, I requested the assistance of an RCMP (Royal Canadian Mounted Police) K9 team from the adjacent jurisdiction to assist. Other attending patrol officers were advised not to attempt to search for the victim, but to secure the area and prevent others from entering until the dog team arrived.

Constable Rob Heppell of the Surrey detachment of the RCMP arrived on scene and subsequently deployed his dog from the point where the subject was last seen. The dog immediately picked up a track, proceeded into the dense forest area a few hundred yards, and located the distraught man, who had rigged a rope tied between two trees about 30 feet apart and approximately 20 feet in the air. He had made a noose with a second rope, which he had secured to the first and placed around his neck. Should he have decided to take his life, we would have been unable to reach him in time, as he would have been dangling between the two trees well out of our reach.

When we arrived, he was very distraught, standing precariously on a branch, and holding a picture of his family in his hand. A dialogue was started by one of the attending officers, Constable Kevin Jones, who learned that the victim was married and had young children. He had recently fallen on hard times, resulting in financial insecurity. He felt he had no way out. He was surprised that he had been located and clearly had no expectation of rescue. Constable Jones was able to connect with him and eventually, with the assistance of the fire department, who had walked in with ladders, the victim was brought safely to the ground, reunited with his family, and provided the professional help he needed. Ultimately, he was able to turn his life around. The fast response and skill set of the RCMP dog team were integral to the success of this operation.

These two events, though over 20 years apart, occurred in similar areas and under similar circumstances, but had two entirely different outcomes. The key to the success of the second case was the invaluable resource of a well-trained dog team.

The Lansing Study on the Efficiency of Police Dogs

In the mid-1990s, Officer Marie Wolfe of the Lansing Police Department, Michigan, produced a study on the effectiveness of police dogs. The purpose of the study was to determine the efficiency of the dogs' olfactory capabilities in performing search-related tasks.

In her study, Officer Wolfe asked different search teams to conduct search exercises. She used two types of teams: patrol officers searching without the assistance of a dog (two to four officers, depending on the size of the building being searched) and K9 teams of one officer and a dog. The officer-only teams consisted of members of the Lansing Police Department's uniform division with assistance from the crime suppression unit, crime scene investigators, and helicopter unit. The K9 teams included dogs from the Lansing Police Department, East Lansing Police Department, Michigan State University Police, and the Eaton County Sheriff's Department. In total, 15 K9 teams participated in the study.

Officer Wolfe's study[1] was driven by three major research questions:

1. How much time and how many personnel are required to conduct a building search for officer teams compared to K9 teams?
2. What is the accuracy of suspect location when a building search is conducted by officer teams versus K9 teams?
3. Are there any significant differences in officers' self-reported certainty levels following a building search by officer teams compared to K9 teams?

The research preparation was brilliant in its simplicity and yielded findings that provide insight into the true efficiency of police dog teams. Several search scenarios were set up in which decoys were hidden inside four different buildings. The buildings ranged from company offices (roughly 5445 square feet) to a large industrial complex (138,995 square feet), providing a variety of building search types and locations, each with its own unique challenges.

The locations of the decoys inside the buildings were unknown to the search teams. These K9 teams, each consisting of a single dog and handler, were then challenged to search and locate the hidden decoys. Tactics were not considered, allowing each team to focus entirely on locating the decoys. The purpose was to determine if the K9 teams, armed with the dogs' olfactory capabilities, provided more efficient and accurate results than the officer-only teams when deployed to search for suspects.

---

1   Information on Officer Wolfe's Lansing study was taken directly from the study report, which she shared with me in December 2020 as I was researching this book. Officer Wolfe originally conducted the study in the 1990s and wrote the paper for her own education. While it was not published, it was widely disseminated at the time it was written.

Figure 1.3. A dog is able to search buildings for suspects and clear them faster and with more accuracy than multiple officer search teams without a dog.

Results were significant, showing the K9 teams outperforming officer-only teams by a considerable margin. The larger the building being searched, the wider the efficiency and accuracy gap between the K9 teams and the officer-only teams. The study thus quantitatively demonstrated the time and cost benefits K9 teams can provide to the departments they serve.

STUDY RESULTS

ACCURACY

Over the course of the study, each team attempted to locate a total of 29 decoy suspects. Of those 29 hides, K9 teams successfully located 27 for an overall 93 percent success rate. Officer-only teams were only able to successfully locate 17 suspects for an overall success rate of 59 percent.

The dogs were 100 percent accurate in three of the four buildings, including the largest building in which the officer-only teams achieved only a 28 percent accuracy rate. As the square footage of the buildings increased, the accuracy of the officer-only teams decreased.

Table 1.1. Officer-Only versus K9 Team Performance Accuracy

LOCATION	SQUARE FOOTAGE	OFFICER-ONLY TEAM ACCURACY	K9 TEAM ACCURACY
Lansing Uniform	5,445	83%	100%
St. Mary's	11,000	100%	100%
BW & L Water Department	40,500	45%	82%
BW & L Stores	138,955	28%	100%

Source: Officer Marie Wolfe, personal communication, December 2020.

TIME

A second measurement of the study consisted of the average time (in minutes) it took for each unit to locate the suspects. A time limit of one hour was established for each building search. Officer-only team time was calculated by multiplying the time it took to complete the search by the number of officers actively searching the building (two to four depending on building size) to calculate the total required officer hours. Within these parameters, K9 teams outperformed the officer-only teams by a wide margin. The table below indicates average time over five searches performed by each team type in each of the four buildings.

Table 1.2. Officer-Only versus K9 Team Performance Time

LOCATION	SQUARE FOOTAGE	OFFICER-ONLY TEAMS	K9 TEAMS
Lansing Uniform	5445	20 mins. 52 secs.	1 min. 24 secs.
St. Mary's	11,000	18 mins. 9 secs.	4 mins. 20 secs.
BW & L Water Department	40,500	60 mins. 30 secs.	14 mins. 15 secs.
BW & L Stores	138,955	148 mins. 15 secs.	15 mins. 51 secs.

Source: Officer Marie Wolfe, personal communication, December 2020.

Wolfe also correctly noted that "additional consideration in cost factor analysis is the time expended by perimeter security that is necessary while the searches are being conducted. Perimeter security typically would involve the assistance of at least two additional officers. Perimeter security time will also multiply as search time increases."[2]

---

[2] Officer Marie Wolfe, personal communication, December 2020.

This study is as valid in today's policing environment as it was when it was completed. While many management teams look at these statistics and see the obvious benefits in time and cost savings, they often do not immediately recognize another value-added benefit: every minute saved puts a minute back into active street patrol.

Police Dog Deployments as Alternatives to Deadly Force

In North America, police dogs are deployed around the clock every day — literally thousands annually — to locate and apprehend suspects for crimes in progress or crimes that have just occurred. Their record of success is unquestionable. Moreover, these deployments save lives, protect property, and apprehend often dangerous suspects, preventing them from committing recurring crimes. In fact, statistics I gathered in the 1980s revealed that during their tenure as dog handlers, K9 officers were 16 times more likely to be involved in an armed confrontation with a suspect than patrol officers during their entire career. Since K9 teams are usually on scene shortly after a crime has been committed and because the primary purpose of the dog is to search for and locate suspects who have just fled a crime, the likelihood of an armed encounter is much greater.

At times when law enforcement comes under scrutiny, one of the arguments brought to the fore by those who wish to have the use of police dogs abolished is the rhetoric that the use of police dogs is equivalent to the use of deadly force. In fact, nothing could be further from the truth. As of the time of writing, there have been only three deaths attributed to the deployment of police dogs throughout the history of their use in Canada and the United States.

The first known incident occurred in 1984 in Nashville, Tennessee. Police responded to an in-progress burglary at a car dealership. Upon police arrival, the dog was deployed in the building to search and locate the suspect, Daniel Briggs. Briggs had attempted to push himself under a vehicle to avoid detection. From descriptions of the circumstances, he was unable to get his entire body under the vehicle, leaving his head and shoulders exposed.

When the dog found him, he contacted Briggs by biting him on the neck. Briggs subsequently bled to death. During a litigation in response to the incident, it was argued that the use of police dogs constituted the use of deadly force. The case, *Robinette v. Barnes*,[3] was heard by the Sixth Circuit Court. The court affirmed that the use of a professionally trained police dog to seize a felony suspect does not constitute deadly force.

The next incident occurred in 1990 in West Palm Beach, Florida. The West Palm Beach Police Department responded to a report of a burglary in progress. The victim, Laurene Macleod, was homeless and had entered an abandoned home to sleep. K9 officers deployed a dog into the building to search for the suspect or suspects. The dog instead located Macleod, biting her multiple times in the groin, abdomen, thigh, leg, and left breast, and causing significant injury and blood loss. She was transported by ambulance to the hospital, where she was treated but was never given a blood transfusion. Fifteen hours later, she stopped breathing and never revived.

The most recent known death involving a police dog occurred in 2018 in Montgomery, Alabama, where suspect Joseph Pettaway was apprehended by a police dog while committing a home burglary. Police deployed the dog into the home after receiving permission from the homeowner. Pettaway was bitten on the upper thigh. The bite severed his femoral artery and he bled to death from the injury.

While each of these incidents is a tragedy, given the hundreds of police dog deployments that occur in North America every day, the notion that the use of a police dog is akin to deadly force is without merit. In fact, most dog bites that result from the physical apprehension of a suspect, while painful, normally result in only superficial wounds, such as puncture wounds from the dog's canine teeth. When treated, these injuries quickly heal.

This is not to say that dog bite injuries cannot be substantial. Much depends on the training of the dog and on how much the suspect fights with the dog during the apprehension. As a supervisor, you must be vigilant about how your dogs are deployed.

---

3   *Robinette v. Barnes,* 854 F.2d 909 (6th Cir. 1988).

You must ensure your K9 teams receive proper training and meet certification standards. Your dogs should be controllable: handlers must be able to deploy them to make an apprehension, but also to successfully call them off on command without the handler having to go hands-on to remove the dog.

DOGS AS TOOLS FOR DE-ESCALATION

It should further be noted that police dog deployment is in many cases a way of avoiding officer and suspect injury altogether. Police dogs are commonly used to de-escalate situations and applied in circumstances that would otherwise result in the use of deadly force. The mere presence of a police dog has been shown to reduce the violent impulses of suspects intent on doing harm. Such situations allow officers to take suspects into custody under circumstances that would otherwise require escalated use of force options, up to and including deadly force.

Anti-K9 activists and politicians, as well as many media outlets, focus on injuries caused by police dogs rather than the thousands of times they are used to peacefully de-escalate potentially lethal situations. These successes go unnoticed because peaceful solutions tend not to make the news. However, the fact remains that situations involving police dogs much more frequently resolve with subjects surrendering peacefully than with a use of force. In fact, statistics gathered by Eden K9 Consulting & Training from over 1500 law enforcement agencies nationwide in the United States show that less than 7.5 percent of police dog deployments result in a suspect being bitten by the dog (Table 1.3).

Table 1.3. Bite Statistics

CATEGORY	WHITE	HISPANIC	BLACK	ALL OTHER RACES AND UNKNOWN	TOTAL (ALL RACES)
Arrests	7115	3009	3678	960	14,762
Bites	511	306	199	79	1,095
Bite ratio	7.18%	10.17%	5.41%	8.23%	7.42%

Note: Data in this table was collected by Eden K9 Consulting & Training between January 2018 and May 2021.

Well over 90 percent of situations where a police dog is deployed to search for and locate or confront a suspect who is potentially violent result in the suspect surrendering. Without a dog, a significant number of these situations would require officers to go hands-on, which carries a higher risk of use of force, officer and suspect injuries, and in some cases lethal force. The benefits of police dogs in these situations are significant: police dogs trained with the ability to intervene in potentially violent situations may save the lives of both officers and suspects.

Figure 1.4. Police dogs are an invaluable de-escalation tool for potentially violent situations and are regularly credited with making the difference between officers taking suspects into custody without incident and having to resort to a use of force. Suspects will often be willing to confront and challenge multiple officers yet will willingly submit to arrest when confronted with a trained dog. Even when the dog is deployed to apprehend an armed suspect, any injury that may occur tends to be less severe than in incidents that do not involve a dog.

KEEPING OFFICERS SAFE: THE SAN DIEGO EXPERIENCE

The San Diego Police Department K9 Unit was founded in 1984 as a direct response to increasing numbers of officer-involved shootings. During that time, officers were seeing an increasing trend in attacks on officers with both conventional weapons and unconventional weapons such as crow bars, baseball bats, hatchets, shovels, and so on. The increase in attacks on officers by suspects using unconventional weapons was a disturbing new trend. The department was also experiencing a high officer mortality rate, believed to be the highest in the United States at that time, with eight officers killed by gunfire over a seven-year time span from 1977 to 1984.

With the inception of the K9 unit, assaults on officers, officer-involved shootings, and officer mortality declined. It was immediately apparent that the deployment of police dogs in many situations was having a considerable positive impact. The city police chiefs recognized the significance of the correlation of the deployment of their dog teams and the drop in officer-involved shootings, assaults, and mortality. They invested more resources to further increase the number of dogs deployed, eventually bringing the number of dogs up to 50 teams. In the 23 years between 1985 and 2008 (when the number of dog teams in the San Diego department reached its peak), only three officers were killed by gunfire.

During the Obama years, there were significant cuts in federal discretionary spending for law enforcement in the United States. Shared funding programs for law enforcement were cut and the asset forfeiture program was suspended. These reductions, coupled with restrictions that the Obama administration placed on the Law Enforcement Support Office (LESO) 1033 Program, affected agencies across the United States. With this loss of revenue from federal programs, agencies had to make budget cuts.

For San Diego, this resulted in a severe reduction in the number of K9 units they could afford to deploy. The unit was cut by 30 dogs, downsizing it to 20 active teams. During this era of cutbacks between 2010 and 2016, assaults on officers increased and three more officers were killed by gunfire.

At the time of writing, the San Diego unit is rebuilding. It has been able to increase to 43 dog teams with a goal of getting back up to 50 dog teams and of operating as a handler control agency.[4]

The San Diego experience shows a direct correlation between the increased use of police dogs and the reduction in officer-involved shootings, assaults, and mortality: assaults on officers decreased with the introduction of dog teams but increased again when the availability of dogs was reduced. This is strong evidence

---

4 The term *handler control* refers to the bite-and-hold or find-and-bite dog training strategy. See Chapter 6 for more information.

in support of expanding the training and deployment of police dogs.

Tracking Dogs

The use of a police dog for the purpose of tracking suspects who have fled crime scenes or locating evidence related to crime scenes has been the primary focus of police dog deployments for over a century. Throughout Canada, and in US jurisdictions including Washington State, Florida, and northern Oregon, on-lead tracking remains the core focus of police dog deployments. Every dog is a multipurpose dog that is trained in all aspects of patrol, with many of them cross-trained for narcotics or explosives detection. The primary purpose of most dogs, however, is to track and locate suspects who have fled from crime scenes.

The tracking profile is one that requires significant time and effort to develop, but the time and effort are worth it as the benefits are significant. Depending on the environment and with the support of patrol teams skilled in proper containment techniques, a good K9 team can successfully apprehend suspects who have fled crime scenes in between 30 and 40 percent of their deployments. The success rate increases when you add air support and patrol containment teams. These success rates are significant, and the benefits are wide ranging.

Law enforcement agencies that provide in-house training for their teams to support police dog tracking skills in their deployment regimen are able to directly control the quality of their training. Most standard police dog training programs within law enforcement agencies are a minimum of 12 to 16 weeks in length. This is the time needed for officers and dogs to fully develop the skills that will allow a team to be successful on the street, including in the tracking profile. Indeed, decades of experience has proven that strong working dog teams for law enforcement take 12 to 14 weeks of daily training to produce. Every week of training that is cut in order to save time and funding results in significantly reduced skill sets.

In Canada, every police K9 handler must complete a 12- to 14-week, in-house training program. Tracking remains the primary form of K9 deployment in Canada and is highly successful. In the

United States, however, the country has seen a significant drop in the number of dogs capable of tracking. The reasons for this are multifaceted, but the influence of vendor-based training cannot be overlooked.

Vendors began taking on a training role in the United States in the 1970s. Most vendors provide limited training programs that operate under time constraints. These short-term handler schools neither allow the necessary time to create strong tracking dogs nor provide the time needed for a handler to adequately develop the necessary competencies to be efficient on the street. Few have the skills to provide a strong tracking profile that meets law enforcement needs. In order to successfully get a police dog on the street, vendors focus their energy on the bare-bones, basic K9 skill set, building search profiles and handler protection routines that are quick and easy to train but are lacking in many areas. If vendors introduce tracking, it is done on an extremely limited basis and will not provide the amount of education a team needs to be successful.

Along with the decline of tracking dog training has come a significant reduction in the number of talented trainers who can train the tracking skill set with all its nuances. This is a direct result of the marketing and implementation of shorter handler schools using "pre-trained" sport dogs as the foundation for potential police dogs rather than handlers training their own dogs from "green," untrained dogs under the supervision of an experienced law enforcement trainer with the appropriate skill set (see Chapter 4). This has also contributed to the unfortunate elimination of the tracking skill set in thousands of agencies.

There are some vendors, however, that do take the time required to provide quality training programs similar to those found in in-house law enforcement agency programs. In these cases, the law enforcement agency itself, as well as you as a supervisor, must be willing to pay the related fees and allow your handler the time required to complete the program.

In all cases, doing your due diligence and researching your vendors to ensure your teams will receive the best training is key.

THE VALUE OF THE TRACKING PROFILE
There are many ways an agency can benefit from a K9 tracking team. Consider the following scenario and the benefits of police

Figure 1.5. The primary function of dogs in law enforcement is to use their innate olfactory ability to detect odors. Properly trained dogs can track fleeing suspects, find lost persons, locate discarded evidence, and detect and pinpoint hidden contraband or explosives.

tracking dog deployments. A suspect commits an armed robbery and flees the crime scene. Police are dispatched and arrive on scene. The shift supervisor, en route to the scene, starts directing patrol units to points of containment, attempting to box the suspect into a specific area while primary units are attending the scene. The K9 unit arrives within 15 minutes and deploys the dog.[5] The dog begins the track, following the scent of the suspect, going over fences and up alleys to a point four blocks away, where the dog indicates a gun in bushes along the route the suspect has taken to flee. The weapon is recovered for evidence and the track continues, leading to a residence where officers make inquiries. This subsequently leads to a search of the residence under exigent circumstances, ultimately leading to the location and arrest of the suspect who is found hiding in the attic.

In this case, the suspect is located within 40 minutes of the crime being committed. Consider the immediate benefits:

---

5 Workable deployment times will vary depending on the conditions and environment; I have done successful tracks with over an hour time delay, successfully apprehending armed robbery suspects in a suburban environment.

1. By locating and apprehending the suspect immediately after the crime, literally hundreds of man hours are saved that would have been expended by major crime detectives to solve the case. This is significant from a cost-savings perspective as well as allowing the detectives to focus on other cases.
2. In this case, the weapon was located on the track. Even if the suspect had not been apprehended, the recovery of the weapon, beyond the obvious public safety benefit, allows for fingerprint analysis, DNA testing, and other forensic analyses. These processes would have opened the possibility of identifying the suspect if the track had not been successful to the point of physically locating the suspect.
3. Stolen property and stolen cash recovered from robberies are frequently recovered on tracks. Over the course of my career, I have recovered hundreds of thousands of dollars' worth of property based on items and evidence recovered on tracks that were ultimately returned to the owners.
4. The evidence provided by the K9 handler is powerful evidence in support of obtaining convictions in courts that allow tracking evidence.[6] Any evidence located on a track by a professionally trained police tracking dog and properly documented (see Chapter 11) can be entered as evidence in court and may play a significant role in obtaining convictions. The dog's ability to track can also be entered into evidence. A conviction is then possible with only slight corroborative evidence.

Detection Dogs

Because of their incredible olfactory capabilities, dogs are often referred to as "biosensors." To date, there is no known mechanical device that can detect contraband or dangerous substances as quickly and as accurately as a well-trained dog. There is no limit to their capabilities. They are used to enforce border laws by detecting illegally imported fruits and vegetables, they support wildlife officers in detecting poached wildlife, and they support law enforcement in locating narcotics and explosives. In the civilian

---

[6] It should be noted that federal courts and most, but not all, state courts, given a proper foundation, allow tracking evidence. In Canada, all courts accept tracking evidence.

world, they are trained by building inspectors to detect mold in buildings. They are trained to locate bed bug infestations and have also been trained to work on farms to indicate when cows come into estrus to enable them to be bred when there is the highest potential for success. Whatever the intended target, so long as it gives off an odor, a dog (paired with a handler capable of interpreting

Figure 1.6. No mechanical device available today has the sensitivity and versatility to detect contraband or explosives as effectively and accurately as the canine species.

its behavior and accounting for environmental conditions) can be conditioned to identify, pinpoint, and communicate its location.

Detection dogs are most commonly deployed in law enforcement for the purposes of drug detection and explosive detection. Narcotic and explosive compounds both can have extensive varieties of odors that a well-trained dog can be conditioned to detect. This makes the use of dogs invaluable in both fields.

Some jurisdictions have decriminalized cannabis; this decriminalization is an ongoing trend. Depending on your jurisdictional requirements, when you work with dogs in narcotic detection, consideration may need to be given to removing cannabis from your detection dog training profile, especially if you are in the process of developing a new unit or adding new dogs to your current unit. If you are currently running dogs that are trained to detect cannabis, ensure that you stay abreast of current case law issues for your jurisdiction. A decriminalization of cannabis or cannabis products in your jurisdiction may impact your ability to use your dog's indications as the basis of search warrants. In jurisdictions

Figure 1.7. A well-trained canine can be trained to identify any target that produces an odor. Conditioning a dog to detect specific odors takes time and repetition.

where cannabis possession remains a criminal offense, it will be difficult in the immediate future to decide whether to train your agency's dogs to detect cannabis products pending potential changes to the drug laws.

Some agencies have experimented with extinction training on dogs that have been trained for cannabis after their jurisdiction decriminalized its use. Extinction training involves retraining dogs to avoid indicating on a specific odor they have previously been conditioned to indicate. In theory it can be done with some degree of success. However, in well-conditioned dogs, extinction training can be a challenge and may not be 100 percent operationally guaranteed. An extinction-trained dog may demonstrate a resurgence of the original behavior, ultimately resulting in failure. To that end, the use of dogs that have been retrained using extinction training techniques is not recommended.

During times of political change, it is always prudent to look to the future. Make the best call you can in terms of flexibility from current to future operations.

CIVIL ASSET FORFEITURE

Operationally, well-trained narcotics dogs play a significant role in taking drugs off the street. More than this, agencies in the United States have historically been able to apply under civil forfeiture laws to use seized assets such as cash that were located and confiscated by narcotics teams to offset agency budget expenses related to detection dogs or even expand detection dog operations.[7]

These laws are currently in flux. Up until 2015, many agencies in the United States funded their K9 detection units with the assistance of RICO (Racketeer Influenced and Corrupt Organizations Act)[8] and civil asset forfeiture procedures. In 2015, the Obama administration severely restricted civil asset forfeiture policies, and various states reduced the powers of police to seize assets. Then, under the Trump administration in 2017, Attorney General Jeff Sessions reinstated police seizure powers that simultaneously raise funding for federal agencies and local law enforcement. On top of this, each state varies in how asset forfeiture laws

---

[7] While there are forfeiture laws in Canada, the funds collected go to the government's general funds and do not directly support detection dog operations or law enforcement.

[8] This act was created in 1970 to fight organized crime.

are applied. In some states, all forfeitures must go to a state fund. In others, seized assets can be used for the initial purchase of a dog, related equipment, and the basic training required to certify. Take the time to research current federal and state forfeiture laws to determine how they apply in your jurisdiction and whether your agency can benefit.

Single-Purpose versus Dual-Purpose Dogs

Single-purpose dogs are those that have been trained to perform all the necessary functions normally required for a specific purpose. Law enforcement dogs are generally separated into two categories: patrol dogs and detection dogs.

A single-purpose patrol dog is trained for tracking, building searches, area searches, evidence searches, and criminal apprehension. These dogs do not do any narcotics or explosives detection. (Keep in mind, however, that many agencies do not have any teams trained in the tracking profile.) A single-purpose detection dog is trained for the sole purpose of detecting various specific narcotics or explosives odors. These dogs are not trained in any skill set required by patrol dogs. A dual-purpose dog is one that has been trained to have all the abilities and functions of a patrol dog combined with the full skill set of either a narcotics detection dog or an explosives detection dog.

There are different schools of thought when it comes to the benefits and disadvantages of single-purpose dogs and dual-purpose dogs. When planning which method of deployment is best for your agency, it will be important to consider several factors.

THE SINGLE-PURPOSE DOG

Many trainers believe that a single-purpose dog will provide the best results. By focusing the talents of the dog and the handler on a specific task, more time can be spent on refining their performance on that task. The handler is able to focus on training that is specific to the assignment, and the dog only needs to be trained in one profile. With repetition, this creates a dog that excels at the specific task.

My experience as a handler and a trainer is that a single-purpose narcotics team that includes a single-purpose dog and a handler who is dedicated solely to finding drugs and taking contraband off the streets will frequently outperform cross-trained teams. The specific focus of the single-purpose teams on interdiction helps them gain expertise and hone their skill set to a point that is difficult to match. However, it is not always practical to operate single-purpose detection teams, nor is it strictly necessary to do so to be efficient.

Single-purpose patrol dogs, despite their single-purpose title, are trained in a variety of profiles to perform a variety of functions. Compared to single-purpose detection dogs, training a patrol dog will take more time and require a much more varied skill set on the part of a handler. Profiles such as tracking require training that involves daily tracking challenges. The difficulty of these challenges is incrementally increased over time, with lengthier distances and increasingly difficult environmental conditions. More difficult

Figure 1.8. A detection dog is rewarded with a wrapped towel to play with as a reward for properly indicating on the correct odor.

challenges require more repetition. Area, building, and evidence searches are less time consuming but are an additional training responsibility.

Criminal apprehension training also requires significant time and skill to ensure the dog is able to bite when appropriate, stay in a violent confrontation as needed, and return to the handler when verbally recalled. In particular, the dog must release a bite on verbal command when a suspect is compliant or under physical control. Unlike a handgun or Taser, a properly trained patrol dog is the only tool that, once sent, can be recalled prior to making contact with a suspect. Due to the nature of the incidents to which patrol dog teams respond, tactical training specific to K9 deployment is also required. Each of these profiles are built through unique, compartmentalized training routines and then put together for a complete patrol package.

THE DUAL-PURPOSE DOG

While single-purpose dogs have the benefit of being highly specialized, dual-purpose or cross-trained dogs have a major benefit, too: with them, you get the best of the detection and the patrol worlds. In Canada and in most police agencies in the United States, police dog teams are trained to be dual-purpose. Dual-purpose K9 teams will often perform equally well in both detection and patrol work, allowing you to get more for your budget dollar. Why take on the costs of two handlers and two dogs that perform two different functions when a single, cross-trained team can be more than capable of performing both tasks well?

One reason is the difficulty of maintaining high performance across all of the dog's profiles. The most frequent problem seen with cross-trained K9 teams is inconsistent performance in the detection profile. It is not uncommon to see an officer run their dog around a car during a search and see little or no proper search behavior from the dog. Even so, the handler may believe that some behavior seen in the dog indicated that the dog had detected the odor of, for example, narcotics, which may lead them to conduct an unproductive search of the vehicle. On other occasions, a cross-trained dog may "walk" the car, giving no indication of any narcotics on board, even when a subsequent search by other means may lead to a significant seizure of contraband narcotics.

Poor performance in detection deployments by cross-trained teams has nothing to do with the inability of the dog to do the job. The issues arise due to unbalanced training or the handler's own lack of interest in the detection profile. Handlers who work cross-trained dogs tend to focus more time and effort on the patrol aspects of the training. They may find profiles such as tracking and bite work more fun. Detection training thus often takes a back seat to the patrol profiles. This inevitably results in poor performance on the detection side.

That being said, I worked cross-trained dogs throughout my career and was able to maintain both the patrol and narcotics profiles to a high standard and was always very productive in both missions. I have also often seen cross-trained dogs perform narcotics detection just as well as, and at times even more efficiently than, some single-purpose drug dogs. It *is* possible, but it takes hard work, balanced training, and dedication.

Patrol profiles will always take more training time than detection profiles. To maintain strong performance in both areas, a handler should average two thirds training time on patrol profiles and one third on detection profiles. In the detection profiles, equal training time should be afforded to each odor the dog is trained to detect. While the ratios are not expected to be exact, they should show a relatively good balance of time spent working the dog on each odor.

As a supervisor, it is your responsibility to ensure that your K9 handlers are maintaining a balanced training regimen in all the profiles your K9 teams are required to perform. When a handler puts appropriate time and effort into both patrol and detection profiles, these teams will perform equally well in both patrol and detection deployments.[9]

---

[9] If you have an electronic records management system, you should be able to monitor the number of hours your teams are putting into their weekly training regimens and how balanced the training is. If you are using the KATS Platinum K9 records management system, for example, there is a report under the "training reports" menu titled *Training Hours by Activity*. This will provide you with details of exactly how much time each team is putting into each training routine. There is also a report titled *Detection Training Balance*, which shows how balanced the detection training is for each type of drug or explosive the dog is being trained on. (See Chapter 11 for more on records management.)

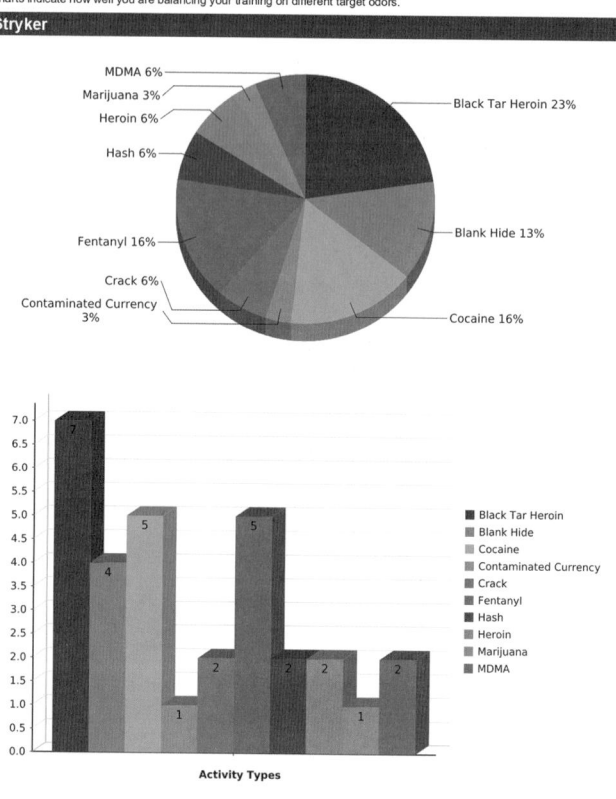

Figure 1.9a. Well-documented training records that back up K9 certifications are the primary focus of the courts when it comes to team credibility. A quality records management system reduces liability and increases credibility in court.

Community Relations

An important aspect of police dogs within an organization is the role they play in the relationship between law enforcement and the community they serve. When exploring the possibility of creating a new dog unit, the focus tends to be on how the dogs will benefit the community through drug interdiction, locating

Training Stats by Activity
KING-COUNTY-SHERIFF

Training Activity	Count	Hours
Handler: EDEN, Bob		
Area Search	9	6.06
Article Search	2	3.92
Bite Work	2	1.00
Classroom	1	3.83
Narcotics Search	8	2.44
Obedience	3	0.71
Track	5	1.34

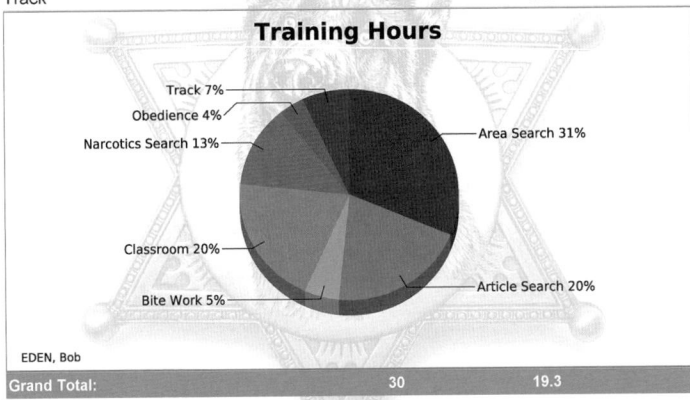

EDEN, Bob

Grand Total:	30	19.3

Figure 1.9b. *Continued from Figure 1.9a.*

and arresting dangerous suspects, finding lost persons, recovering property for victims, and protecting the officers to whom they are assigned. Overlooked is the powerful community relations ambassadors police dogs become once they are introduced to the community.

Building trust between your law enforcement agency and the community you serve is so important. An officer who is good at public speaking and willing and able to spend some one-on-one time sharing experiences with community groups or schools can begin to build this trust. Add a police dog into the mix and the interaction can be even more powerful.

I know how deeply a community can connect with a K9 because I have experienced it. As a handler, I was frequently asked to provide public demonstrations. I was also asked periodically for interviews by the local news. As my career continued, I realized that people on the street knew the name of my dog. They did not have a clue who *I* was, but they sure knew the name of my dog! One time, I even had an elementary school girl show me a small scrapbook that she kept with pictures and articles of our K9 unit that she had collected over the year, including copies of each K9 team's collectable trading card, which we gave out to kids when doing demonstrations. There is no doubt that community outreach K9 teams are an invaluable bridge between police and

Figure 1.10. Public demonstrations are an ideal venue to connect with the community and share your agency's core values.

the community they serve. If you want the community to connect with your department, the K9 unit is the right choice for the job.

RONNIE AND LANCER

Even the suspects we deal with have a certain amount of "connection" with police dogs. This became apparent to me in a situation that occurred following a vehicle pursuit we had in our jurisdiction. The suspect abandoned his vehicle at the edge of the highway and fled into a thickly forested area nearby. My fellow handler, Constable Walter Eng, deployed with his police dog, Sultan, to locate the suspect. The night was pitch black and vision was particularly difficult underneath the forest canopy. The team had tracked into the bush a few hundred yards when Sultan started to exhibit behavior to indicate that they were closing in on the suspect. Suddenly the suspect stood up from where he was hiding with his hands high in the air and called out, "Don't bite me Lancer, it's me Ronnie!"

Ronnie was a career criminal: one of our regular burglars, an auto thief and into whatever other crime you can think of. He was often drunk and was almost always up for a fight when we dealt with him. I had dealt with Ronnie many times, and my dog (Lancer) had recently apprehended him on two of those occasions. In the darkness, he thought it was me and my dog coming for him again. He knew my dog by name and called out to the approaching team as if he had a personal relationship with my dog, thinking it was Lancer coming in on him. Needless to say, he was taken into custody without incident. Long story short, even the "bad guys" pay attention to what goes on with the K9 unit. After a few contacts, some even respect past outcomes to the point where they are willing to surrender on the presence of the dog.

Any agency that runs a dog program knows only too well the number of calls they receive from various community organizations asking for a police dog demonstration. Scouting groups, service clubs, schools, church groups, and more frequently request the attendance of a police dog team for their events. Children of all ages, as well as most adults, will immediately connect with a dog when provided an opportunity to spend even a small amount of time with it. This is especially true of a dog they perceive to be their protector. People love to hear stories of the dog's experiences and see demonstrations of its skills. They are curious about

Figure 1.11. Well-designed trading cards are one of the most cost effective and popular ways to connect with children during public and school demonstrations. They introduce the team, provide a memorable souvenir, and are always well received.

the dog's training and the various situations in which it has been deployed. Demonstrations showing how the dog loves to play hide and seek (e.g., by finding narcotics a volunteer helps to hide for the demonstration) or how the dog apprehends a suspect are always crowd pleasers. The dog becomes a bridge between the community and the police.

POLICE DOG COMPETITIONS

Police dog competitions are another venue at which you can create a strong bond with the community. My own agency, the Delta Police Department in British Columbia, created an event that brought in K9 teams from the United States and Canada to compete in a three-day competition. While the first day's activities — involving tracking, narcotics, and area searching profiles — were not conducive to public view, we welcomed the public on the second and third days.

The second day of events involved basic obedience, agility, and criminal apprehension profiles. When not competing, officers and their K9 partners were available for pictures with citizens who were in attendance. The third day's event was a timed and incredibly fun obstacle course. The course involved driving a K9 car in reverse through a miniature slalom course and traversing a small pond in a canoe while decoys actively tried to entice the dog to jump out in attempts to tip the officer into the pond. Both the officer and the dog had to complete the obstacle course together. There was no end of sabotage from one K9 team to another, making the whole event highly entertaining for all.

One year, we bussed in a group of special needs children and their families on the third day. These were children 12 years old and younger who had challenges such as Down Syndrome, Autism, and various visual and auditory impairments. With the help of supportive news teams who had worked hard on our behalf to notify the local communities of the competition, parents had applied for special access to the K9 officers on their children's behalf. Each officer was assigned two little fans. The children were given event T-shirts. As the day progressed, the children cheered on their chosen K9 team and it was obvious everyone on all sides loved the events.

When the bus first arrived, our forensic unit attended and photographed each child with their chosen K9 officer and dog. During the awards ceremony at the end of the day, our special little supporters each received copies of their photographs to take home with them as mementos. Every K9 officer also gave the children their K9 trading card and other personal mementos, such as shoulder flashes.

Events like these create a connection between the community and the police and are also a lot of fun for the officers. They are a morale booster and allow the officers to take pride in what they are able to do with their K9 partners. Their families have an opportunity to see them perform, and the public sees the challenges and the skills these officers and dogs perform daily. When a handler goes back to their home agency with trophies and awards from a strong performance, the department can put their media relations team into action. News releases for local papers and news interviews about the events always bring positive press and allow the community to have a sense of pride in their dog teams. In short, these public-facing events can be an astounding success and a public relations coup for your agency.

CONSIDERATIONS FOR K9 DEMONSTRATIONS

There are some things to keep in mind when assigning a K9 team to attend a public demonstration. Every event is an opportunity to better the relationship between the police and the community they serve. It is a chance to develop trust with every age group if approached in the right manner. While the focus of the demonstration is the K9 team, questions will often be asked regarding other aspects of policing — everything from why police issue tickets to police hiring practices and what education is needed to join the department. For this reason, officers who attend need to be community minded, understand the core values of the department, and be open to sharing experiences on a personal level. Select a team with a very stable dog and a strong handler who is a talented public speaker.

The default performance at K9 demonstrations is sending the dog to apprehend a decoy suspect. People love to see the dog's performance and are often awed by it. When demonstrating the dog biting a decoy, however, it is imperative that the handler be able to recall the dog from the bite or even recall the dog just before the bite to emphasize the control the team has. These control demonstrations also never fail to impress the crowd.

I always recommend that public K9 demonstrations show more than just a dog's bite work. It is important to show that these dogs' roles in policing are much more diverse than just their bite. When I did presentations, I would always leave any subject apprehension demonstration to the last part of my routine, beginning instead with a presentation about the multifaceted roles police dogs play in serving the community, adjusted for the age group I was speaking to. I would perform some fun obedience routines, show how responsive my dog was to commands, and do two or three searches for narcotics in the room. For each of these demonstrations, I would use someone from the group to help me hide the training aids.

Finally, during any public demonstration, it is crucial that any interaction between the dog and the public is strictly controlled. A handler must always maintain positive control of the dog, and those in attendance must understand they can only approach and pet the dog if the handler agrees and gives them direction. Some dogs are simply not social enough to interact with the public directly. If your agency is one that does not have a social dog, this does not preclude you from doing demonstrations. However, appropriate measures need to be in place to ensure there is no chance

Figure 1.12. Children appreciate any opportunity to meet a K9 team. One-on-one time helps ease children's anxieties about police and provides them with a better awareness of the human side of police officers.

of an accident. Such measures may include restricting the audience from petting or approaching the dog.

UNINTENDED BENEFITS

The presence of a police dog can provide many unintended, but significant benefits. A dog can be a great ice breaker; it can, for example, help calm certain people down when they otherwise might be hesitant to speak to police. Dogs can even help you to connect with youth and people going through difficult times.

I experienced one of these situations when working in my K9 unit. The obstacle course and training field for our K9 unit was at the back of our headquarters, in a building shared with the courts. The judge's offices overlooked the area, and it was not unusual to see court staff or a judge in the windows between sessions, observing our training. One afternoon, while working my dog in the training area, I received a radio call saying that one of our judges wished to speak with me and had requested that I see her in her chambers.

On speaking with the judge, she advised that she had two young children attending court that day on a family court matter having to do with family separation and custody. They were having a difficult time, and she asked if I would be willing to introduce my dog to the children and spend some time with them in an effort to help reduce their anxiety. It was a pleasure to be able to do so, and to be able to provide a distraction for these young children. I introduced my dog to them and gave them some time to pet him and ask questions. If only for a moment, we were able to provide some respite from the emotional trauma they were experiencing. While this was not a typical "call" for a K9 team, it was an important job, and one that we were suited to. This was not the first and would not be the last occasion in which my K9 partner and I provided a distraction for children and even teenagers feeling distressed.

A Swiss Army Knife on Four Legs

The benefits of well-trained police dog teams are clear. They can search for and locate lost persons or suspects who are hiding after committing crimes. They can work in difficult terrain. They can recover evidence that can be submitted to court and support convictions. While many criticize the cost of running a K9 program, it is evident that the proper application of K9 teams can save thousands of hours of follow-up investigation time and free up officers for other duties. The quick and effective deployment of a dog after an in-progress crime often results in an immediate arrest in situations where the perpetrator may otherwise never have been found due to lack of evidence.

Indeed, police dogs may even have an effect on the number of crimes being committed. Though it can't be measured, a well-marked police dog unit patrolling high-crime districts no doubt has significant impact on community policing and has a high deterrent value.

A well-trained dog also levels the playing field when officers find themselves in highly dangerous or violent situations. Many officers owe their lives to the courage and effectiveness of their K9 partners. Along with these benefits are the dogs' added value as ambassadors for their departments and their ability to bring police and the community they serve closer together.

The cost effectiveness of good K9 teams is well established and cannot be understated. Dollar for dollar, a K9 unit provides law enforcement with one of the most cost effective, multifaceted crime fighting tools available. A police dog is truly a Swiss Army Knife on four legs.

2

Ensuring K9 Unit Success

There are many ways a K9 unit can fail. Issues in a unit may begin with a problem handler or dog. Ongoing training and performance issues may grow into unit-wide issues that eventually take the unit down. Ultimately, when an objective assessment is done on an agency that has consistent personnel issues, has lawsuits related to the deployment of their dogs, or has seen their K9 units disbanded, all roads lead back to one place: the management team.

When starting a new K9 unit, it is wise to research and understand what you are getting into before you dedicate time and resources to the project. Whether your unit consists of a single dog team or 20, it is imperative that you are proactive in determining any problems that threaten your unit's viability. Once problems have been identified, you must take appropriate action to address them to transform your K9 unit into an effective agency asset.

Five Fundamental Factors for Success

There are five areas of management responsibility that K9 supervisors need to consider when managing any K9 unit:
1. Administrative support
2. Budget
3. Handler selection
4. Dog selection
5. Initial and ongoing training program selection

Each of these areas builds on the others, collectively contributing to the K9 unit's success or failure. As a K9 unit supervisor, your key to success is to minimize downsides and potential risks by striving for excellence in all five of these fundamental areas of responsibility. If you deal with each of these five aspects and achieve high marks in all of them, you will reduce your liability and have the right formula for success.

1. ADMINISTRATIVE SUPPORT

K9 officers are as tenacious in searching for dangerous suspects as they are in searching for a lost hiker or Alzheimer's patient. They are often first in on high-risk deployments and will never fail to meet the call when needed. They are more prone to encountering and confronting armed suspects than any other member of your department. They train daily to ensure their skill set remains strong and, due to the nature of the position, are dedicated to caring for their four-legged partners 24/7. Your role as the supervisor of your police dog program is to bridge the gap between your K9 teams and the management team. While you need to be cognizant of the larger picture often faced by management, you must advocate for your officers, the work they do, and the support they deserve.

You will find no officers more dedicated to their jobs than those who choose to work police dogs. However, without strong administrative support, any K9 unit is destined to struggle and will likely fail in the long run.

Administrators play two key roles in K9 units. First, administrators address liability concerns for the unit. To ensure the success of a unit, it is important for managers to be liability aware, but *not* liability scared. That is, efforts to minimize liability in your K9 unit should not lead to operational restrictions that are so stringent that they interfere with the ability of your officers to perform their jobs effectively.

Second, when a K9 team is backed by both a supervisor who is sincerely invested in the unit's success and by the full support of its administration, it effectively buoys morale and sets the stage for high productivity. The results are evident and cannot be understated.

Unfortunately, there are a number of unintentional roadblocks to administrative support because of the necessary organizational structure of a department. For one, it is often difficult for K9 unit supervisors to find the time to connect with their K9 teams given, for example, shift schedules that do not align with the supervisor's working hours. As well, some supervisors are unable to devote their full attention to K9 unit management because the unit may not be their sole assignment. A single supervisor may oversee the K9 unit as well as other support sections of the department, such as the air unit, crime prevention unit, SWAT/ERT, or traffic enforcement teams.

Managing such a wide range of responsibilities requires the supervisor to learn about the distinct needs of each section being managed and how they operate. This alone can be a daunting task given the wide spectrum of responsibilities. Each of these assignments involves the management of personnel, equipment, budget, and related paperwork. These units, as complicated as their operations can be, deal with straightforward issues that are normally limited to those specific areas of responsibility. K9 operations, however, are distinct from other units, in part because they involve live animals. This fact opens a litany of issues unique to the K9 unit, which the supervisor needs to be aware of and prepared to deal with.

A DOG IS A DOG, NOT A PIECE OF EQUIPMENT
For instance, it is important in K9 units to consider how the dog differs from other officers and from standard law enforcement equipment. Some unit managers consider the dog as simply another tool for law enforcement, but this does not take into consideration the emotional attachment at play between the handler and dog. I have, for instance, seen management teams make unscrupulous decisions to use the dog as a form of punishment by removing it from the handler and their family for some issue that, under normal circumstances, would have been dealt with in an entirely different manner. In one case, a dog was removed from service and housed for six months at a kennel facility until the situation was finally arbitrated in the handler's favor.

Supervisors must take into consideration that decisions made concerning the dog will affect both the handler and anyone else connected to the dog — for instance, the handler's family, who will inevitably also become emotionally attached to the dog. In no way do I mean to suggest that a K9 handler's family should have a direct say in a K9 supervisor's decisions. However, the supervisor needs to be cognizant that decisions made about the dog affect more than just the handler and are often more complicated than a simple officer re-assignment.

Still, difficult decisions must often be made. If training issues arise, K9 supervisors must decide whether to keep a dog in service or to replace it. If a dog suddenly acquires a chronic illness, decisions must be made as to whether to treat the illness, replace the dog, or in some cases, euthanize it. These can all take a heavy emotional toll on the handler and their family. Such decisions require a strong administrator who can make wise and objective decisions in the department's best interest, while also keeping in mind the importance of being able to support the handler and their family.

VEHICLES, EQUIPMENT, AND MORALE ISSUES

Management teams who lack interest in supporting their K9 program are often far removed from the line officers on the streets. They either do not have the time or will not take the time to understand the experience of the K9 officer. Historically, this has been reflected in how some law enforcement management teams have approached K9 programs. The relationship between less-supportive management and K9 officers has sometimes been adversarial; K9 programs may be viewed as a necessary evil. This obvious lack of support is demoralizing and always has a significant negative effect on officers.

Lack of managerial support also tends to materially affect the K9 unit, which in turn further contributes to morale issues. For instance, patrol cars assigned to K9 units are often hand-me-down cars that have maxed out their allowable time in other assignments. These cars' inherent mechanical issues are inherited by the K9 unit. I experienced this myself as a young handler back in the 1980s. It was not uncommon for our cars to be offline for weeks with major repairs such as a transmission replacement. We would be assigned to patrol without a dog while we waited for the car to be fixed. In our department, it took over a decade to have a change of policy that mandated the issue of better vehicles to K9 teams.

ACCESS TO VEHICLES SURVEY

Writing this book, I began to wonder how K9 officers experience these issues today. In late 2020 and early 2021, I reached out and did a brief survey of K9 officers on the topic of administrative support and, in particular, access to quality vehicles. The question was:

> Do you have an administration that struggles in supporting you? As an example, are you assigned older, hand-me-down patrol cars as a K9 unit because management won't provide a new car as it will be used to carry the dog?

Many officers responded from agencies large and small across different parts of the United States. I expected to find the problems that I experienced in the 1980s to be partially addressed but not fully resolved, with some departments still operating under old-school management reasoning. I was surprised and discouraged, however, to see the extent to which many of the same problems have gone unaddressed. The officers' frustration and disappointment about how they have been and are being treated was apparent. The following are a selection of the responses I received:

> They want the program, but they only give the minimal. I paid out of pocket for KATS K9 records management this year. They did provide a police SUV Interceptor, but I had to pay to outfit it. I have to buy my own explosives kit, which puts me $2500 out of pocket each year.

> Last year [2019] I got a $4000 2006 Ford Crown Victoria to put my $9000 dog in. We are the bastard children of the job though, so I wouldn't expect anything else.

> I can't even log my mileage because my dash is digital, and the lights won't work.

2014 Tahoe. 160k on it. 2nd motor, 2nd transmission, 3rd radiator. Was a supervisor vehicle before me, shared by four supervisors.

Document every issue that's wrong with the car to cover you if anything happens.

I have requested for years that we get cruisers with rear climate control for the dog…falls on deaf ears.

First car was a 2012 Crown Vic with 125,000 miles. Ran it up to 140k and got upgraded to a 2009 Explorer with 133,000 miles. It does have way more room and 4wd [four-wheel drive] though. Our K9 vehicles were retired county/sheriff vehicles.

My current car was given to me four months ago with 105,000 miles…my last one, 128,000. To quote my city manager, "I'm not putting a stinking dog in a brand-new car." It's hard to stay motivated when you have to fight for even the most basic equipment.

Oldest car in a 250-vehicle fleet. Bitching does no good. If they don't care, they don't care. A 2013 with 125,000 miles.

We are the biggest city in our state. Most of our handlers are driving 2009 models with 170,000 or more miles.

This is just a small sample of concerns and common complaints about access to suitable cars that can be found throughout the profession. These officers' feelings of discouragement are palpable; it is clear they don't feel supported by their administration. In 2021, some of these officers were driving cars that are 12 years old with extensive mileage.

Figure 2.1. The cabin of a modern K9 team's vehicle bristles with the equipment needed for everyday law enforcement operations and K9 response. The efficiency and morale of your K9 teams is significantly impacted by the quality of the equipment available to them.

It is important to appreciate that K9 officers understand what is required in order to do the job. Even when working with less-than-supportive management, K9 officers do what they need to in order to make it work. This level of dedication and positive attitude was highlighted in one response to my survey:

> An officer in another agency close by and I both have many similar struggles. As handlers, we just have to keep our heads held high and keep doing our thing. Hopefully, in the end, the administration and politicians will see it and offer better funding.

Without this level of dedication, many K9 programs would not exist. But a unit cannot succeed on the dedication of the officers alone. K9 officers are asked to perform a high-risk job and are expected to meet particularly high standards and expectations of professionalism while receiving insufficient support and little appreciation from their management team. This is an unsustainable model for any workplace.

Thankfully, there are departments that strongly support their police dog program and provide the training and equipment they need. One respondent to my survey clearly explained the transition from old-school thinking under one sheriff's administration to the positive changes and growth of the unit under a more forward-thinking management team:

> We started out that way, 3 cars for 6 dogs. They were turned over to us after about 60,000 miles. We used wood for floorboards in the K9 compartment and a backing. Dogs were deployed out a rolled down window. We had several bad bites because of that. Our now-retired sheriff fixed that for us about 14 years ago. We now have the best cars in the fleet. We are assigned new units at 95,000 miles. We have 12 dogs and 17 cars; 5 are for when the unit needs repairs. We are well taken care of, equipment wise.

This department and others like it understand the value of strong, well-educated, and well-equipped K9 teams. They understand the positive public relations and crime fighting value that these teams provide. They ensure their K9 teams have the training they need to be highly productive on the street.

TENURE OF SUPERVISORS

K9 supervisors tend to have a short tenure. In my career, I have taught many K9 management programs, often returning to areas where I've taught in the past. It has not been uncommon for me to teach new K9 unit managers for the same agency every year. This high rate of turnover has a significant negative impact on many K9 units.

Dedicated supervisors who take interest in their teams and take the time to learn the unique characteristics of managing a K9 unit require up to two years' experience to fully and effectively understand and manage their K9 teams. Unfortunately, many agencies have managers that are in and out in less than two years — indeed, often after just one year of service. Just when they are reaching a point where they are in a good position to understand their teams and push the unit forward, they are replaced with a new supervisor who starts the learning process over again. To make the assignment even more difficult, many K9 supervisors serve multiple roles, allowing them only limited time to dedicate to the dog program. Senior handlers are often required to pick up the slack until the new supervisor is able to attend an appropriate K9 manager's program and gain the hands-on experience required to understand the unit's unique needs and operations. These short-term supervisor assignments also have an impact on K9 officer morale, leaving them feeling like the agency is not seriously committed to the unit.

Morale issues and lack of experienced K9 supervision are the most prominent, though certainly not only, issues to consider when it comes to administrative support. Moreover, *administrative support is the cornerstone that supports all the other elements required to maintain a successful unit.* Without administrative support, the four remaining factors of K9 unit success are almost unreachable. However, if you, as a K9 supervisor, effectively manage the remaining four factors, success with limited liability and highly productive teams will be the standard for your agency.

2. BUDGET

While cars seem to be the paramount management-related issue, it is far from the only one. For instance, K9 budgets are often extremely limited; officers are frequently left to pay out of pocket for necessary materials. Some officers struggle to pay for equipment such as the custom cage to house the dog in the car and the training kit required to train the dog. Some agencies even require officers to pay for the K9 records management software required to track training and deployments. What other section in any police department requires its officers to pay for the equipment and records management systems required to do their job?

This not only affects your officers' pocketbooks but wears on their morale.

Before the 1980s, police K9 units were budgeted entirely through the agency's annual budget. Just like patrol teams, SWAT/ERT teams, detectives, and virtually every other part of the law enforcement team, K9 units were factored into the law enforcement budget of the city, county, or state they worked for. K9 teams went through a minimum three-month training program before hitting the street, and the training budget was allotted accordingly.

Most large agencies today still include their K9 unit as part of their normal budgeting process. However, since agencies began using private commercial vendors for training, this is no longer the norm. While the rest of the police department is budgeted through formal budgets, many departments provide minimal and, in some cases, no financial support to their K9 units.

Figure 2.2. Good training takes many hours of dedicated work and a significant budget. Despite the unparalleled value of dogs in law enforcement responses and community engagement, K9 units have been historically underfunded.

Never in my career have I experienced any department that required its officers to raise funds to pay for operational patrol training and equipment, SWAT/ERT training and equipment, or any other aspect of law enforcement responsibility. Quite the opposite. SWAT/ERT teams, for example, are provided significant funding, extensive time for training, and the latest technology to enable them to do their jobs safely and effectively. In many cases, these teams are from agencies that may require SWAT response only two or three times a month, if that. Conversely, K9 teams are the tip of the spear responding to in-progress calls, often with armed suspects. They respond to these calls on a daily basis, and even multiple times per shift. Statistically, K9 officers are involved in more armed confrontations than any other officer by a considerable margin. They also provide support to SWAT/ERT teams, for instance in locating known armed and dangerous suspects. Despite this, K9 officers in many agencies have to scramble to find ways to finance their operations.

Some agencies begrudgingly move forward with creating a K9 unit but will require the officers who are submitting proposals to ask for public donations rather than supporting the addition of a dog team by properly budgeting for the quality of dog required to do the job. It is not uncommon for officers who want to implement a K9 team within an agency to be advised that they will be "supported" by the department, but that this support will not be monetary. They must be entirely self-funded. It is, in other words, left to the enthusiasm of dedicated officers and charity organizations to raise the funds necessary for the basic functioning of the unit. The quality of the dogs, the necessary equipment, and the training programs — as well as, ultimately, the safety of these K9 teams — depends on the success of fundraising campaigns and the goodwill of the community that contributes to them. It is not uncommon to find K9 officers out selling T-shirts or doing public demonstrations during their off-duty time to raise money for their unit to function. They must literally beg for funding to function so they can protect the citizens they serve while maintaining a professional standard, deploying daily or nightly, and taking more high-risk calls than any other member of the police department. This sets the tone for the unit before it even has a chance to launch. The frustration of K9 officers who are in this position is palpable and, sadly, quite common.

Inadequate budgeting has hurt both the quality of dogs that can be acquired and the amount of training dogs and handlers get before being deployed. This has created a void in training over the past few decades that has negatively impacted law enforcement K9 operations. It also greatly impacts the morale of many officers who dedicate significant time and effort to developing their units.

The most significant impact an administrator can have in support of a K9 unit is to provide the unit with a budget large enough to support a professional level of training and service that meets the expectations of the community and is representative of the core values of your department. This is not to suggest that a K9 unit should not fundraise, but rather that fundraising should not be relied upon to provide the basic needs of your unit. All primary funding for equipment, training, and dogs must be the responsibility of the law enforcement organization (ultimately financed by the city or county they serve) and should be given the same priority as every other unit in the department. Command staff that support their units and ensure they have the finances needed to function will reap the benefits in better staff morale, reduced liability, and highly productive teams. Administrative support and proper budgeting go hand in hand when developing and maintaining a successful unit. This is one of the most significant issues in today's K9 policing operations.

3. HANDLER SELECTION

Like any police investigation, dog handlers are required to make wise, split-second decisions based on fluid and often dangerous deployments. Every dog deployment is a potential liability, but it can also be the difference between success and failure during in-progress crimes. Significant risk is mitigated with sensible deployment decisions by a well-vetted K9 handler.

The right handler for the job is a person who exhibits the traits of self-initiative, good decision-making, patience, courage, and self-discipline. They should be an officer with a history of being a hunter on the streets. Physical stamina is a must. A strong selection process that evaluates these characteristics plays an integral role in the development of a K9 unit. (See Chapter 7 for more on handler selection.)

4. DOG SELECTION

Finding the right dog is one of most difficult aspects of developing a K9 unit. The Belgian Malinois, Dutch Shepherd, and German Shepherd breeds are the most common patrol dog breeds. Each breed has its own unique characteristics. Malinois and Dutch Shepherds have fewer medical issues and frequently can work more years than German Shepherds. However, they also tend to be more difficult to train and handle due to their natural born intensity. Experienced trainers will understand this and be able to assist in the proper selection of dogs that will suit your agency's needs.

Genuinely good dogs are hard to find. Ninety-five percent or more of the dogs offered for sale from European vendors to American vendors and police departments are dogs that do not meet the high standards of European breeding and training (see Chapter 4). Many dogs will have training problems the new trainer and handler will inherit. Strong testing by a qualified and experienced trainer is imperative to selecting the best candidate animal. It takes a skilled trainer to survey potential dogs to determine which dogs have the best characteristics for law enforcement. The scarcity of quality dogs means that they can be very expensive. As a K9 supervisor, you need to be prepared for this cost. After all, as the saying goes, you get what you pay for.

Poorly selected dogs will result in potential liability concerns or dogs that will not meet the performance standards needed to work the streets. If these poorly selected dogs manage to certify — that is, if they manage to be formally approved for law enforcement dog work — these issues will come to the street. Unfortunately, it is not uncommon for poorly selected dogs to certify, particularly with private commercial vendors who certify their own dogs (see Chapter 10).

Having poorly selected dogs in your K9 unit can result in liability, failure to perform, and handler frustration. Eventually, it will create problems that make the unit untenable. Always take the time to locate the dog that best meets the highest standard. If at all possible, do not let cost dictate the quality of the dog you purchase. Money spent up front on a quality animal that is social and has all the characteristics needed to do the assignment will save money in the long run. The financial and time losses that result from a failed selection can be significant. (See Chapter 7 for more on dog selection.)

5. TRAINING PROGRAMS (BASIC AND MAINTENANCE)

The type of training program you choose to develop your K9 teams will determine the strength of your unit's foundation. Even if the previous four criteria are perfectly met, your K9 teams cannot be successful without excellent training and maintenance programs.

It takes 12 to 16 weeks of dedicated, daily training to train a rookie K9 handler and a well-selected, untrained dog. Unfortunately, the days are gone when all agencies were able to provide high-quality, in-house training that was consistent across most of North American law enforcement agencies. In some areas of the United States, private vendors are now the norm in law enforcement dog training, making it a competitive, commercial business. Vendors can provide significant benefits in some areas if they have the necessary experience, especially for departments that don't have the resources to provide their own quality training. That being said, the private vendor landscape is a maze to navigate when looking for qualified training options and can be a minefield of potential liability and unit failure (see Chapter 4). Consistency in training, training philosophy, and certification standards is another issue (see Chapters 5 and 10).

It will be up to you to explore all options available to you and to vet each option thoroughly to help you make the right decision for your agency. This is one of the most important decisions you will make, and it can make the difference between success and failure for your unit.

The same holds true for weekly maintenance training programs. The current industry standard is a minimum of 16 hours of maintenance training each month for every team. You want to ensure that you are working with trainers that provide you the highest quality training regimens during your ongoing maintenance routines. Keep in mind that while 16 hours of monthly maintenance is the minimum, the more training you provide, the less liability and greater success on the streets you will have.

The quality and success of your unit depends on each of these five elements. Each is as important as the next. I have learned much from my experience traveling and training with thousands of handlers and conducting K9 unit audits over the years. Though I have seen K9 units survive despite shortcomings in one or more of these areas, that survival always comes at a cost. Not surprisingly, these costs are consistent from agency to agency, and include lack of productivity, conflicts within the unit, conflicts between management and the K9 officers, and increased liability and lawsuits related to inadequate training or supervisory support.

By critically applying the five factors of success, you can create an effective K9 unit with high productivity and operational success that will impact crime rates in a positive manner, provide better protection for your officers and the citizens they protect, and significantly increase the efficiency of your agency. When effectively managed, this can be achieved with limited liability and be cost effective.

3

Understanding Liability

Too many agencies and agency managers restrict units from operating efficiently and from deploying in situations where the use of the dog would be invaluable. The reason: perceived liability concerns.

Liability is always a concern when you are deploying police dogs to apprehend suspects. There are concerns over accidental bites, bites that occur on suspects that are subsequently litigated by attorneys, and litigation as the result of an inappropriate deployment decision by the handler. These concerns are often aggravated by well-intentioned city attorneys. In their desire to minimize risk, they provide advice that can be very restrictive. They often have the power to mandate when and how the dogs are deployed even though they have no background in law enforcement and an insufficient understanding of how the dogs are trained and managed. This can become frustrating for your K9 teams and, over time, can become self-defeating.

It is pointless to create a K9 unit that has the tools to provide better law enforcement service to your community and more effective results for your organization only to restrict the unit with policies that prevent them from using their specialized skill set effectively. What's more, it is possible to run a very proactive K9 unit with a broad deployment policy when you have taken the proper steps to minimize your risk. Proper dog and handler selection, good policy, strong support for your team members, a solid understanding of their concerns, and proper basic and ongoing training will significantly mitigate risks.

Two basic points frame the discussion in the chapter:
1. **Be liability wise, not liability scared.** Policy outlines for K9 units need to be practical. They need to keep in mind potential risks but not so much as to make your unit ineffective. Often, when policies that aim to reduce liability are too restrictive, they can make your agency *more* susceptible to liability. Keep agency policy in line with current case law regarding deployments along with current industry best practices, and you will benefit from having proper protections in place while allowing your teams to be effective on the streets. K9 liability is minimized by simply managing the risk related to the use of police dogs.
2. **Poor deployment decisions by K9 officers are the primary cause of lawsuits.** Lawsuits are most common in the application of dogs trained in criminal apprehension. It is critical for handlers to understand that the use of the dog is a valuable asset to law enforcement and that misuse of the dog or lack of critical thinking before using the dog in any use of force can result in significant repercussions. This is true not only for the handler and their agency, but for the entire industry. Every handler has a responsibility to be ethical and judicious with every deployment. All incidents that may result in a physical apprehension by the dog must be carefully assessed by the handler prior to any deployment. It is your job as a supervisor to monitor your teams and ensure that they deploy their dogs using sound judgment that upholds the core values of your department.

K9 Deployment and Training Standards in Case Law

Several US court decisions affect when and how police dogs are deployed in the United States, particularly in circumstances that may result in injury to a suspect. These include *Graham v. Connor*,[10] *Tennessee v. Garner*,[11] *Robinette v. Barnes*,[12] and *Kerr v. City of West*

---

10 *Graham v. Connor*, 490 U.S. 386 (1989).
11 *Tennessee v. Garner*, 471 U.S. 1 (1985).
12 *Robinette v. Barnes*, 854 F. 2d 909 (6th Cir. 1988).

Palm Beach.[13] Every K9 supervisor and police dog handler should already be familiar with these cases. We will discuss two of them below.

GRAHAM V. CONNOR

In *Graham v. Connor*, the US Supreme Court ruled that excessive force must be analyzed under the Fourth Amendment's objective reasonableness test. This test is meant to determine if the use of force is reasonable based on an analysis of the totality of the circumstances surrounding it, including:

- The severity of the crime at issue
- Whether the suspect poses an immediate threat to the safety of law enforcement officers or others
- Whether the suspect is actively resisting arrest or attempting to evade arrest by flight

To paraphrase *Graham v. Connor*, objective reasonableness applies to that moment in time during an incident when an officer decides to use physical force or deadly physical force. The "reasonableness" of a particular use of force must be judged from the perspective of a reasonable officer on the scene rather than with the 20/20 vision of hindsight. The calculus of reasonableness must include the understanding that police officers are often forced to make split-second judgments about the amount of force that is necessary in circumstances that are tense, uncertain, and rapidly evolving.

KERR V. CITY OF WEST PALM BEACH

CASE OVERVIEW

During the events that led to *Kerr v. City of West Palm Beach*, the City of West Palm Beach had two police dog teams that had been sent to a 12-week, 480-hour police dog program. However, upon returning from training, the handlers were left on their own with no direct supervision and no policy in place for a regular training regimen. The incidents that subsequently resulted in bringing this case before the courts clearly show how lack of supervision set up the K9 teams for failure and contributed to an abusive culture that was not conducive to the professional deployment of police

---

13   *Kerr v. City of West Pam Beach*, 875 F. 2d 1546 (11th Cir. 1989).

dogs. Unit and agency accountability played a significant part in the jury's decisions.

The case presented three different individual instances in which police dog deployments resulted in significant injuries to the individuals apprehended. In one instance, the subject apprehended was a person (Josh Terrell) who was intoxicated and had fallen asleep in the bushes at the side of a house. Police were in the area searching for a burglary suspect. During the search, the dog located Terrell. The dog handler (Officer Pontieri) intentionally sent the dog to bite Terrell. The dog bit Terrell on the arm and pulled him out of the bushes. After the dog was removed, Terrell began to walk toward the K9 handler, who subsequently struck Terrell on the head with a flashlight, knocking him to the ground. The K9 handler then handcuffed Terrell. The dog attacked Terrell again after he had been restrained and bit him on the thigh. Terrell was not, in fact, the suspect the police were searching for.

The second case involved a subject (Jimmy Jerome Arnold) who had stolen fishing rods from a parked vehicle. Upon hearing what he thought were police vehicles in the area, Arnold climbed up a nearby tree to hide. The same K9 team that was involved in the Terrell incident was brought in to search for Arnold. They eventually located him in the tree. Officer Pontieri commanded Arnold to come out of the tree. When Arnold did not comply, Pontieri grabbed his leg and pulled him out of the tree. Arnold fell and was forced onto his stomach by Pontieri, who then stepped away, leaving Arnold lying spread-eagle on the ground. At this point, the dog bit Arnold, seizing him by the arm. Arnold screamed and asked Pontieri to call the dog off. Pontieri commanded the dog to release the bite, but the dog failed to comply. The dog released the bite only when Pontieri hit it over the head with a flashlight.

In the third case, Uwaine Kerr was walking through a park observed by K9 Officer Chestnut. Officer Chestnut exited his car and ordered Kerr to speak with him. Kerr panicked and began running. He exited the park and, believing that he had eluded the officer, stopped to urinate against a building. While doing so, Kerr heard someone behind him say "Sic him." He was subsequently attacked by Chestnut's police dog, who took him to the ground. Kerr suffered wounds on the upper thighs of both legs and was taken to the hospital for treatment. No charges were laid.

During the trial, the jury was presented with direct evidence that the city was aware of the problems within the K9 unit. Chief William Barnes testified at the trial. Chief Barnes had become the acting chief of the West Palm Beach Police Department in October 1984, shortly after one of these incidents, replacing Chief John Jamason, under whose leadership these cases occurred. Chief Barnes testified as follows:

Q: When you [became] acting chief in 1984, did you make any changes regarding the West Palm Beach Police K9 unit?
A: Some.
Q: Why did you make those changes?
A: One of the reasons, one of the things that I was told to do when I came back was to look into the K9 situation. The city manager felt there was problems and he wanted me to look into it and do something about it.
Q: Did you become aware of problems with the K9 unit from any other source other than the city manager's office?
A: Well, it was just general conversation around that maybe we were having too many bites and it should be looked into to see what I thought about it.[14]

The jury found against the City of West Palm Beach and Chief Jamason, citing that the K9 unit had been inadequately trained and supervised and had "encouraged an atmosphere of lawlessness"[15] that ultimately resulted in the plaintiff's injuries. The jury was presented with specific yes-or-no questions to answer regarding their findings. Table 3.1 presents only those findings relevant to police dog supervision.

The circumstances leading up to *Kerr v. City of West Palm Beach* clearly show failures on multiple levels:
- Inappropriate deployment decisions by the K9 officers to the point of abuse that were not dealt with by agency supervisors
- Lack of supervision that allowed a "bite culture" to evolve and flourish within the unit
- Failure to properly train dogs and the inability of officers to control their dogs

---

14 *Kerr*, 875 F. 2d at 1557.
15 *Kerr*, 875 F. 2d at 1558.

Table 3.1. *Kerr v. City of West Palm Beach* Jury Findings Relevant to Police Dog Supervision

QUESTION TO JURY	JURY ANSWER
Was there a failure on the part of Defendant Chief Jamason to have the police dogs or their handlers adequately trained or supervised?	Yes
Was there a failure on the part of the Defendant City of West Palm Beach to have the police dogs or their handlers adequately trained or supervised?	Yes
Was there a failure on the part of Defendant Chief Jamason which encouraged an atmosphere of lawlessness on the part of the Defendant Officers?	Yes
Was there a failure on the part of the Defendant City of West Palm Beach which encouraged an atmosphere of lawlessness on the part of the Defendant Officers?	Yes

Source: *Kerr*, 875 F. 2d at 1558.

- Lack of adequate documentation or any system to monitor bite ratios on deployments or measure training performance that would have identified subpar performance prior to deployment
- Failure to instate a K9-specific policy that specifies the conditions of when and how dogs should be deployed

RESULTING CASE LAW

Kerr v. City of West Palm Beach resulted in case law that spoke to the deployment of police dogs and what standards a police dog program is expected to meet. It should be studied in detail by every K9 officer and supervisor.

Lack of a regular training regimen and failure of the officers to maintain control of their dogs became an issue during the case. The severity of injuries resulting from the application of the dogs also came into focus. Specifically, it was emphasized that the severity of injuries to a suspect can be reduced if the handler has complete control over the actions of his dog. A handler must be able, when necessary, to recall or restrain the dog before a bite occurs. Alternatively, if the dog has made contact, a handler must be able to quickly remove the dog from the suspect, minimizing injuries to the suspect. Since a police dog apprehending a fleeing suspect is often far in front of its handler, the ability to use oral commands to remove the dog from a bite at a distance is paramount. *Kerr v. City of West Palm Beach* clearly showed that the K9 teams at the center of the case failed to meet these requirements. Indeed, the case is a classic example of failure to train.

The department K9 policy afforded significant latitude regarding the offenses for which the K9 handlers could deploy their dogs in order to apprehend a suspect. In fact, the trial revealed the agency had no written policy. They only had what was referred to as an "oral policy"[16] that allowed officers to deploy on concealed persons suspected of a serious misdemeanor. This oral policy did not define what constituted a serious misdemeanor. In fact, testimony revealed that the dogs were apprehending subjects for petty theft, prowling, drunkenness, prostitution, traffic offenses, and even for such minor offenses as being in a city park after hours. The latitude of this oral policy encouraged an "atmosphere of lawlessness"[17] among the defendant officers.

This case also spoke to the necessity of a proper, detailed records management system to monitor K9 training performance and bite ratios. The case noted that police dogs require continual training to ensure they will perform appropriately and remain responsive to their handlers. A strict monitoring system is necessary to ensure the dogs receive prompt corrective training when they need it. For instance, high bite ratios have been found to be an indicator of a problem dog. Bite ratios were significant in the dogs related to the case. At the time, however, the department had no internal procedures for monitoring the performance of the K9 unit for either deployments or training.

Reducing Deployment Liability

Poor deployment decisions are often the result of attitudes driven by a culture that tends to evolve in some training groups. Most handlers, by their nature, are strong alpha personalities. Often, the focus of the training becomes skewed towards aggressive tactics. An aggressive culture within your unit will lead to abuse or simply

---

16 *Kerr,* 875 F. 2d at 1550.
17 *Kerr,* 875 F. 2d at 1548.

Figure 3.1. Dogs are often deployed as the default method to deal with a potentially violent suspect. Properly equipped officers can provide a multitiered approach. One officer acts as team leader to communicate with the suspect, while providing lethal overwatch and directing officers as to which option to deploy if needed. This prevents confusion for both the officers and suspect. K9 teams can be used as an alternative to multiple officers going hands-on or implementing other solutions such as OC spray, a bean bag gun, tasers, and other intermediate uses of force.

inappropriate decision-making by handlers. It is important that you are aware of the training strategies, attitudes, and mindsets within your unit, and that you ensure your K9 unit's culture does not evolve to glorify the use of the dogs to bite suspects — what we called above a "bite culture" (see also Chapter 5). This is and has always been an issue that needs to be managed.

Aggressive attitudes and mindsets can often be exacerbated by programs designed around more aggressive training that tends to focus on the bite. Some vendors in the private commercial industry have proliferated this bite culture. It is also prevalent with some agency trainers. The fact is, it is much easier to market a training seminar to a handler based on biting and fighting with a decoy in scenarios that may involve challenging tactics than it is to sell a program that focuses on dog control and critical thinking. While these are all invaluable handler skills, keeping the emphasis on the latter is imperative for keeping the bite culture in check. Handlers tend to lose sight of the fact that the primary purpose of the police dog is to use its olfactory capabilities to search for and locate suspects and contraband. The use of the dog as a method of

Figure 3.2. Being able to direct and control your dog while dealing with a potential threat is paramount in any training regimen. Here teams are working on the first steps of a controlled movement exercise, learning how to manage their dog without taking their eyes off the threat. Control is key in every aspect of police dog deployment. The more control handlers have on their dogs, the more tactically sound they will be.

distracting and apprehending suspects to facilitate an arrest is a vital but secondary mission. When selecting courses, place emphasis on those that include training in critical thinking and dog control.

Of course, there are times when a dog must be used to apprehend a suspect. Indeed, this has always been a necessary skill for any dog working the streets. The dog's abilities to establish a strong bite, to incapacitate and distract a suspect, and to stay in a fight with a violent subject, when needed, are significant equalizers and can be life savers. As already noted, K9 officers have significantly higher contact with violent offenders than most patrol officers. This being the case, there is a significant need both for your dogs to be able to meet the challenges of criminal apprehension and for your K9 handlers to attend tactical training programs that challenge their decision-making regarding deployments in high-stress situations.

THE VERBAL RECALL AND THE TACTICAL OUT

The handler must be able to reliably control their dog, including verbally recalling the dog off a bite from a distance. Some trainers feel this skill is unnecessary, and many handlers resist it. This ambivalence is often because the dogs they train are incapable of being recalled from a bite. In real deployment situations in which a dog must apprehend a subject, however, the inability to verbally recall the dog results in the handler having to go hands-on to remove the dog from a subject. This is impractical in many situations (for instance, when the dog is far ahead of the handler) and dangerous in many circumstances. Any quality trainer knows that dogs normally react to hands-on treatment by biting harder, exacerbating the injury to the suspect. Moreover, any time a handler is forced to go hands-on to remove the dog from the suspect due to a lack of ability to control the dog, it is the dog and not the officer who is dictating the tactics of the situation. This creates an unsafe situation for all involved.

Do not be deceived by handlers or trainers who believe it is unnecessary to have a verbal recall from a bite. They may not understand the tactical advantage of this skill, be incapable of managing or correcting the dog's behavior, lack the training skills to develop a well-controlled police service dog, or have an unwise philosophy on police K9 deployments. Virtually every K9 certification standard in Canada and the United States requires the verbal recall and has done so for decades. Handlers and trainers who espouse the opposite are pushing against every certification standard known.

USING THE TACTICAL OUT

While the verbal recall is imperative, there are situations in which a properly trained, hands-on bite release can be useful and appropriate. If an agency does employ a hands-on bite release, it must be an augmentation of rather than a replacement for the verbal out. This is called a "tactical out." A professionally trained and employed hands-on bite release is not a matter of choking the dog off a bite. *Choking the dog will exacerbate the intensity of the bite.* By contrast, a hands-on tactical out, when done properly, reduces the dog's natural tendency to bite and fight harder. Unfortunately, many trainers and handlers fail to understand this concept. *In fact, many handlers are inappropriately taught that a choke-off is a tactical out, which it is not.*

A proper tactical out involves the dog voluntarily releasing the bite on command of the handler while the handler has their hands on the dog's collar. The handler holds the collar to manage the dog as it releases its bite in order to prevent the dog from biting the suspect again or from redirecting onto nearby officers, who may be taking the suspect into custody.

Inappropriate hands-on bite releases are recipes for lawsuits. Many lawsuits have resulted from handlers being unable to control their dogs and unable to remove the dog from a bite. This results in unwarranted or excessive injury from the dog biting a suspect longer or harder than is necessary. *Any time a dog remains on a bite after the suspect has surrendered is a continued use of force no different than any other use of force tool.* Once a suspect has surrendered and is under control, it is imperative that officers move in and take custody as quickly and safely as possible.

ACCIDENTAL BITES

Accidental bites do occur. Every situation is fluid, and circumstances can change very quickly: An innocent pedestrian can come around the corner directly into a team that is tracking in the

Figure 3.3. Preparing to perform a tactical out. A tactical out is *not* choking the dog off a suspect. Rather, the handler has the dog release on command while they hold the dog's collar to prevent a further bite on the suspect or a redirected bite on any nearby officers controlling the suspect.

opposite direction. A jogger running nearby can suddenly attract the attention of the dog, and the dog may believe that this person is the intended target.

Many trainers train their dogs to immediately exit the patrol vehicle and engage a suspect when the vehicle door to the K9 compartment is opened via a remote car door opener. This strategy is commonly used during vehicle stops when a handler, without their dog, is dealing with a subject who suddenly becomes assaultive.

While this training can be effective in such situations, it may also increase the risk of accidental bites. In numerous instances, officers have accidentally triggered the car door. In these cases, the dog behaves as trained: it exits the car and, once loose, makes contact with and bites the first person it sees on the street.

While I was working on this book, I saw a post on social media that showed an arrested and handcuffed suspect being escorted out of his home by two officers for transport. The K9 handler was driving a car that had no K9 markings. He was still in the suspect's home when the two escorting officers walked the suspect out to the K9 officer's car, not realizing it had a dog in the backseat.

Thinking they were about to place the arrestee in a transport vehicle, one officer reached out and opened the rear, driver-side door, inadvertently releasing the dog onto the street. Initially, there was no issue, and the officers called out to the K9 handler to let him know the dog was out. Before the handler could respond, however, the dog walked to the handcuffed, passive arrestee, sniffed at the subject, then engaged him by biting him on the hand.

This incident was obviously an accident with no ill intent from anyone involved. Indeed, it's a situation that K9 handlers and trainers could not anticipate. Regardless, training that requires the dog to be verbally called out by the handler, whether the dog is intentionally or unintentionally released from the vehicle, would do much to mitigate this type of accident.

Although — thankfully — accidental bites are not frequent, K9 supervisors must take them seriously. They must have a process in place for how to deal with accidental bites both to help mitigate future risk and to maintain positive trust with the public. In some cases, accidental bites are simply the result of a perfect storm of unfortunate events. Other times, they may indicate a shortcoming of your training or deployment policies.

Every time an accidental bite occurs, it needs to be properly investigated. The investigation into an accidental bite should be done with a focus on reducing the likelihood of similar events in the future. To that end, supervisors and units must self-critically analyze both the specific incident and the impact of training, policies, and practices in effect at the time of the incident. Consideration must be given to any recommendations or changes in training or deployment policies that may help mitigate the risk of similar accidents. This process should also involve remedial training directly aimed at any issues uncovered in the accidental bite investigation and a thorough return-to-duty evaluation.

Supervisor Approval for K9 Deployments

Use of force is expected in K9 deployments because the dog is often used to search for suspects, some of whom are planning to do harm or engage in lethal confrontations. By the very nature of its job, the dog draws officers towards potentially violent and dangerous situations.

Every use of force must come under scrutiny. When a dog is used to apprehend a suspect, the supervisor will normally receive an after-action report along with a use of force report. The reports are scrutinized for accuracy and to ensure the handler adhered to department policy.

After the K9 supervisor has read and acted on these reports, every agency follows its own routine. Some agencies simply file the reports for future reference. Others require copies of the use of force reports to be forwarded up the chain of command. Still others require they be sent to the professional standards branch for further scrutiny.

In every case, the primary focus is the justification of the use of force — that is, whether the application of the dog is necessary to arrest the suspect and if the deployment meets the *Graham v. Connor* standard.

For most agencies, decisions to deploy a dog on a case that may ultimately result in a use of force have historically been left up to the discretion of the K9 officer. Supervisors have rarely been involved in the decision. In many cases, the supervisor is unaware of circumstances leading up to a K9 deployment until they read the after-action report. When you consider the exposure of K9 supervisors or road supervisors to vicarious liability, however, it raises the question of whether leaving the deployment of the dog to the sole discretion of the K9 officer is, in fact, best practice.

Some agencies, particularly those with large K9 units, have policies in place that require supervisory approval prior to K9 deployments. These policies come from experience and have proved effective in helping to reduce liability exposure. However, not everyone agrees with their implementation. Arguments against supervisory approval include the following:

- The supervisor has no experience or background in police dog deployments.
- There is not always a supervisor available to obtain approval.
- The dog is often deployed in circumstances that occur so rapidly it is impractical to obtain any approval.

While each of these points is valid, they are shortsighted. K9 handlers may be opposed to taking this extra step and relinquishing some of their decision-making autonomy, but there are significant benefits to the handlers themselves when a pre-deployment approval policy is implemented.

It is incumbent on the agency to ensure the K9 supervisors and any road supervisors who are responsible for the direct supervision of any K9 team are educated in K9 procedures. This helps to alleviate concerns that handlers have about supervisors not having K9-related experience.

BENEFITS OF PRE-DEPLOYMENT SUPERVISORY APPROVAL

When it comes to liability, there is wisdom in having a second opinion on the decision to deploy. Handlers may resist supervisory oversight because they feel they should have total control over deployment decisions. However, when a handler makes a unilateral decision to deploy a dog that results in a use of force, the responsibility of that deployment decision lies solely on the shoulders of the handler. A policy that includes a supervisor in the decision to use the dog for a potential use of force application provides the handler additional protection from possible liability.

When a road supervisor or K9 unit supervisor is notified of a potential dog deployment while the handler is en route to a call, it provides the opportunity for both the handler and the supervisor to scrutinize the decision prior to deployment. If the supervisor or handler has any doubt whether the decision to deploy the dog is justified given the circumstances of the call, either has the option to abort the potential deployment.

It is important that these decisions be understood not as the supervisor undermining the decision-making of the K9 handler, but as a team effort to reduce liability and increase protection for the handler, supervisor, and agency. Both the supervisor and the handler are equally dependent on the other for guidance and support in fast-moving, fluid situations. Deployment thus becomes a shared responsibility, adding an extra layer of protection for both the handler and the supervisor. That being said, keeping a supervisor appraised of a pending deployment in no way reduces the liability responsibility of the handler. The handler is always responsible for the deployment decisions they make.

Another key benefit of employing a policy to obtain pre-deployment approval from the K9 supervisor or a road supervisor is that it allows the supervisor to be ahead of the curve on the deployment rather than having to rely entirely on the after-action report. Instead, the use of force review in effect begins prior to the deployment of the dog. The decision to use the dog and the potential use of force is validated prior to deployment, thus reducing concerns regarding the handler's decision to deploy. This approach has been well received by the courts. Furthermore, should there be a litigation, it shows a jury that the agency is proactive in its approach to K9 use of force policy.

CAVEATS TO SUPERVISOR PRE-APPROVAL

HANDLER'S RIGHT OF REFUSAL
The K9 officer must have the exclusive right to refuse to deploy their dog in any given situation. This right is inviolable. Only the K9 handler knows the true capabilities and limitations of the dog they are working. If, in the handler's judgment, the use of the dog will unnecessarily place the dog in jeopardy, put civilians or officers at risk, or inflame a situation with little or no likelihood of success, then the handler's choice not to deploy must be respected.

EXIGENT CIRCUMSTANCES
Often, events will occur where obtaining supervisory approval for K9 deployment is impractical due to supervisor unavailability or other exigent circumstances. In these situations, a policy recommending pre-approval for K9 deployments must allow handlers latitude to make operational decisions unilaterally. The policy should in no way impede K9 officers from using their dogs when necessary.

Reducing After-Action Liability

AFTER-ACTION INVESTIGATION
In any deployment that results in a suspect being bitten by a police dog, the supervisor should attend the scene and ascertain the circumstances leading up to the deployment of the dog that resulted in the suspect being bitten. In some cases, the suspect will have been transported to a nearby hospital for treatment of any injuries. When this is the case, the next step is to attend the hospital to check on the status of the person who was bitten. Ensure pictures are taken to document all injuries and speak to the involved party.

Photo documentation should be done after the cleaning of the wounds to ensure clarity of the injuries. Photos should include the entire body of the involved person so the total physical condition of the person at that time is documented, including any bruising or injuries that are in the process of healing and not the result of police interaction. This is important to protect against false accusations. There have been situations in which, subsequent to law enforcement interaction, suspects have caused further, self-inflicted injuries and accused police of the additional injuries or have attempted to use prior injuries to make false accusations.

AFTER-ACTION DEBRIEFS
After-action debriefs involve speaking both with the handlers involved in an incident and, if possible, with the injured party. If the injured party is cooperative, interview them regarding the circumstances surrounding the dog deployment in order to ascertain the situation from their perspective.

When reading K9 incident reports, supervisors need to ensure that all deployments meet the elemental requirements of case law that affect how and when police dogs are deployed. I recommend that the program supervisor conduct a routine on-site or after-action debrief with the handler in any case where a service dog has been used to physically apprehend a suspect and in every case where an accidental bite has occurred. Debriefing allows you to have the handler articulate their reasoning for the use of the dog and at the same time offers an opportunity to discuss whether any other options may have been considered.

There are countless cases that are widely available online that show K9 handlers deploying dogs under circumstances that clearly do not warrant the use of the dog. For instance, does a dog need to be sent to take a subject into custody when there are multiple officers on scene that can go hands-on rather than sending the dog? In such cases, a dog can still be ready to deploy to assist if the officers are unable to gain control; however, it would be hard to justify using the dog as the first line of action. Always remember: the primary causes of K9-related lawsuits are poor deployment decisions by the handler. Remember, too, that a properly managed police dog program can be one of your most valuable public relations assets. If left unmonitored or improperly managed, however, it can become an albatross.

Handler decisions to use the dog to apprehend a suspect must be within the constitutional framework of current case law. Self-control is paramount for police officers in any incident. Some K9 officers believe that attending a serious offense gives them greater latitude when it comes to the deployment of the dog. This is not the case. On-scene circumstances will further dictate what action is warranted. The seriousness of the offense is far from the only factor at play in a decision to use the dog in situations that may result in the dog making physical contact with the suspect. The officer must also consider whether the suspect poses an immediate threat to the safety of law enforcement officers or other citizens, the potential danger to bystanders, and whether the suspect is *actively* resisting arrest or attempting to flee. Above all, the handler must decide whether the decision to deploy the dog is morally and ethically sound.

Questions to consider when debriefing handlers include:
- Was the application of the dog needed?
- Was it the appropriate decision given all the circumstances and using an objectively reasonable standard?
- Was the use of the dog over other available options the most reasonable choice, taking into consideration the safety of the officers, citizens, and suspect?

In no way should debriefs be conducted with the intent to restrict your K9 teams. Incident debriefs allow you and your K9 teams to develop critical thinking around deployments and discuss any ideas that could improve tactics while keeping everyone involved keenly aware of the importance of being judicious in the use of the dog. When these debriefs are common practice, the discussions are top-of-mind for officers when responding to calls. This encourages them to be cognizant of their responsibilities with each deployment.

Reducing Supervisor Liability

UNDERSTANDING SUPERVISOR LIABILITY

When a K9 deployment results in a use of force, there is potential liability not only for the K9 officer who was responsible for the use of the dog, but also for the agency administrators and supervisors. There are two legal doctrines that come into play in these situations.

The first doctrine is *respondeat superior*.[18] This doctrine dictates that the agency is responsible for the actions of the officers it employs if the action taken by the officer was performed as a course of their employment. In lawsuits of this type, the agency becomes liable for the actions of an officer, even though the agency was not directly involved in the actions taken.

The second doctrine is vicarious liability. Vicarious liability is imposed on a person for the actionable conduct of another, based on the relationship between the two parties. In other words, it is indirect legal responsibility for the acts of another person — for example, the liability of a supervisor for the actions of a person they supervise.

To protect yourself and your agency, manage your program with the following eight areas of liability in mind:
1. Negligent appointment
2. Negligent retention
3. Negligent entrustment
4. Negligent assignment
5. Negligent direction and failure to direct
6. Negligent training and failure to train
7. Negligent supervision and failure to supervise
8. Failure to discipline

As a police dog program manager, you must also factor in each dog that is assigned in your program. In many cases, similar issues need to be considered for both the dog and the handler.

1. NEGLIGENT APPOINTMENT
The first step in assigning a dog or a handler to your program begins with quality screening procedures. There must be a standard selection process in place for applicants that explains the expectations and requirements needed to qualify for the handler position. The same holds true for the selection and assignment of potential

---
18 To be found liable under *respondeat superior*, the plaintiff must prove that the agency, administrator, or supervisor was the "moving force" behind the constitutional rights violations. To prove this, the plaintiff must show that the agency, administrator, or supervisor had a policy of deliberate indifference.

police service dogs to the program. (For more on handler and dog selection, see Chapter 8.)

2. NEGLIGENT RETENTION

When a handler is found to have repeated issues such as refusal to ensure their training is up to standard, lack of discretion in how they deploy their dog, or other repeatedly documented deficiencies, consideration must be given to removing the handler from the program. The same concerns may apply for a dog that exhibits dangerous or uncontrollable behavior.

Supervisors should be reviewing all training documentation and, when possible, attending training events to ensure that agency training requirements are being met and that each handler is attaining the minimum number of training hours mandated to maintain efficiency. Regular consultation with the agency trainer can also be valuable in ascertaining any current deficiencies. Along with training, all deployments also need to be scrutinized. Conduct annual reviews to ensure the K9 teams are being certified annually and that all dogs are receiving annual veterinary checks.

3. NEGLIGENT ENTRUSTMENT

An easy example of negligent entrustment is assigning a K9 position to a handler who has a history of excessive force complaints or who is physically incapable of the strenuous requirements of the assignment. If a handler is unable to perform, and there is a failure to act or to succeed because of the physical or mental ineptitude of the handler, such events can result in unnecessary injury to officers, civilians, suspects, or even the K9 handler. Every handler must be able to deal with potentially violent suspects, manage the dog, and make solid, common-sense decisions in the heat of the moment.

4. NEGLIGENT ASSIGNMENT

Negligent assignment is the assignment of a K9 team to circumstances that are not within the scope of the training that has been provided or not within the expected abilities of the team. Often, out-of-scope decisions are made by handlers who feel pressured to use the dog in circumstances such as the following:
- Deploying the dog in an application for which the dog team has received no training (e.g., deploying the team on

a SWAT/ERT assignment when they have never trained with SWAT)
- Using the dog in lieu of more practical applications (e.g., deploying the dog into a building to apprehend an armed suspect when the situation clearly calls for a SWAT/ERT team)
- Assigning the available on-duty K9 team to patrol duties unrelated to their stated assignment, resulting in the dog being unavailable to be used for their stated assignment

5. NEGLIGENT DIRECTION AND FAILURE TO DIRECT

A supervisor may authorize a deployment or choose not to deploy the dog. However, just because a supervisor has authorized a deployment doesn't mean the dog must be deployed. The handler must always have the authority to not deploy the dog. The supervisor's direction of a handler to deploy when such deployment is not warranted is a typical example of negligent direction.

The failure of a supervisor to order that a dog be removed from service for remedial training after consistent failures on the street is also an example of negligent direction. Another example is the failure of a supervisor to stop a deployment when a handler is making a poor decision.

6. NEGLIGENT TRAINING AND FAILURE TO TRAIN

There are three areas of concern related to K9 training that are raised in court cases involving police service dogs:

1. **K9 Training Standards**. Ensure your agency has a training standard that sets out expectations. A number of states require standards that are developed through the state's Peace Officer's Standards and Training (POST) or equivalent. If your state does not have a mandated standard, you have the option of selecting a standard that has been developed by another state or by national law enforcement K9 associations and is recognized by the courts. In some cases, standards developed in-house have also been accepted as standards by the courts. These include standards developed by the RCMP in Canada and the Los Angeles Police Department (LAPD) in the United States.
2. **Training**. All training routines must meet or surpass the minimum requirements laid out in the training standards

your department has chosen to adhere to. Keep in mind that a standard is only a guide that provides the minimum standard of efficiency required by your dog teams in order to pass certification. Good trainers will always train to exceed the minimum standard.
3. **Certification**. Every organization that has a mandated standard will have a testing process to test the proficiency of its K9 teams. Your job as a supervisor is to ensure that all of your teams are certifying to the chosen standard. The certification process should be done by someone who is impartial and independent of your agency. If the certification is done in-house, evaluations conducted either by a trainer who has not been directly involved with the development of the team or by an independent trainer from outside the agency lend credibility to in-house certifications. (For more on certification, see Chapter 10.)

While these issues are often considered separately from the other, they are inextricably entwined. The accepted industry standard is a minimum of 16 hours of training every month. A lawsuit against a team that shows this minimum training requirement was not maintained exposes the officer and agency to potential liability. A supervisor who checks training reports regularly for completeness, ensures the officers are receiving 16 hours a month of quality training, and attends periodic training events as an observer will easily avoid any allegation of failure to train or failure to supervise.

7. NEGLIGENT SUPERVISION AND FAILURE TO SUPERVISE
One of the more common reasons K9 programs fail is due to supervisors who are not committed to the program and lack dedication to the unit. Supervisors who technically manage the unit but do little in the way of monitoring and being involved in team member activities often contribute to program collapse.

When there have been no specific complaints about the K9 unit, some supervisors may leave the K9 officers largely on their own, failing to monitor training and deployment reports for quality and completeness. When they are served a subpoena for records relating to a dog bite case and are required to produce historical records of all training for a specific team, they suddenly realize the officer has not been keeping sufficient training notes. Only then do they become aware of problems with the team.

While it is the responsibility of the K9 officer to maintain detailed notes of all training regimens and deployments, it is also the responsibility of the supervisor to ensure that training is occurring and that thorough notes of all training and deployments are being submitted and scrutinized. K9 records management systems are a priority in today's modern K9 units in order to manage K9 training and deployment records. (For more on records management, see Chapter 11.)

Documented post-incident debriefs with your handlers, especially for any deployment that results in a bite, are also indicative of strong supervision and help to suppress any accusation of inadequate supervision.

8. FAILURE TO DISCIPLINE

As stated previously, poor deployment decisions by K9 officers are the primary cause of lawsuits. It is imperative that supervisors take appropriate action, when necessary, to ensure that handlers maintain the highest ethical standards regarding deployment decisions and that teams meet expected training regimens. Any lapses in the integrity or responsibilities of the handler in regard to deployments or training expectations should be documented and action taken to ensure corrective measures are put in place.

K9 SUPERVISOR TRAINING PROGRAMS

A recommended best practice for every K9 supervisor, regardless of prior experience, is to attend and participate in at least one training day each month. For agencies that have implemented supervisory pre-deployment approvals, where the K9 unit supervisor is not always available for pre-deployment approvals, in-service training should be provided by the unit supervisor and one of the senior handlers to any and all road supervisors who are responsible for the K9 teams. As a team, they can provide the fundamentals needed to prepare the road supervisors to assist with the policy as needed and will be able to answer any questions that arise.

The K9 supervisor may summarize information they obtained when attending a K9 management course and pass it on to the road supervisors as reference material. Road supervisors should be assigned to attend one or two K9 training events to help them better understand K9 operations and build trust with the K9 teams.

There are numerous K9 management and supervision courses available. These programs provide updated information on current case law, policy development, dog and handler selection processes, methods of dealing with problem handlers, and interactive training that involves decision-making related specifically to police dog deployments. Every K9 unit manager and senior K9 handler should regularly attend courses such as these and should take refresher courses regularly to ensure they are up to date on any new developments in the industry.

It is, of course, essential as a supervisor to know the legal requirements for deployments. It is also important to know the abilities of the teams you are supervising and what limitations, if any, each team might have. The only way to accomplish this is for you to regularly spend dedicated time with the handlers so you know and appreciate the unique abilities each team brings to the table. Having a supervisor who connects with the handlers on a regular basis is something that handlers appreciate and will help create opportunities to coordinate on continuing team development.

I have worked with police departments where the supervisors had zero hands-on experience with working dogs. Once assigned to manage the K9 unit, however, they became actively involved with their teams and attended weekly training events whenever possible. They learned how to lay tracks and decoy for their teams. They attended K9 management programs to gain a better understanding of K9 operations. The relationships between supervisors like these and the K9 officers they supervise tend to be relationships of mutual respect and appreciation, with each member of the unit having their own responsibilities. This rapport binds the unit as a close organization and alleviates officer concerns about inexperienced K9 supervisors.

When properly trained, K9 officers are subject-matter experts in their field. As a supervisor, your officers should always be your go-to resource when in need of guidance or advice regarding K9 operations or training matters. Ultimately, they are the ones who know the capabilities of their dogs and, if they are doing their job well, they will be up to date on current practices. Entrusting them with your concerns and getting feedback will help to build your working relationship with the teams. If you feel you need more impartial guidance in some situations, you can always request advice from K9 unit trainers in another agency.

Supervising personnel is always a challenge. The addition of a dog to the equation adds an entirely different dimension to that challenge. You are supervising an officer that has specialized knowledge and skill sets that are outside the scope of most normal policing operations. Managing a K9 team is significantly different and can be more challenging than managing other units because you are dealing not just with your officers but also with your dogs: other living beings that require constant care and training and have their own unique behaviors and idiosyncrasies. It may seem overwhelming at times, but the rewards for the agency are significant. The K9 unit is one of the most versatile and productive tools available to law enforcement today. When effectively managed, liability risks associated with K9 units can be limited.

4

Modern Development of Police Dogs in North America

Whether you are a new administrator just taking over the management responsibilities of an established police service dog program or a potential administrator currently researching the possibility of implementing a new K9 unit, it is imperative for you to understand the current trends in law enforcement K9 training.

This chapter covers information gleaned from my personal observations and experience over four decades, as well as knowledge shared with me over the years by several of my mentors. It encompasses the era between 1970 and 2021, which has critically impacted law enforcement K9 units, particularly in the United States.

While dog training has changed much and advanced exponentially over the last 50 years, these changes have not all been beneficial for law enforcement. To make educated decisions about the path you want your unit to take and how to best manage it, it is critical to understand how the police service dog training industry has evolved and the direction that evolution is currently taking.

I refer to dog training in the field of law enforcement as an "industry" because that is precisely what it has become. In fact, it is big industry. From purchasing potential police dogs to obtaining the equipment and training required to put a team on the street, K9 training is a worldwide business that brings in hundreds of millions of dollars annually. It is extremely competitive. That competitiveness has impacted how we develop our K9 units in both positive and negative ways.

Standard Police Dog Operations Before 1970

Before the mid-1970s, virtually all law enforcement K9 teams in Canada and the United States were trained in-house. In other words, every police dog was trained by a police officer who specialized in K9 training. Smaller agencies that did not have the benefit of having their own in-house trainer would send their teams to a larger agency that had the appropriate training facilities and expertise. Most training was standardized, with most agencies running basic K9 training programs that were 12 to 14 weeks in duration for dual-purpose dogs (i.e., dogs that are trained primarily to track suspects, with a secondary function of either narcotics or explosives detection; see Chapter 1). In fact, there are many agencies that still follow this time-proven practice, including most, if not all, agencies in Canada.

A new handler would be assigned a potential police dog that had little or no training (often referred to as a "green" dog). The dog was selected by a trainer who put the dog through a series of stress and behavior tests to ensure it met the minimum requirements to enter the training regimen. This ensured the dog selected would have the best potential to pass the extensive and challenging program required to produce a quality team.

The officer and dog, together referred to as a "K9 team," would then begin a rigorous training routine that, in most circumstances, involved 8 hours of training daily for 12 to 14 and even 16 weeks, with the officer learning everything from grooming and care of the animal to the basic, intermediate, and advanced levels of training their dog for every aspect of police service. When training was completed, most teams would be fully patrol capable with extensive tracking profiles. Each team would also be proficient in detection, specializing in either narcotics or explosives.

Each handler became a skilled dog trainer under the direct supervision of "master trainers": police dog handlers who had extensive experience in both training K9 teams and handling dogs of their own on the streets in real-world law enforcement deployments.

This system of training was invaluable. When a team trained in this way hit the streets, they were very well prepared to handle the wide variety of scenarios that confronted them. Further, because the handler had been involved in every part of the process, from selection to becoming a street-ready team, they had an excellent skill set and an understanding of how to further develop the dog once out of training. They also understood how to correct deficiencies should any arise. Every handler was knowledgeable in the various behavioral aspects of their dog and became an expert at providing courtroom testimony on their dog's ability to track and locate suspects and/or search for and find contraband or explosives.

During this period, continued support of K9 units, including all training and development and all financial support, was an essential part of an agency's annual budget, whether it be local, state, or federal. This all changed with the introduction of private vendors.

The Introduction of K9 Vendors

In the mid-1970s, the savvy operator of Mandelyn Kennels in Bakersfield, California, recognized the rate of exponential growth of the number of police agencies in need of potential police dogs.[19] At the time, law enforcement trainers would spend significant time searching for potential police dog candidates. It was becoming increasingly difficult for kennel operators to locate dogs that could meet the strict requirements of law enforcement.

While there was an ongoing shortage of quality candidate animals in the United States and Canada, Europe was a different story. Europe's vast and well-established dog sport industry made it easier to find good quality dogs there.

LOOKING TO EUROPE AND SPORT DOGS

Dog sports have been an important part of European culture since the early 1900s. The Schutzhund sport originated in Germany and was developed as a test for the German Shepherd breed to determine its suitability as a working dog. Similarly, the IPO sport (*Internationale Prüfungsordnung*, German for "international

---

19 The kennel operation noted was very reputable and successful for many years. It is, however, no longer in business.

examination regulations") began testing dogs on their tracking, protection, and obedience abilities. Both tests were developed to ensure the German Shepherd breed remained strong. They therefore involved dogs with known pedigrees. In 2004, these two organizations — Schutzhund and IPO — came together under the same standards. In 2019, IPO became *Internationale Gebrauchshunde-Prüfungsordnung* (IGP), meaning "international working dog examination regulations."

Another discipline, the KNPV (*Koninklijke Nederlandse Politiehond Vereniging*, Dutch for the "Royal Dutch Police Dog Association"), was first developed to organize the training and development of potential police dogs for Dutch police in the Netherlands. It later became a civilian sport. KNPV focuses on the protective capabilities of the dog. The discipline does not include tracking as part of its PH1 or PH2[20] certifications; however, a separate examination is offered that includes scent discrimination exercises.

These are the most common civilian dog sports that are capable of providing an abundant supply of potential police dog stock, though there are others.

UNDERSTANDING SPORT DOGS

Dog training is all about conditioned behavior, and the competitive application of dogs in the various European dog sports are designed to test a dog's ability to perform certain tasks. In general, dogs that score high in these competitions exhibit the traits required for law enforcement K9 service in the United States and Canada. These traits are tested by putting the dog through competitive tasks where the dog must successfully perform actions that are similar, in some respects, to the actions performed by police dogs. Each sport has its own philosophy, standards, and structure; the specific challenges a dog must face during training and competition depends on the sport in which it competes.

For example, a strong Schutzhund- or KNPV-trained dog must perform bite apprehensions on a skilled decoy who will challenge it and test its level of courage. Each sport approaches this event differently with different expectations; however, the results of the

---

20 PH here stands for *Politiehond*, Dutch for police dog.

performance in either sport provide a measure of how well the dog will bite and stay in a fight when confronted. A dog that successfully completes these exercises exhibits high levels of courage and a strong ability to manage a threat. The dog's ability to track may also be assessed through competition results, depending on the sport. IGP requires obedience, protection, and tracking skill regimens for each level of testing requirement. KNPV, as already mentioned, is more focused on the skill sets of personal protection and obedience. These are the default skills taught in this sport, though optional tracking and scent discrimination profiles are offered.

The competitive tests in these sports allow dogs to earn "titles." With each title earned, a dog advances to a higher skill set and is trained at a higher level of difficulty for subsequent testing. For example, in IGP, there are three levels, which coincide with basic, intermediate, and advanced levels of achievement. Further, three levels of FH[21] titles can be achieved for a more advanced tracking skill set along with several other title options depending on the skill set being tested.

People involved in the various dog sports in Europe are interested in training their dogs to excellence. Obtaining the highest possible title for their dog, whether in IGP, KNPV, or another dog sport, is proof of that excellence. The higher the dog's title, the more value it has. Members of these clubs take pride in the number of title certificates they have earned. (This is apparent when you travel the various clubs and see the walls of title certificates on display.) Understanding the extent of this focus on titles helps us to understand the mindset of these trainers and how they choose which dogs to put on the market. It is important to these dog owners to retain their strongest and best dogs for the purposes of breeding high-quality standard stock. These dogs, therefore, are rarely up for sale. Moreover, if a dog fails to perform to a standard that allows it to achieve a title, then the owner will put the dog up for sale even before it has its first competition. They have no interest in furthering training on a dog that will underperform.

Consequently, these underperforming dogs are often sold into the law enforcement market in the United States (and sometimes

---

21 FH here stands for *Fährtenhund*, German for "tracking dog."

in Canada). In other words, law enforcement is often purchasing civilian handlers' rejects. This does not mean dogs coming out of Europe are all bad dogs. On the contrary, the expectation of European trainers is extremely high. Even among these rejected, pre-titled dogs there is a good pool of dogs to choose from. That being said, it is important to understand that there are also large numbers of dogs that truly do lack the proper temperaments for police service. It is incumbent upon the receiving agency to ensure the dogs are properly vetted before accepting delivery.

It is also critical that every police administrator understand that an IGP or KNPV dog, regardless of whether the dog is titled, *does not meet* the criteria of a fully trained police service dog in America. They may have basic characteristics necessary to be developed into a well-trained police service dog, but a sport dog is not, in and of itself, a police dog. Just because a dog can bite or track in the sport does not mean it will perform as expected on the street. This difference is profound, yet may not be obvious to the untrained observer.

THE BASICS OF DOG BROKERAGE

With the shortage of quality dogs in 1970s North America, having access to an unlimited supply of dogs offered an excellent business opportunity. The Bakersfield kennel operator therefore took advantage of the European resources and began to import dogs from Europe into the United States, significantly increasing the supply of potential police dogs.

Soon, other kennel operators began to follow suit. They traveled to Europe to seek out dogs in various sports clubs, observing and testing dogs to find those that would meet law enforcement requirements in the United States. At that time, dogs could be purchased in Europe for a fraction of what they could be sold for in North America. Even shipping costs from Europe were minimal, as any dogs being shipped in crates were simply considered excess baggage for which operators needed to pay only small fees. There were, moreover, very few limits on the number of dogs a passenger could transport back to North America. Kennel operators took advantage of the high margins of return and made large profits on the resale of imported dogs to law enforcement agencies in need.

Vendors in search of potential police dogs for sale to North America and elsewhere in the world will spend days, sometimes weeks, traveling to European dog sport clubs in search of dogs to purchase for resale. European vendors do not restrict their sales to North American clients. As such, it is important to understand that any vendors or law enforcement agencies traveling from North America to purchase dogs from European vendors are purchasing in an extremely competitive global market. From an agency point of view, this is one of several reasons not to be stingy when it comes to buying your dogs. Vendors will always give priority to agencies willing to spend the most money.

If a dog owner offers to sell a dog the vendor is interested in purchasing, they will negotiate a price. Most of these dogs are purchased without titles. In other words, they have not yet achieved a title in their given sport, and the owner has decided that it is not worth investing any more training in the dog. In some cases, titled dogs can be purchased; however, their IGP, KNPV or other recognized title will earn them a higher price. Moreover, depending on the circumstances of your agency, a titled dog will not always be the best choice.

In dogs that have been bred by their owners for the purpose of competition, the foundational building blocks of basic training have already been started. They have been taught their basic obedience profiles, been tested for their tolerance to the sound of gunfire and have learned how to bite. In some cases, they will have received a formal foundation in the sport methods of tracking and scent discrimination. Their level of advancement in each category will depend on whether they are a titled dog and to which degree they have been titled.

Once a vendor has tested, selected, and obtained the number of dogs they need to fulfill their quota, they will then transport the dogs to their kennel facility.

Depending on the vendor and how they operate, some will almost immediately put these dogs up for sale on the open market. Others will put the dog through a short cycle of training, as little as a week or two, in order to condition the dogs' behavior so it will pass the known temperament and stress tests that are common in the law enforcement industry, to whom they intend to sell the dogs.

THE PRE-TRAINED POLICE DOG CONCEPT

For a while, the brokering of quality dogs was the only service kennel operators provided to law enforcement agencies. Then, that same Bakersfield kennel operator who had kicked off the brokerage industry saw a further opportunity: marketing not just quality dogs, but "pre-trained" police dogs and corresponding short-term handler training schools.

There has been a dramatic shift in police dog training since the 1970s. Today, this multimillion-dollar industry revolves around the development of civilian businesses that, in many areas of the United States, have replaced professional law enforcement dog trainers when it comes to the selection and training of police dogs. (This trend has not made any significant inroads in Canada, as of this writing.)

The ideal candidate dog to select for K9 training is a dog that is like a fresh, unpainted canvas: a dog that has no formal training, a "green" dog. A strong green candidate for police work will be social and responsive to those around him. Initially, however, agencies were not purchasing green dogs, preferring instead titled sport dogs already trained for sport profiles in obedience, tracking, and personal protection. Vendors marketed these dogs as "pre-trained police dogs."

Vendors sold the idea of pre-trained dogs to police agencies by offering a six-week training and certification program for new K9 officers. Vendors suggested that there was no need to put these dogs through 12- to 14-week training schools to develop a team. Because the dog was already trained, it was argued that all they had to do was send their handlers to the vendors' schools for a short training course alongside the dog for the officer and dog to be "certified" as a fully trained law enforcement K9 team. Moreover, because their programs were half the length of a standard training program, agencies' officers would be back on the street in half the time.

To any administrator with little or no background in fundamental police dog training, the concept of not having to pay for a full-time, in-house trainer, along with the quicker turnaround of the K9 officer returning to duty, made sense. However, significant differences can be seen today in the quality of training between agencies that still choose to educate their own officers as professional trainers and handlers and those who purchase pre-trained dogs and short-term handler courses from outside vendors.

Beware of making decisions regarding the training and development of your K9 unit based on financial expense. Look past the bottom line and think about the fact that every officer who works a dog is at the front line of more dangerous situations than any other member of your department. They must have training that emphasizes the ability to track down dangerous suspects, and they must have the tactical skill set to bring dangerous situations to successful, safe conclusions. This means that they must be supported in all aspects of their job — or, rather, their two jobs. First and foremost, K9 officers are police officers. They are, however, also dog trainers and handlers. These two skills must be combined at the highest level for a K9 team to be effective.

A PRE-TRAINED SPORT DOG IS NOT A TRAINED POLICE DOG
As mentioned above, it should not be assumed that successful sport dogs will make good police service dogs without further training. The requirements and expectations of sport training on their own do not meet the needs of law enforcement in North America.

That being said, in many respects, the pre-trained dog concept is like the European dog training philosophy of the KNPV sport itself, which trains dogs in order to sell them to police agencies where their training will be completed. The difference is that many officers in the Netherlands are raised in the KNPV sport and are knowledgeable in the development and training of the dogs they receive. When they receive titled KNPV dogs, they complete the training using skill sets within their own organization. In the United States, on the other hand, handlers receiving pre-trained dogs rarely have any such experience. They are, in effect, as "green" as an untrained dog. Nevertheless, thousands of agencies throughout the United States have become entirely dependent on vendors to provide both dogs and training for their K9 teams.

Any vendor that purchases a sport dog and then "flips" that dog, selling it as a fully trained police dog with a short-term handlers' course is disingenuous and dangerous. Still, many agencies continue to purchase packages that include the sale of the dog and the training of the handler with a training course that may be as short as 10 days. The shortest training course I have seen was only 3 days, though such short courses are rare. More common are 2- to 3-week K9 handler schools that subsequently "certify" the team as street ready. This is particularly common for patrol dogs. Simply put, this is nowhere near enough time to train a proficient police service dog *team* — that is, both the dog and the handler — regardless of how much pre-training the vendor has put into the dog.

THE APPEARANCE OF COMPETENCE

A pre-trained dog should by no means be automatically considered a competent law enforcement K9 candidate without being

Figure 4.1. Proper selection testing by an experienced evaluator is paramount to securing good potential candidate dogs.

properly vetted by a knowledgeable trainer. As already mentioned, training is based on conditioning, and almost any dog can be carefully conditioned to give the appearance, to the untrained or unskilled eye, of having the appropriate genetic traits and basic skills to become a police dog.

This can cause a number of problems. For one, this training can hide genetic weaknesses that may jeopardize the dog's ability to do the job. Some dogs may also be conditioned to extreme levels that create control issues. For instance, some vendors will put the dogs through as much as three months of intense bite training in every possible environment. In most cases, this ensures the dogs will perform adequately on basic tests. However, the vast majority of these dogs have not been taught to release a bite on command but to retain a bite at all costs, only releasing when forcibly choked off by the handler. This is one of the most prominent and difficult issues with dogs being sold to North America.

It is, therefore, imperative to have a skilled trainer perform exhaustive testing on every dog that is offered for sale to ensure the dog actually has the basic qualities of a potential police dog and is not simply going through the routine behaviors for which it has been conditioned.

TESTING PRE-TRAINED DOGS

It is crucial to test seemingly pre-trained dogs as stringently, if not more stringently, than untrained dogs. Exhaustive testing will detect weaknesses that may be hidden through repeated training routines that temporarily diminish unwanted responses through conditioned behavior.

Whether testing a trained pre-title or titled dog that has been purchased from a club or a young, untrained, green candidate, the same basic tests and challenges should be conducted to determine the potential viability of the dog. You should conduct the tests in an area unfamiliar to the dog and using trainers the dog does not know. This way, you'll be able to see the true heart of the dog. Only then can you be confident that you are getting an adequate analysis of the dog's performance.

Every dog should be tested for the presence and severity of genetic issues (such as innate fear of being challenged) and

Figure 4.2. Dogs must be environmentally sound and able to work in any situation, whether it be in dark, tight spaces, on slippery floors inside buildings, around aircraft, along highways, or in deeply wooded areas.

environmental issues (such a dog's hesitation or fear around slippery floors or stairs). It should also be vetted by a trusted veterinarian to independently ensure its health. When potential genetic, environmental, and health weaknesses have been exposed, an educated decision can be made to determine if the dog is a good candidate. (For more information on dog selection, see Chapter 7.)

The Good and Bad of Vendor-Based Training

DISADVANTAGES OF VENDOR-BASED TRAINING

The introduction of the pre-trained police dog to the United States was the beginning of a largely civilian-based industry that has become prolific and has had significant influence on the training and deployment of police dogs today. In many ways, this influence has been negative.

Police K9 training in the hands of private vendors without law enforcement experience now largely serves the business needs of outside trainers who significantly influence young handlers with their own perceptions of how police dogs should be trained and deployed. This in turn influences the culture and tone of law enforcement police dog operations. The needs and philosophies of vendors only rarely reflect the true needs of law enforcement.

Over the last four decades, this transition to a reliance on vendors has had some benefits but has also resulted in significant damage to professional police dog operations and capabilities. In many cases, law enforcement agencies are no longer in command of the quality of teams they deploy as they are totally dependent on the services of outside vendors.

DEEMPHASIS OF THE TRACKING PROFILE

Dependence on vendors has resulted in inadequate training time, dependency on pre-trained sport dogs, and reduced operational capability due to limited training profiles such as tracking. The tracking profile was at one time the primary use of police dogs in most of North America. As vendor dependency increases, however, tracking profiles within agencies decrease. Informal surveys that I have conducted over the years have indicated that almost 40 percent of agencies in the United States no longer include tracking as a primary mandate.

Vendors rarely offer training in the tracking profile because of the extensive time commitment required to develop and maintain it. Those that do offer tracking usually base their programs on sport tracking and have little or no concept of the specific requirements of police dog tracking. Sport-based tracking is the ability of the dog to follow a track left by a person in a sterile environment without distractions. The dog is usually trained using food as enticement. While sport training can lay a foundation for police dogs, it can also create idiosyncrasies and training issues that need to be overcome for law enforcement applications. The technique tends to produce a dog that is slow to track, which is not practical in police work.

Well-conditioned police dogs track at a fast pace, allowing the team to close in quickly on suspects. The training teaches the dog to work in heavily contaminated urban and suburban environments and to work through the many distractions common in normal, everyday working conditions. Most agency-trained teams today will have a stronger foundation in profiles such as tracking, which cannot be developed in the time allotted for most vendor-trained K9 teams. The difference in skill set and street readiness is dynamically different.

Deficiencies exist, too, in terms of training the handler in the tracking profile. Most vendor-trained handlers have limited knowledge of the basic science of scent. When it comes time for a handler to explain to a judge and jury how their dog is able to reliably track and locate suspects or find contraband, they are unable to give a clear or convincing explanation.

OVEREMPHASIS OF HANDLING OVER TRAINING

Vendor dependence also tends to limit K9 officers' opportunities to reach their full potential as trainers and handlers on the street. Crucially, they may lack training in problem-solving, which is a crucial skill when working with police dogs. Much depends on the types of programs a vendor offers, the length of the programs, and whether the programs focus on teaching the officer how to handle a pre-trained dog or how to actually train the dog and gain the expertise needed in order to maintain and correct training issues. The resulting skill set will also depend on how many training profiles the handler is exposed to.

There are distinct differences between training a dog and handling a dog. A well-trained dog can be handled by giving it appropriate direction and working with it regularly. However, an officer cannot train a dog simply by learning how to handle it. Programs that provide handlers with pre-trained sport dogs don't allow the handler the opportunity to develop a whole range of skills and knowledge that they would learn through training their dog from the beginning.

Most handlers who receive a pre-trained sport dog and short-term handler training through a vendor have minimal, if any, ability or experience in training dogs from scratch. As K9 handlers, this severely limits their ability to understand their dogs, to problem solve, and to address training deficiencies. These handlers are consequently "vendor dependent," needing to return to the vendor to remedy any deficiencies.

On the other hand, a handler who is required to learn every aspect of K9 development and training over a 12- to 14-week patrol dog school leaves that program knowing how the dog is trained because they have done the training themselves under the supervision of an experienced trainer. They have developed the dog and therefore have the skill set to recognize and resolve training issues as they arise. All of this equips them to be a significantly better handler.

Training a dog from the beginning of a partnership also allows the trainer to understand their dog on a deeper level. A qualified dog handler must understand how their dog thinks, how to communicate with the dog, and how to read and understand the dog's behavior. The handler needs to be able to interpret everything the dog does in order to react appropriately in any given situation. This is a prerequisite to their tactical training. For instance, certain subtle body movements in the dog can indicate imminent danger to the well-trained handler. The only way a handler can learn all the skills required to communicate adequately with their K9 partner and to correct training issues is for the officer to train the dog from the start of the partnership and have the time needed to develop the proper skills.

INADEQUATE TRAINING TIME

As I've said often — but the point bears repeating — it takes 12 to 14 weeks minimum of strict daily training at a basic patrol school for a dog and handler to come together as a team and develop the skill set required to function in a street environment. Simply stated, the reason major law enforcement agencies take three months or more to train is because it takes that long to develop a police dog team to true street readiness, regardless of how many years' experience an officer has previously had as the handler of another dog.

Figure 4.3. Techniques that allow the officer to train the dog from scratch, teach them to understand canine behavior, and include specific education on K9 policing tactics provides them with the skills needed to resolve fundamental training issues and continually improve the dog's capabilities.

In a traditional, in-house basic training program, a handler is given a green, untrained dog to train from scratch. They are required to develop a strong skill set under the direct supervision of a qualified trainer. In Canada, 12- to 14-week training programs are still the norm. In the United States, organizations such as the Washington Police K9 Association require that a handler pass a minimum 400-hour or more training program with their dog before they can be certified. In Florida, full K9 training programs may be as long as 460 hours before a team can hit the streets. There are even professional agencies such as the Baltimore police department in Maryland that provide up to 640 hours (16 weeks) of training before a team graduates for service. Prior to commercialized training, this is what the industry standard was, and in fact still is, for most in-house law enforcement K9 programs.

Training programs also need to dedicate time to handler decision-making and problem-solving. Officer tactics change significantly when a dog is involved. Training that is scenario-based, including decision-making centered on situational circumstances and founded on legal doctrines of deployment and law enforcement experience, is vital to success.

Most vendors will neither dedicate the amount of time nor develop the breadth of skill set required to develop a law enforcement K9 team. Most offer programs that produce "finished" teams in three to six weeks, or 120 to 240 hours of training. Moreover, many vendors are civilians and are not experienced with law enforcement. The difference in the training between in-house and vendor-based programs is significant; this difference has severely impacted many law enforcement K9 teams.

THE EFFECT ON INDUSTRY DEMAND

There are a couple of caveats to this. The first is that, since the inception of vendor-based training, police agencies have increasingly demanded that vendors train their dog teams quickly and only provide their teams with short time frames to complete training.

As time has gone on, agencies have become accustomed to short-term training programs and the associated financial and time savings. These programs have become the new norm for many. Some quality vendors who are willing to offer longer-term schools are unable to do so because law enforcement agencies have become accustomed to short-term programs and are not willing to spend the money or take the officer off the street for the amount of time required for quality training. This is an unwise practice and has had significant negative impact on the quality of K9 law enforcement, ultimately reducing the quality of training and limiting the capabilities of their K9 teams.

To meet the demands of these agencies, vendors have no choice but to find ways to give as complete a training regimen as possible on a short time frame to produce somewhat workable teams on the street. To accomplish this, the vendor provides only a basic training regimen that lacks certain training profiles or gives only limited introductions to them — for instance, dropping the tracking profile and focusing instead only on area search techniques for locating suspects.

Some vendors provide even less training, selling an agency on short-term programs championing the (usually sport-based) pre-training of the dog as the reason they can complete the dog in such a short time frame (see "the pre-trained police dog concept," above).

Shorter training programs leave your handlers with disadvantages that can increase liability and reduce the success rate and efficiency of your dog teams. This is the tradeoff that comes with limiting your vendor to offering short-term handler schools. Ideally, vendors would provide the same 12-week-minimum training that traditional in-house trainers provide to new, inexperienced handlers.

The second caveat is this: there are vendors who *do* have the ability to develop a strong tracking profile, even specializing in offering tracking programs. These vendors can provide tracking training as part of their basic training programs, but it is incumbent on law enforcement agencies to actively ask for this type of training and to provide the time and funding necessary to complete it.

Teams that go through longer, more rigorous, and more complete training programs developed by law enforcement agency

Figure 4.4. Police dog teams trained by fellow law enforcement officers benefit from their knowledge and real-world experience. A trained dog coupled with a police officer does not make a police service dog team. Sound and safe deployments originate from the synergy of policing experience and K9 training specifically designed for law enforcement applications.

trainers or vendors with previous law enforcement experience will be more tactically sound and have a greater skill set. They will make wiser deployment decisions. The ultimate outcome is less liability and more arrests that result in convictions.

Law enforcement agencies need to return to full-package training programs that provide training in all profiles, which have historically produced controllable dogs and productive teams. This is a decision that they can make. Agencies also need to lobby for the time and funding needed to achieve the training requirements in all the profiles in which their teams work. Until this happens, substandard performance will continue to be the norm in many agencies and continue to have a negative impact on K9 policing as a whole.

PENNY WISE, POUND FOOLISH
As previously noted, the most limiting factor in failing K9 units is budget. Pre-trained dogs and short-term vendor training became popular when it was sold as a cost-savings method for law enforcement agencies. Agencies anxious to save money easily bought into the concept based on the belief they were receiving the same caliber of teams as they would receive from their agency-led, in-house 12- to 14-week training programs. Following through on this promise is, as it turns out, next to impossible.

A team that has a strong basic training foundation obtained through a full training program will be productive on the street, more tactically sound, and less prone to lawsuits. Do not be sold on the cheapest program simply because it's cheap. Money spent up front results in both financial and time savings, whereas short-term programs result in the need for extensive follow-up training courses at additional cost to complete the full spectrum of training a team needs to be fully productive.

BENEFITS OF VENDOR-BASED TRAINING
While it is important to understand the pitfalls of vendor-based training, it is just as important to understand the benefits. Vendors who provide dogs and training to law enforcement in the United States do have a significant role to play in the industry. They have become and will continue to be the primary source of potential police dogs in North America. In many corners of the country, they have also taken over the role of training dogs and handlers for

law enforcement and providing the maintenance training required to keep the teams up to standard.

Small departments that do not have a large and well-established K9 program will benefit from having access to a well-established and qualified vendor. When you can't get guidance and training assistance from within your agency, access to a vendor with strong training regimens that meet the high standards and certification requirements of police service will be vital to the success of your unit.

The primary and most beneficial role vendors play in the K9 industry is providing well-vetted potential police dogs that are ready for training. Whether you are trying to locate a young, untrained dog for your in-house program or looking for a dog that has some prior sport training, a quality vendor will be able to provide you with a good selection of dogs to choose from.

There is also real value to what vendors can bring to the table in training specialties such as controlled aggression training. Vendors who are reputable and have significant experience can and do provide a critical advantage since they often have the decoy experience to understand and manipulate dogs' behaviors. A decoy, also referred to as a "helper" or "quarry," is a person who is trained to take bites from a dog using various pieces of equipment. This is a vital skill set required for proper K9 bite development and control work. The value of well-trained decoys cannot be understated. They play a significant role in the training of any police dog because they can understand the dog and perform the precise maneuvers needed to support the dog during an engagement. The decoy understands the fundamentals of reading K9 behavior and knows when to put more pressure on the dog and when to reward the dog for specific behaviors.

Vendors also have the benefit of having experience with significant numbers of dogs. Many are also involved in the various K9 sporting events such as IGP and KNPV, which provides them with significant hands-on experience in taking bites and manipulating K9 behavior. This can be a benefit, as long as the vendor also has a vetted background in law enforcement training and can bring in the proper resources to either train your teams or fill in any gaps in their training. Remember: sport training alone is not adequate for law enforcement needs.

Figure 4.5. Vendors provide valuable training relating to apprehension and controlled aggression techniques and can be very skilled in problem solving.

Selecting the Right Vendor

It is critical when researching vendor-run training programs (and, for that matter, training through another law enforcement agency) that significant time and effort be put into researching and evaluating every option. However, researching all your available options can feel like navigating a maze, especially as the number of private, commercial vendors continues to grow significantly in the United States.

Narrow down your options by looking for programs that fulfill more than basic skill sets, and that focus on the dog as a search or tracking tool rather than primarily as a use of force tool. When it comes to bite work, programs should focus on handler control of the dog.

Look, too, for vendors who will provide an absolute minimum of 8 weeks or more of training. Ideally, the best option is to encourage your vendor to provide 12 to 14 weeks of training that includes all aspects of police dog deployment, including both tracking and detection work. By supporting vendors who are willing and able to provide full-length programs, you immediately improve your potential for success, provide a more versatile team for the street, reduce potential liability, and make a positive impact in the industry.

Finally, look for a vendor that understands how to train both dogs and handlers to work as a team in a law enforcement role that requires them to respond to dangerous calls daily and within a legal framework. Training a team involves teaching more than just the basics of dog handling. It must also teach the fundamentals of dog training and how to make ethical and tactically sound

Figure 4.6. Good decoy work is vital to problem solving. In fundamental training, the decoy can make or break a dog. Ideally, every police officer working a dog should have significant work experience as a decoy. Decoys learn canine behavior and how to manipulate that behavior to get the best performance out of the dog.

decisions about applying the dog in law enforcement situations according to the law and department policy.

ASSESSING VENDOR BACKGROUND

Another place to start is to think about who you want to be training your dogs. Think, for instance, about the law enforcement experience the trainers have, if any. While dog training talent can be provided by civilian operators, they typically cannot on their own provide all that is needed to sufficiently prepare a K9 team for street deployments and potential street combat situations. Dog training is one skill set. Law enforcement training is another. When combined, they must work seamlessly together as a coordinated unit with all that comes in both capacities. Vendors without law enforcement background do not have the benefit of street-level police experience to draw on when developing potential law enforcement K9 teams.

There are exceptionally good vendors with excellent training programs that are operated by or employ active or retired police personnel with many years of police K9 experience. They bring law enforcement knowledge and practical street experience to the table, which can provide your teams with scenario-based experiences that will prepare them for the streets and give them a foundation in the principles of legal doctrine.

There are also some particularly good civilian vendors and trainers who have developed, over the years, a good understanding of the law enforcement application of police dogs. In many cases these vendors can also provide robust training programs. But be aware: just because a vendor has a law enforcement background or extensive experience with law enforcement training does not guarantee that they are the best available trainers.

In fact, there are vendors out there who are less than reputable. Some have criminal backgrounds and others simply do not have the skill set and expertise required to do the job. The subsequent fallout has seen K9 officers that are often ill prepared to hit the streets with their dogs when they are "certified" after their training by a private company.

If one of your K9 teams is involved in a bite incident resulting from either a poor handler decision or the handler's inability to control the dog, the lawsuit will most likely not name the vendor who trained your teams, but you, your agency management team, and the handler will most certainly be named.

Due diligence is key when researching private industry training options. Quality vendors will have a strong track record, which can be verified by other law enforcement agencies. It is up to you as a K9 unit manager to screen potential vendors to ensure you select a reputable vendor with solid law enforcement references, a clean criminal background check and, preferably, a strong law enforcement background.

BUYER BEWARE

It is important to note that no state or federal standards or regulations exist in the United States to ensure these vendors meet any form of minimum qualification standard. Basically, anyone can start up a business, advertise as a police dog trainer, and begin selling dogs and training programs to police agencies. It falls, therefore, to the department or agency itself to research these vendors and make sure they offer quality dogs and training.

There are many "trainers" with fancy websites marketing themselves as police dog trainers who have little or no experience in training law enforcement teams and no background in law enforcement. In fact, some have become "certified" police dog trainers by other businesses that have offered "police dog trainer" courses who also have zero experience in law enforcement or in anything other than sport dog training.

The need to execute exhaustive background checks, including numerous references and comparisons with multiple vendors, cannot be understated. Vet your vendors carefully.

A CASE FOR VENDOR BACKGROUND CHECKS

You're researching vendor-based training programs for your K9 unit. The owner and trainer at one police dog vendor states they have seven years' experience in dog training. Cursory research shows that this trainer took a civilian dog training course, graduating with a certificate issued by the business naming him a "Master Dog Trainer." This certificate is given after successfully completing only 10 weeks of training that involved no content related to law enforcement or military K9 training. Upon graduation, this trainer was immediately hired by a police dog training company as their head trainer, even though his only qualification was the 10-week civilian dog training course. That vendor subsequently went out of business within the year. The trainer then went to work for another police K9 vendor where he worked for a little over a year, at which time he opened his own business as a police dog trainer and vendor, which is still in operation.

This vendor has no law enforcement background, minimal K9 experience, and no tactical experience or workable knowledge of K9 case law or courtroom procedures. The fact that he has only seven years' experience — less time than a K9 officer would spend with his first dog — should in and of itself be a concern.

Unfortunately, this is not a major aberration. Virtually anyone can put out a shingle and call themselves a police dog trainer. Without properly looking into backgrounds, checking references, and comparing vendors, you risk founding your K9 program on shaky ground and having K9 teams that are unprepared for the task. This raises officer safety issues as well as potential liability concerns.

Don't let marketing fool you. Be cautious when choosing K9 vendors.

Making a Case for Expanded Basic K9 Training

It truly can't be said too many times: it takes a minimum of 12 to 14 weeks to train a K9 team with a dog that is well selected and meets the high standards of law enforcement.

I began my career when training programs in the United States were 12 weeks minimum. In many areas in both Canada and the United States, they had expanded to 14 weeks by the time I ended my career as a K9 officer. Over the last few decades, trends have taken us from 12- to 14-week training programs to accepting — and sometimes expecting — 4- to 8-week programs. In some cases, programs that provide as little as 10-day to 3-week schools are offered. These programs are dangerously inadequate and should be avoided at all costs. Ostensibly, cost savings is the significant driver of this trend, but in the end, short-term programs are not truly cost effective, nor do they produce efficient and well-trained teams.

Consider a comparison: Would you put your children through school to grade 4, then turn them loose in the world and expect them to be successful in a career? In many respects, this is exactly what we are doing when we are sending our K9 teams to a 4-week training school.

What's more, placing the officer through a full training program realizes long-term savings and produces teams that are superior on the street to those that have only received a basic handler's program. A successful team will encounter more armed suspects and be at higher risk simply because of its success rate. The sheer level of high-risk deployments these officers face emphasizes the need for more complete training programs. A full training program also allows the officer to learn legal frameworks and tactical training crucial to a K9 team.

Ideally, trends will change in the future, and in-house agency training and private vendor-based training programs alike will pursue more comprehensive schools that provide handlers with the 12 to 14 weeks of foundational training needed to put out professional teams. A minimum training standard that provides a more substantial skill set for handlers will have a significant positive impact on the quality of K9 law enforcement in the United States. Further, it will enhance officer safety and tactical abilities, while significantly reducing liability and personal risk.

5

K9 Unit Culture and Training Trends

Police agency administrators must pay attention to the culture of their K9 unit to ensure it develops in a healthy and productive way. Law enforcement police dog programs tend to employ handlers with alpha-type personalities. This can lead to a competitive atmosphere, cultivate an "us versus them" attitude, and sometimes develop into a cynical mentality when it comes to dealing with suspects. These types of attitudes and mentalities can contribute to poor deployment decisions.

As a supervisor, you must be cognizant of your unit's culture to ensure your teams do not lose touch with their primary mission: using their skill set to search for and locate suspects to bring them before the courts while maintaining the highest standards of professionalism and ethics. There will always be times when a dog is required to physically apprehend suspects. A dog is the ultimate "distraction device" when dealing with potentially dangerous subjects and is an effective equalizer when the person being apprehended is significantly violent. However, any decision to use the dog for this purpose needs to be judicious, considering all the circumstances of any given situation. A bad deployment is never inconsequential and has potentially far-reaching effects.

Bite Culture, Litigation, and Conflict

LAWSON V. GATES

History has proven this in the past. In June of 1991, *Lawson v. Gates*[22] was filed against the LAPD by the American Civil Liberties Union of Southern California, the NAACP Legal Defense and Education Fund, and two private law firms. The plaintiffs demanded the LAPD's 17-dog K9 unit be shut down until "the dog handlers and dogs are adequately selected, trained, supervised and disciplined."[23] In other words, the culture within the K9 program of the department had been identified as a contributing factor in unnecessary injury to numerous subjects and had to change.

There was significant evidence of improper use of police dogs in numerous agencies in Southern California at the time. However, the LAPD ended up in the spotlight and became the focus of the lawsuit. At the forefront of the allegations were accusations of misuse of police dogs especially when the suspects were Black or Hispanic.

In the time leading up to the lawsuit, the deployment of dogs had become questionable. There was a clique of officers within the K9 program that promoted an aggressive mindset. Bite ratios were significant. In some areas, 45 percent of searches by police dogs resulted in dog bites — a rate so high that, when a dog was used on a call, it was expected that the deployment would result in a bite. This "bite culture" was embedded within the unit and flourished there. It was this mindset, which underlay the deployment decisions and actions of the K9 officers, that ultimately resulted in *Lawson v. Gates*.

Faced with a significant lawsuit, the LAPD chose to make significant changes: it decided to deal with the bite culture within the unit and adapt. Under the recommendations provided by K9 unit trainer Sgt. Donn Yarnall, a settlement was agreed upon. The settlement included a monetary payment to 54 plaintiffs along with injunctive relief through revision of LAPD policies. It should be noted that while the settlement was in the form of a private agreement, it included a court enforcement provision.

---

22 *Lawson vs. Gates*, 1991 CA Super. Ct. County of Los Angeles, BC031232.
23 *Lawson*, 1991 CA Super. Ct. at §106C.

Significant changes were made to how and under what circumstances LAPD K9 teams could deploy. Policies were put in place to change the culture within the unit and provide more supervisory oversight on deployments. Before a dog deployment, on-scene supervisory approval and a K9 sergeant's approval were required. Initially, deployments were only permitted on crimes against persons and violent felonies. Deployment requirements have since changed to allow searches for felony suspects and for misdemeanor suspects who are reasonably believed to be armed.

The settlement also required the agency to change from its apprehension policy of "bite-and-hold" (also called "find-and-bite" and "handler control") to one of "guard-and-bark" (also called "find-and-bark"). E-collars were mandated for all deployments and progressive warning announcements were required prior to the deployment of the dogs. At the time, the agency began requiring quarterly and annual reports from the K9 unit, including the number of searches conducted broken down by division, number of suspects located, bite ratio reports, and hospitalization records that would be scrutinized by the American Civil Liberties Union. This oversight by the ACLU ended in 2000.

The culture within the unit at the time of the lawsuit was such that half of the K9 officers were unwilling to work within the guidelines of the new mandate and subsequently chose to leave the unit. It was also determined there were service dogs that could not be retrained and subsequently had to be replaced. New officers and dogs were brought into the unit. Under the new mandate and new ideas regarding training and deployments, the agency earned a much more positive reputation.

Since that time, the LAPD K9 unit has become one of the more professional units in the United States and is known for its high standards. The agency maintains strong training regimens assuring high performance supported by strong moral and ethical standards in an admittedly hostile environment.

CONFLICT WITHIN THE UNIT: THE PHOENIX EXPERIENCE

In 2003, the Phoenix, Arizona, police department also experienced a significant breakdown in its patrol dog program. The unit consisted of two squads, each managed by a different trainer. Philosophical differences between the trainers created inconsistencies in training and deployments as well as two significantly different cultures in the unit. The two squads had almost diametrically opposing viewpoints on training and deployments, creating friction within the organization. The conflict got to the point where the program had become untenable, and consideration was given to disbanding the K9 program altogether.

As a result of these issues, the chief elected to reorganize the unit by assigning a lieutenant and sergeant to oversee and redevelop it from the ground up. I was asked to take on the task of working with the unit to develop and implement a new training program. The unit obtained new dogs and, over a period of 13 weeks, we introduced new elements into the unit's training regimen, including the tracking profile, which allowed them to be more diversified in their methods of deployment. By bringing the teams under a common command with a common training routine, they began to work together with common goals, resulting in a much more productive unit. This did not come, however, without some internal conflict. While phasing in the new training, there was resistance by some officers that ultimately resulted in some personnel changes, similar in nature to what LAPD experienced.

These examples show how attitudes and a set culture within a program can create significant problems to the point of making it ineffective. Negative attitudes, attitudes that are counterproductive, and attitudes that do not meet the highest professional and ethical standards, when not dealt with, will lead to a K9 unit culture that becomes self-destructive.

Trainer Philosophies and Agency Expectations

One benefit of having training managed by an in-house trainer is that you have more control over the ethical principles of your K9 teams. They are in an environment that is compatible with the vision and core values of your department and not affected as strongly by outside influence. You can shape your handlers' mindset and set expectations and ethical standards pertaining to the training and deployment of your officers. This enables you to better manage how they ultimately apply their skill set on the street.

Even so, regardless of in-house training, differences can occur within the unit. In large agencies where there are multiple trainers — as in the example of the Phoenix police dog program — there may be philosophical differences between trainers that create conflict. There may also be training issues that become obvious to the handlers. When the trainer fails to deal with the issues or is reluctant to go outside the agency to look for assistance from a fellow trainer, fractures can occur that result in conflict.

It is important to be aware of potential issues and to understand that differences of opinion in training routines can be diverse, whether your training is done in-house or by an outside vendor. It is essential that K9 supervisors be ready to mitigate any problems as they begin to gestate and before they damage the cohesiveness of a unit. A cohesive unit culture based on high ethical and moral standards and expectations will be both highly productive and reduce liability.

Training provided by a vendor can significantly influence the culture of the K9 team(s) within your department. With a well-selected vendor, this influence can have a strong positive impact that supports camaraderie within your unit or training group and gives your teams the strong ethical standards and controlled training techniques they will need to deploy safely on the streets.

Policy differs from place to place and agency to agency. One jurisdiction's standards may be significantly different or nonexistent in another. In particular, great care needs to be taken when it comes to deployment philosophies that could potentially result in a physical apprehension by a dog, especially in states that are not covered by qualified immunity. Training must emphasize a high degree of discretion when it comes to deployment decisions and must reflect the requirements and standards of your particular location and department.

Most knowledgeable vendors understand this and will work with your agency to maintain the integrity of your standards and culture; however, not all vendors have this same philosophy. As with any free market industry, different providers offer different perspectives. Just because a vendor professionally trains dogs does not mean that their training philosophy aligns with the best interests of you and your agency. It is prudent to research numerous vendors to ensure the philosophies they impart and promote to your K9 handlers are in line with the core values of your department and service dog program (see Chapter 4).

RECENT DEVELOPMENTS IN TRAINING PROVIDERS

In recent years, a younger generation of vendors has begun to break into the industry. Many of these vendors are high-speed trainers who pique the interest of the newer generation of handlers through strong marketing programs and a strong presence on social media platforms. Some focus on hardcore dogs and the aggressive aspects of being a K9 handler. New, young handlers tend to be attracted to this aspect of training because it is intense and, to put it simply, more fun. However, some of these vendors lack the foresight to recognize that the priority function of a police dog in the case of patrol deployments is to search for and locate suspects. They instead emphasize the dog as a use of force tool. This can set the wrong tone for your teams and may not align with the core values of your agency.

There has also been a recent increase in private vendors operated by military veterans who promote tactics based on their experiences overseas. Agencies buy into the programs because the instructors have strong CVs based on their overseas deployments in a theatre of war. Most of these veterans have excellent backgrounds and extensive experience in K9 deployments with a strong emphasis on explosives detection training. Dog handlers are drawn to the programs provided by these veterans due to the obvious skill set they have to offer.

While retired military veterans can indeed provide excellent training and invaluable experience, it is prudent to understand that tactics and deployment methods employed in military operations are not in step with methods of deployment for civilian law enforcement. Indeed, there is a significant difference between the two. Many military-based trainers understand this and adjust, providing quality training regimens to law enforcement. Others, however, promote training and tactics that lean more towards military operations, which can conflict greatly with accepted practice for civilian K9 operations.

When researching vendors or training instructors with military backgrounds, ensure they are grounded and well versed in civilian operations and policy and that the training offered is consistent with both your own agency training requirements and industry norms.

It is important when discussing your agency needs with any potential vendor that you make it clear what your ethical expectations are. The training philosophies of the vendor you choose must fall within your agency's vision and ethical standards. While there is nothing wrong with intense training — in fact, such training is recommended — it is always important to remember that the trainer you choose will have a strong influence on the culture within your unit. A training regimen and philosophy that strongly promotes bite work over the primary purpose of a police dog — that of using its olfactory abilities — puts your unit at risk of developing a bite culture and should be avoided.

Figure 5.1. Classes that promote intense situations and training challenges are encouraged but should not be the main focus of your training regimen. Fundamentals and balanced training routines in all profiles, with a focus on search regimens, strong tactics, and control work will produce top working teams.

The Influence and Impact of Social Media

TRAINING TRENDS

Social media influence has both positive and negative ramifications. Connections to handlers worldwide can provide distinct benefits. Connections can be made that result in long-term sharing of new training techniques, ideas, and events. At the same time, social media is, in many ways, "the great equalizer" — and not always in good ways. It can become a platform for virtually anyone to have influence on the industry, whether they are qualified or not. Often, information uncritically shared and consumed has the potential to be damaging.

Consider the example of mindsets around the application of dogs in law enforcement contexts. While most handlers understand case law requirements regarding the deployment of a dog in situations that could result in a bite, many deploy dogs in less-than-tenable circumstances. Case law is only a part of the equation. Police dog handlers must be absolute experts in case law, local requirements, and department policy and should always operate under the more restrictive of these.

However, across the United States, we have recently seen distinct shifts in handler mindsets around the application of police dogs. Often, these shifts are connected to social media posts by well-meaning vendors and influencers. Handlers will often justify their deployments with information provided by outside trainers who post their ideas online but are not connected with a particular department. They may have unique perspectives on how case law will back up certain types of deployments. These interpretations, however, often fail to recognize or acknowledge the importance of local requirements and policy. They also tend not to account for the way in which societal perceptions in current times can profoundly affect what is considered acceptable. Indeed, just because a deployment can be justified under case law does not mean that it is morally and ethically correct under any given circumstances.

Many of these outside opinions come from trainers on social media who have no significant background in law enforcement. They may be proliferated by other trainers or handlers who have been unduly influenced. Counsel your officers to be critical consumers of K9-related social media and to always measure what they hear on social media against their knowledge of case law, as well as local and departmental policies and requirements.

As an example, some trainers work with the philosophy that there is no reason to teach a dog to release a bite on a live deployment. They employ a tool referred to as a "bite breaker" or "break stick": a device inserted into a dog's mouth in order to force the dog to release its bite on a suspect. This flies in the face of sound tactical advice and decades of training police to verbally recall their dogs off suspects. When used as the go-to strategy, break sticks are essentially meant to overcome a lack of training and, in some cases, to promote the philosophy of those who are incapable of training to the highest standards of control and bite management.

Common sense dictates that it is not always tactically sound to go hands-on to force a dog off a bite. For example, some deployments involve tight quarters — crawl spaces under mobile homes, for example — that are extremely dangerous for an officer to enter. If a dog deployed in such a situation contacts and bites a suspect, the officer must be able to verbally recall their dog and have the suspect come out to where officers can take him into custody. Any dog that is unable to perform in this manner should not be working the street until retrained and proven to be responsive to the handler's direction without the need for hands-on compliance.

None of this is to say that handlers should not carry a break stick as part of their tool kit as a backup should the dog fail to comply with a command to release a bite. In fact, it is far better to have the handler trained in its use than not. If the handler does have a break stick as a backup tool, however, they should be trained to use it properly. This means understanding that the break stick is not a replacement for good training and a responsive dog. It is vital that every dog respond to the handler when commanded to release a suspect.

BITE CULTURE AND HANDLER CONTROL ON SOCIAL MEDIA

One issue at the center of *Kerr v. City of West Palm Beach*[24] (discussed in Chapter 3) was the bite culture that had become predominant within the K9 unit. The attitudes within the unit were obvious to the jury, and in referring to the circumstances of the case, the jury found that both the chief and the city were aware of but did nothing to prevent the rise of bite culture within the unit. It was found, in fact, that they "encouraged an atmosphere of lawlessness on the part of the Defendant Officers."[25] In response, the decision included the expectation that handlers be able to recall

---

24 *Kerr v. City of West Palm Beach*, 875 F. 2d 1546 (11th Cir. 1989).
25 *Kerr*, 875 F. 2d at 1558.

Figure 5.2. A breaker bar, also known as a bite breaker, can be a valuable asset for exigent circumstances on live deployments where a dog refuses to release a bite on a suspect. This Sirius K9 breaker bar has a design similar to a pocket knife, making it easy for handlers to carry and deploy. It should always be considered a backup tool when needed and not the primary method of bite release. Every street level police dog should always have a reliable verbal recall.

their dog from an apprehension prior to a bite and call the dog off a bite on a suspect from a distance.

As *Kerr v. City of West Palm Beach* shows, bite culture can become a big problem. It can create liability, reduce officer safety, and cause increasing numbers of lawsuits. Particularly when filmed, these incidents spread rapidly on social media platforms and affect the public perception of how police dogs are used.

We frequently see videos on social media where the dog is sent in on a suspect when other means of taking them into custody are available. Other frequent media postings include videos of police dogs biting suspects for extended periods of time while the handler struggles to force the dog to release the bite on a suspect who is clearly under the control of the officer and often handcuffed. In these cases, there is obviously no control on the dog. Struggles such as these, often involving a choke-off technique that further exacerbates the issue, tend to cause significant injury beyond what would have been caused by the initial bite.

Many comments from handlers on social media imply that they have no issue with such bites or injury to the suspect. These comments also imply a lack of understanding on the part of the handlers of the negative impact those posts can have on public opinion.

It is unsurprising that officers feel the need to defend their profession, especially given the stress involved in K9 deployment and the fact that K9 officers are deployed on more dangerous calls annually than any other unit. In some cases, this also involves dark humor, which can appear particularly unempathetic. For some, this can be a way to release the stress of the job. However, to the public, it is unprofessional and unacceptable. It is a culture we as an industry do not need and should avoid at all costs. Officers need to be reminded that these types of comments are detrimental in any public forum. They should be keenly aware of what they say on social media and understand that any comment or post an officer makes on a social media platform can leave them and their department open to scrutiny. In particular, they should never post individual situations that involve bites. Anyone who has access to their posts on social media can copy the post and the comments attached to it to use against the officer in later litigation.

Addressing Public Perception

THE APPEARANCE OF EVIL

There is a saying that the appearance of evil is often worse than the evil itself — a phrase that has its beginnings in the Bible: "Abstain from all appearance of evil."[26] Unfortunately, we live in times of extreme political correctness in which small-interest groups and (often left-wing) organizations advocate for defunding police departments. Periodically, incidents occur that ultimately result in segments of society vilifying law enforcement despite the fact that these incidents are an aberration to the hundreds of thousands of calls handled with courage and integrity by professional law enforcement officers around the globe. In other words, the "evil" seen by the public is very far from an accurate representation of police work.

Still, there is always someone who believes that any action being taken by the police is wrong. Society in the United States and Canada is, at the moment, hypersensitive to police actions. Right or wrong, this is the reality in today's world of policing.

Every professional and ethical officer, regardless of position, understands that from the time they submit their application to become a law enforcement officer, their lives are scrutinized for traits of integrity. From lie detector tests given during the application process to the ongoing scrutiny of supervisors as to how every case is dealt with, officers are continually monitored for their honesty and work ethic. They are held to the oath they swore: to uphold the law without fear or favor. Due to the nature of their work, K9 officers are susceptible to higher scrutiny than most.

Historically, society has trusted police officers because, quite simply, it knew them to be dependable and of high integrity. Those of us in the job know that dependability and high integrity are still the heart of policing. Moral standards are central to the job and are the guiding principles according to which the vast majority of officers operate.

Those who choose to defy law and order are, unlike K9 and other law enforcement officers, not bound by legal constraints or moral standards. The fact is: A large number of the criminal

---

26 1 Thessalonians 5:22 KJV.

elements we deal with are dangerous and only understand violence. Dangerous situations are part of policing. But regardless of who they are dealing with, police are bound by the law. Their moral standards are such that they approach every situation cautiously, with the desire to help those in need, even those who would do them harm. They will do whatever it takes to deal with any situation they face with courage and integrity in order to bring about a successful conclusion in a manner that preserves life and prevents harm wherever possible.

There are those who fail over time — those who lose integrity. These few do incredible damage to the trust that society has in those who protect them; consequently, a broad brush is often used to paint all officers the same as those who have breached that trust. This, however, is not only unfair to those officers — the majority — who uphold the highest moral standards, but it makes officers hyperaware of the perceptions of others: always concerned that someone might misconstrue their actions.

Many of those misconstruals are made by those who are critical of law enforcement without caring to understand the true nature of police work. Some of these people dedicate no small effort to vilifying police, basing their arguments on broad generalizations, increasing the amount of misinformation about law enforcement, and making it more and more difficult to have fact-based conversations. This creates an atmosphere of increased tensions between law enforcement and the public. Working in environments in which officer-community trust has been destabilized puts law enforcement in a very precarious position and makes it more difficult for officers to do their jobs. Overcoming this tension requires extraordinary effort and risks becoming, quite literally, a deadly spiral.

MARKETING YOUR UNIT
Police dog programs are ripe for the picking when it comes to use of force and excessive force complaints, justified or not. Lawsuits on dog bites are commonplace and often make headlines, especially if the bite on a suspect is particularly severe or the person bitten was determined to be an innocent bystander. News articles and social media releases about the deployment of police dogs that result in bad bites on suspects overplay the few cases that are an

aberration to normal operations. Unfortunately, the K9 industry has inadvertently exacerbated the problem through the marketing of items such as T-shirts and challenge coins with images that play up, rather than down, the narratives that critics cling on to.

To be clear, there is absolutely nothing wrong with having team T-shirts or challenge coins created for your unit. There are thousands of designs that present a professional appearance and promote the integrity of what K9 teams do. A quick Google search using the keywords *police k9 t-shirt designs* will bring up many well-designed shirts with artwork and phrases that any agency would be proud of. The same holds true when searching various challenge coin manufacturers. The problem is with the messaging of the designs on both the coins and shirts that have become popular among officers, which promote an aggressive, and in some cases sinister, message. While understandably acceptable to those who wear them, the connotations involved are highly offensive to those who do not understand the underlying dark humor that is common to those who put their lives on the line every day. Those who demand political correctness take advantage of the negative impressions of such designs to vilify K9 law enforcement. A common example popular with law enforcement is the "punisher skull," which is prominent on many police T-shirts and coins.

Figure 5.3. T-shirt and coin designs depicting photos and characterizations of aggressive dogs and slogans are popular with K9 officers; however, they send the wrong message to the public and can result in negative media and uninformed stereotyping. Shirts and coins with slogans such as these are irresponsible and damaging to the industry given today's anti-police rhetoric.

Figure 5.4. Principles of vigilance, courage, loyalty, respect, and excellence in service combined with artwork that promotes those principles send a message that promotes professionalism and serve to foster confidence and trust.

In October of 2020, a large city newspaper in Canada published a story that spoke specifically to this issue. The author included a picture of a city police department challenge coin. The coin was manufactured for the department firearms training team. It depicted a front-facing skull with a bullet hole in the forehead along with the name of the agency, three weapons, and the words *Saving Lives* inscribed on it. The coin was brought to the attention of city council, who deemed the coin unacceptable, and the police chief subsequently banned distribution of the coin. The local newspaper jumped on the story with the headline "Unbelievably Inappropriate, Police Prohibit Distribution of Offensive Coin."[27] Shortly af-

---

27 Sammy Hudes, "'Unbelievably Inappropriate': Calgary Police Prohibit Distribution of 'Offensive' Coin," *Calgary Herald*, October 16, 2020, https://calgaryherald.com/news/local-news/unbelievably-inappropriate-calgary-police-prohibit-distribution-of-offensive-coin.

ter, the story appeared in a national news publication, *The Georgia Straight*, with the title "Challenge Coins Reveal Disturbing Side of Policing."[28] At the time of this writing, a photo of this coin and others is prominently displayed on the blog of an organization that promotes defunding the police.[29]

While not a K9-specific coin, it is a current and excellent example of how just one design on a coin can have significant and far-reaching negative influence on public perception, providing ammunition for anti-police segments of the population that thrive on vilifying law enforcement.

When designing T-shirts or challenge coins, consider ways to promote your unit in a positive manner. Find creative ways to express the professionalism and integrity of your unit without providing ammunition to those who will push negative narratives about policing.

Shiny Object Syndrome

There is a phenomenon in the K9 world that I refer to as "shiny object syndrome." It comes in multiple forms and is propagated through slick marketing and the desire of handlers to have the best and newest in training and equipment, whether they need it or not. The problem is often exacerbated by the competitive alpha-personality-based culture that seems prevalent in some police dog training circles.

GEAR

Let's start with "trendy" gear. When certain equipment is requested, supervisors need to be able to distinguish between that which is necessary and that which is just "shiny." This is especially true considering that restricted budgets for K9 programs are, sadly, the norm for many agencies, despite the fact that proper equipment to do the job is required for any K9 team to function safely and efficiently. As a supervisor, you'll need to ask: Will this equipment assist my officers in doing the job in a safer manner? Is the

---

28 Dana Larsen, "Dana Larsen: Challenge Coins Reveal Disturbing Side of Policing," *The Georgia Straight,* October 26, 2020, https://www.straight.com/news/dana-larsen-challenge-coins-reveal-disturbing-side-of-policing.
29 Project Calgary. n.d. "Does the Calgary Police Service Think Calgarians Are the Enemy?" Accessed May 6, 2021. https://www.projectcalgary.org/d2f_cps_coins

piece of equipment being purchased because it is needed in order for the team to do its job, or is it being purchased because, for lack of a better description, it looks "Gucci" on the dog or performs a function for a unique incident the team may encounter once or twice in the lifetime of a career? Would the money be better spent on more basic gear that provides a daily function and allows for improved performance?

Take the example of a harness. You have two options:
1. A standard, leather tracking harness with quick-attach clips that can be put on the dog in a few seconds and allows the dog plenty of freedom to move
2. A camouflage vest with multiple zippers and patches sewn on it that is specifically designed for rappelling out of helicopters and is three times the cost but looks three times as "cool" at five times the cost

On a day-to-day basis, the two harnesses perform the same function, and will be going on and off the dog multiple times a day (the normal routine for most tracking teams). Which harness is the more practical use of your limited budget, especially if you never rappel with your teams?

There are times when high-end equipment is called for, depending on the individual mission, and should be acquired. However, it is important to understand the true needs of your teams. Take into consideration how often the gear being purchased will actually be used and if the equipment is necessary to perform the mission. Balance that off with budget priorities.

TRAINING

Shiny object syndrome also has an impact on training. I have taught at training events where handlers attend who have every fancy piece of equipment available and an impressive list of training under their belts. No expense has been spared on the dog or the handler, yet the handler lacks some fundamental K9 handling skills and knowledge. Not only do they not understand the proper use of some of their equipment, but there are severe deficiencies in the training of the dog and handler when it comes to fundamental training or deployments.

The "shiny object" draw to intense training programs is understandable; however, it is necessary to consider what is more important. How many times are your dogs required to search a building for a burglary suspect, track from an armed robbery, or pursue the driver of a dumped stolen vehicle? These are all scenarios dog handlers deal with on a daily basis. These deployments require strong fundamentals and good control of their dogs with the ability to recall the dog from a bite or prior to a bite if needed. This is where the training priority needs to be.

How many times are your teams engaged in intense gun battles or situations where the dog is required to stay on the bite for an extended confrontation with a suspect? Generally speaking, with limited exceptions, *police dogs bite suspects in less than 7.5 percent of their deployments,* and in most cases these engagements last only a moment before the dog is recalled and the suspect is taken into custody. Gun battles, while more frequent for K9 officers than most patrol officers, occur much less frequently than bites.

If this is the reality, then why is there so much focus by so many trainers on the bite and on high-end tactical training, when the fundamentals are what is needed?

The draw to so many tactical schools that include intense combat training without the appropriate balance of strong fundamentals will create control issues for your teams and increase liability. They will not provide the tactical advantages they should unless the fundamental training and maintenance of the dog are up to an appropriate standard. By keeping priorities in perspective and balancing the training accordingly, your success rates will be better and the risks lower.

LOSING SIGHT OF THE BASICS

I've witnessed many examples of shiny object syndrome at play in handlers' training. One handler who attended one of my training events, for example, had been to numerous tactical programs, was well kitted, and was working a 5-year-old German Shepherd that was a difficult dog. When attending my exercise, the officer had three different types of collars on his dog, including an e-collar, flat collar, and pinch collar. According to the handler, each had a specific purpose and were, in his opinion, needed to manage the dog.

The exercise I was teaching involved a scent problem in a building search for a suspect in which the handler set up at the entrance to the building and called out standard verbal challenges into the building prior to releasing the dog. Once released, the dog was to locate and bracket the odor of a hidden decoy, staying focused at the strongest source of odor, indicating where the decoy might be. If the dog performed well, stayed on the odor, and barked for an adequate amount of time, the decoy would step out from his place of concealment and reward the dog with a bite. This is a simple and standard exercise that any patrol dog team should be able to perform easily.

Upon approaching the building and setting up in a ready position to start the search, this particular handler's dog was immediately out of control, barking and trying to enter the building. It even spun in a circle periodically while the handler tried to call out his verbal challenges. Training had to be walked back to basic steps in attempts to make the dog understand that he was not going to be able to move forward into the building until he was down and quiet. While time consuming, we managed to get one instance where the dog was quiet during the verbal warning, at which point the dog was released.

When sent to search, the dog entered the building, eventually showing good indications at the source of the odor. However, rather than staying and barking at the source of the odor, the dog did everything possible to gain access to the decoy to initiate a bite. After only a few minutes, the dog became frustrated and left the odor source to look elsewhere for an easier mark. Again, action had to be taken to show the handler the proper steps to develop the desired responsive behavior in the dog.

At the completion of the exercise, I observed the dog as it bit the decoy in the final phase of the exercise. The dog hit hard with a deep bite but would not release the bite when directed. The handler attempted to correct the dog using the e-collar, increasing the power intensity as the dog continued to fight through the pain and bear down harder on the decoy. Only after hooking up to the pinch collar and lifting the dog off while continuing to nick the dog with the e-collar was the dog finally removed from the decoy.

I interviewed the officer after the exercise to learn more about the background of his training and his dog. His department had a strong budget, providing him with every conceivable piece of equipment a handler could have. They had also sent him to some very well-reputed schools around the country that were known for "high-speed" training, including deployment with SWAT, bite development schools, tactical schools, programs that included rappelling, and other more hardcore programs. The officer believed the training he attended was needed in order to give him the best skill set for street operations. In his opinion, he had a tough dog that was ready to deal with any confrontation. He had worked the streets with this dog for more than three years and, while frustrated with the ongoing control issues, had never reached out to have them addressed.

Every part of the exercise described in the story above involved what should be basic routines. When a dog approaches a building and is placed in a position to prepare for entry into the building, the dog should be down and quiet while the handler calls out warnings into the building. The dog needs to be quiet so the handler can hear any response that may come from the building being searched. The person on the premises could be the owner, a worker, or have a legitimate reason to be there. If the dog is barking, it could drown out a response from an innocent bystander. The only time the dog should bark at this point is if directed to do so by the handler.

The dog should do a systematic search until it finds the source of human odor, at which time he is to stay at the strongest source of that odor and bark until otherwise directed by the handler. If the dog is rewarded with a bite on the decoy, there should be no issue of recalling the dog off the bite back to the handler, who, if doing proper tactical training should remain behind cover. If the officer is intending to remove the dog physically, they should do a proper approach with a backup team. In short, the team above *looked* sharp and was well equipped, but after three years of road service, they could not perform a foundational and common deployment. The priorities for this team were not where they should have been.

Shortly before writing this book, I encountered an officer who fit a similar profile to the one described in "Losing Sight of the Basics." He came to me and asked me if I would spend some time with him to get his dog to release his ball. He had always had difficulty using a ball as a reward to work and interact with the dog as the dog was extremely possessive. He had attended courses teaching him to rappel down the side of a building with his dog. His dog would nearly go through a wall to take down a suspect. The dog would engage under heavy gunfire and stay in the fight to extreme levels. He had every piece of equipment imaginable and had been to many vendor-provided "tactical" schools, yet he was unable to simply have his dog relinquish his ball when directed to do so. It soon became apparent there were a number of other, related issues as well, including the dog's refusal to release a bite and its complete inability to perform a productive search. The dog was out of control and almost completely unproductive on the street.

While I have selected specific instances of handlers I recall, these instances are not anomalous. Similar scenarios play out at least a few times if not more at many training events. They are testaments to the lack of understanding by handlers and their supervisors of what the priorities should be when it comes to police dog training. It is also a failure on the part of the trainers who are responsible for these teams.

FOCUS ON THE FUNDAMENTALS

Handlers love to attend what I've referred to as high-speed training events because they are challenging, fun, and satisfy what seems to be that innate alpha-drive common to almost every handler in the industry. Fixing bite issues, developing control on the dog, and being able to recall the dog from a distance after engaging a suspect are activities that don't have the same intrigue and excitement as kicking in doors, taking down aggressive suspects in a tear gas environment, or fast roping with your dog out of a helicopter.

There is, of course, nothing wrong with learning well-developed tactics and going to more high-end training events. However, the focus should be on honing the day-to-day skills before advancing to more high-end routines. Such routines should wait until the fundamentals are strong and the teams' workability on the street is proven. Fundamentals are what truly make a team more tactically sound and better at their jobs. While they don't have that "shiny object" appeal to handlers, a dog that can be maneuvered into place quietly and deployed efficiently in a controlled manner should always be the ultimate goal. This is always where your training priority should be.

Strong fundamentals and solid control on your dogs will reduce your liability risk and lower the level of stress your handlers are under. Moreover, a team that performs well because of solid foundational training will also excel should they choose to advance into more intense training routines; thus, a strong foundation makes the advanced tactical training that much better.

THE IMPORTANCE OF CONSISTENT TRAINING

There is more than one way to train a dog. However, there are a lot of wrong ways to train a dog. Every trainer who has any credibility understands this. One trainer may have an entirely different solution for a training problem than another, but each may have the same capability to resolve a problem or train a skill set successfully.

Regardless of training method, the key to success is always consistency in training routines. What makes a trainer outstanding is the ability to understand fundamental canine behavioral and training issues and to be able to reliably produce good results with their training regimen.

Consistency is also important when it comes to finding training routines that fit with the needs of law enforcement and with your agency's culture and expectations.

Young K9 handlers are often enthusiastic and looking for the next best thing when it comes to training techniques or equipment in an effort to become better at their jobs. It is always important for both trainers and handlers to stay open-minded to new ideas as we continue to learn more about canine behavior. The study of canine behavior and exploring new ideas in tactics is an ongoing process. Due diligence must be practiced, however, to separate out techniques that are beneficial for the purposes of law enforcement and those ideas that may in fact be detrimental or even harmful. It seems common for younger officers to get caught up in trends being promoted by companies that cater to law enforcement, without recognizing that the training school or equipment being marketed may not fit with their normal training regimen and could be detrimental to their performance and safety.

I have seen similar issues with officers who choose to attend sport dog clubs and become more dependent on sport- or military-experienced trainers than their mandated agency trainers. There can be significant benefits to the experience a sport club decoy can provide, or even the knowledge that can be learned from an IGP, KNPV, or military-experienced trainer (see Chapter 4), but these training techniques and philosophies can sometimes conflict with civilian law enforcement training, resulting in confusion for the dog and potentially detrimental street performance.

Any training provided by outside organizations should be evaluated and considered by the program administrator or trainer before participation. It would be wise to have policy in place to ensure that any outside training of significance is authorized by the department.

6

Apprehension Methods: Bark or Bite?

Police dog training methods used by departments in Canada and the United States are progressive and diversified, borrowing heavily from European methods that have been used for many decades. Until the 1980s, law enforcement employed bite-and-hold methods of apprehending suspects who were violent, resisting arrest, or actively fleeing crime scenes. This method involved sending the dog to physically apprehend and hold a suspect until taken into custody.

As a result of numerous dog bite lawsuits against departments in Southern California, agencies began to look for other, less intrusive options for safely apprehending suspects. The LAPD pioneered the process and looked to Europe for a solution. They ultimately adopted a method rooted in the dog sport of Schutzhund (now IGP; see Chapter 4) called "guard-and-bark." Soon afterward, other agencies also began exploring this same deployment philosophy.

Guard-and-bark routines were originally employed by border patrol guards in Europe as a method of protecting their working dogs. Before the implementation of these routines, the dogs worked off-lead, far out in front of their handlers, searching for smugglers and other criminal elements who were illegally crossing the borders. When the dogs located a suspect, they would bite and hold the suspect until officers arrived and took them into custody.

Over time, the criminal element began to defeat the dogs by "feeding" them an arm wrapped in a thick jacket or similar padding. Once the dog took hold, the suspect would stab the dog to death and escape. To combat this problem and protect their dogs, authorities introduced a brilliant solution. In the new training routine, the dog harassed the suspect while staying out of harm's way by barking at the suspect from a distance just out of arms' reach. The barking would identify the location to the handler and officers would quickly move in to take the suspect into custody. Under these circumstances, this was an ideal method of apprehension. It was successfully used to combat a specific threat and its application significantly reduced the unnecessary loss of good service dogs.

Guard-and-bark and bite-and-hold are the most common terms for these apprehension styles that you will come across in the law enforcement K9 world in the United States. Because of the prevalence of this terminology, I use these terms throughout the chapter. It should be noted, however, that these two methods of K9 deployment are more accurately described as "find-and-bark" and "find-and-bite."

Guard-and-Bark versus Bite-and-Hold: The American Saga

The LAPD embraced this guard-and-bark method of training and deployment. Vendors also adopted it, marketing guard-and-bark routines to North American law enforcement agencies. Vendors sold this training method as a way of potentially reducing the number of bites that occur during criminal arrests, suggesting it would reduce liability concerns.

As the guard-and-bark concept grew in North America and was promoted by dog vendors, it began to fracture what had previously been good relationships between agencies with different training philosophies. Those agencies that adopted guard-and-bark deployments for their operations were often in conflict with those that retained bite-and-hold training. The traditional bite-and-hold apprehensions began to be questioned in court cases, which deepened the rifts developing between agencies.

During this time, the term *guard-and-bark* went through various name revisions, including "find-and-bark," "bark-and-hold," "circle-and-bark," and "harass-and-delay." For a period of time, the term *reasonable force* was popular — a term that implied that bite-and-hold apprehension methods were inherently unreasonable force. In response to the use of the term *reasonable force*, bite-and-hold handlers began using the term *handler control* to describe their own approach. This term was meant to emphasize that bite-and-hold dogs were under the direct command of the handler and would only bite when directed to do so by the handler. Because bite-and-hold dogs would bite by default when encountering the suspect on a search, the argument was that these dogs were not deployed unless the situation justified a dog bite. The term *handler control* was also meant to point out that guard-and-bark dogs would, at this point in time, frequently fail, biting suspects when doing so was unwarranted. Indeed, the only academic study to date that directly compares guard-and-bark to bite-and-hold dogs found that "it is clear that 'bark and hold' dogs will produce much higher bite ratios than 'bite and hold'...This is contrary to the findings of the Department of Justice and has serious implications for the future."[30]

I have spoken to German, Canadian, Norwegian, English, and American trainers and handlers who are or have been under mandates to train in the guard-and-bark style but will admit in trusted company that this training philosophy has a high degree of failure. I have, however, also spoken to handlers who have deployed guard-and-bark very successfully. Failures with dogs trained in the guard-and-bark style happen for a reason, as do failures with dogs trained in bite-and-hold. What, then, is the difference between successful and unsuccessful guard-and-bark deployments? More specifically, why would dogs trained in guard-and-bark from large agencies such as the LAPD have high success rates, whereas guard-and-bark dogs from small agencies have increased bite ratios?

The difference is two-fold, having to do both with the application of dedicated training to the profile and how the dogs are deployed. The LAPD puts significant resources, time, and training into their dogs on an almost daily basis, securing the proper

---

[30] Charles Mesloh, "An Examination of Police Canine Use of Force in the State of Florida," (PhD diss., University of Central Florida, 2000), 158.

techniques to maintain their dogs and handlers to a high standard. They train for real-world deployment and are not limited to weekly maintenance training. Smaller agencies do not have this luxury, often train with vendors who only have sport training backgrounds to draw on, and in many cases are only able to attend maintenance training once a month. They are often very restricted in their training budgets and simply are not given the mandate needed to maintain conditioning on a guard-and-bark dog, leaving them more susceptible to failure.

GUARD-AND-BARK TODAY

The Schutzhund sport (now IGP) was developed from German police training methods. Schutzhund trainers and private K9 vendors have commonly sold Schutzhund-based dogs to agencies in the United States under the guise they are police-ready guard-and-bark dogs. However, just as Schutzhund methods of tracking are not practical for real-life police tracking situations (Chapter 4), Schutzhund methods of apprehension are not practical for street applications. There is a distinct difference between professionally trained German police methods of guard-and-bark and the Schutzhund-trained skill sets of the sport dogs that are still heavily marketed in North America.

The demonstrations of vendors who sell these dogs clearly illustrate this. They are able to show potential buyers that their dogs will not bite a suspect, but only if the suspect stands still. There is little or no tolerance built into Schutzhund training for street applications in which, for example, it is unlikely that the suspect will not move. This training gap gives rise to the liability concerns around unnecessary bites from guard-and-bark dogs.

It should be emphasized, however, that this is a training *gap*, and not a training impossibility. Schutzhund-based guard-and-bark training is not true law enforcement guard-and-bark training. It is sport-level training and incompatible with the needs of law enforcement. Training adjustments and conditioning consistent with law enforcement needs must take place to prepare a dog for use as a police dog under guard-and-bark guidelines. Further, deployment adjustments also need to take place on the street to ensure guard-and-bark viability.

BITE-AND-HOLD IS NOT AN INHERENT LIABILITY

Recently, bite-and-hold training methods have again come under fire, largely due to misinformation about the root cause of inappropriate bites.

It is wrong to assume that the liability associated with K9 use originates with the bite. The bite is only the end result of the deployment of a dog in a given set of circumstances. In other words, liability arises from improper application of the dog (i.e., poor deployment decisions by the handler) and lack of proper training or control of the dog. Failure to follow policy and procedure laid out by the department, inadequate record keeping, and a host of other reasons can result in lawsuits.

Litigation and liability are ever-present factors in K9 use. Whether you have a guard-and-bark dog or a bite-and-hold dog, liability is always a factor when the dog is improperly deployed. Improper or inadequate training in either style is potentially dangerous. Regardless of the training method, it is essential that the dog react to situations appropriately as directed by the handler. The end result should be identical in either method. If it is necessary for the dog to bite in order to take a suspect into custody, then a bite will occur regardless of apprehension philosophy.

Policies and procedures backed by strong training and deployment records are your best defense against liability. Each case will be judged on its own merits, comparing the facts against a standard. When your standards are high and expectations have been met and properly recorded, you may still lose a case due to the aberrant actions of an individual or other unavoidable circumstances, but you will not be shown to have been negligent.

Many agencies have properly applied the guard-and-bark techniques. The dogs used by these agencies are not Schutzhund titled dogs sold as police dogs. They are dogs that have been conditioned by police officers or professional, private vendors specifically for law enforcement applications.

To Switch or Not to Switch?

The use of guard-and-bark dogs has become popular with some administrations because of lawsuits generated by improperly trained bite-and-hold dogs or misapplications of such dogs that have injured people without just cause. The misconception is that such incidents are the fault of the bite-and-hold method of deployment rather than the handler's application of the dog or lack of proper training. This causes the uninformed to believe that switching methods of training and deployment — for example, turning to the guard-and-bark profile — will solve the problems.

Simply switching to guard-and-bark applications without making other changes will not solve your problems. The belief that moving to guard-and-bark teams will on its own reduce the number of physical contacts by police dogs is incorrect and short-sighted. It is the responsibility of K9 officers, regardless of their training profile, to keep the work ethics and standards high, and always within the scope of department policy. Should your agency choose to move its program to a guard-and-bark profile, it is vital for the program to be properly implemented.

As any trainer worth their salt will advise you, it takes trainers with significant expertise and it takes significantly more time to train and maintain the guard-and-bark profile than it does to train and maintain the bite-and-hold profile. Compared with bite-and-hold, guard-and-bark requires more maintenance training with professional decoys who are well versed in understanding K9 behavior. Should your agency move to guard-and-bark training, you will need to choose trainers who are experienced in guard-and-bark techniques specifically and can provide instruction that is designed for law enforcement, not for sport. In other words, proper, high-quality guard-and-bark training will take more time and financial resources to implement than high-quality bark-and-hold training.

Groups such as the ACLU, which advocate training police dogs in the guard-and-bark profile, cause difficulties for small agencies that cannot afford training budgets to accommodate the higher costs of guard-and-bark training and maintenance — and as we have already seen, improperly trained guard-and-bark dogs may pose a greater bite risk than properly trained bite-and-hold dogs. Ultimately, both guard-and-bark teams and bite-and-hold teams that deploy improperly or without just cause will still result in unwarranted injuries to suspects or citizens.

If you choose to make the switch to guard-and-bark, you should first ensure that you are able to commit adequate time and resources to this training profile. Making the switch with limited resources, and inadequate funds and training and maintenance time may, in fact, increase your liability and ultimately result in failure.

BOTH DEPLOYMENT METHODS HAVE MERIT
Any deployment using dogs trained in either the bite-and-hold or guard-and-bark profile can be used for law enforcement. Regardless of which apprehension technique you employ with your agency, the result should be identical so long as your training and deployment decisions are sound. In situations in which the dog is required to physically apprehend the suspect in order to take them into custody, the dog's specific training profile is irrelevant.

With this in mind, it is imperative that we as police officers *embrace both types of training* and not ply one against the other. Interagency conflicts based on training profiles only serve to weaken law enforcement.

7

Creating the Right Team

Creating a new K9 unit or adding teams to an already established unit starts with selecting the right candidate officers and the right dogs for the job. While that concept sounds simple enough, many variables need to be considered in the selection process. Not least, the dog and handler must, to some degree, be compatible. While a well-selected handler can, in most cases, work with almost any dog, this is not always the case. In cases where problems arise, the issues can almost always be traced back to poor dog or handler selection.

Selecting the Right K9 Handler

A K9 assignment needs to be carefully considered. The selection process needs to ensure that you are getting the most qualified person for the position. To accommodate a fair and thorough vetting process, a written selection standard should be an integral part of your K9 policy.

Your K9 policy selection criteria should set the standards, basic requirements, and desired traits the department is looking for in a successful applicant, including, but not limited to, the categories listed in Table 7.1.

Beyond the basics, you can also employ recruitment processes that allow you to find candidates who are truly up to the challenge. One such process involves having the candidate attend training

Table 7.1. Handler Standards, Basic Requirements, and Desired Traits

Standards (defined in agency policy)	Desired Traits
• Minimum length of service required • Limited use of force complaints • Minimal citizens' complaints • Demonstrated responsible use of sick time	• Self-initiating • Comfortable with dogs • Above-average work ethic • Patient • Able to create strong interpersonal relationships • Good public speaker (for K9 demonstrations)
Basic Requirements • Current First Aid certificate • Home compatible with housing a dog • Stable home life • Good physical condition • Strong report writing skills • Willingness to be flexible with shifts	

in which they must take bites under the direction of the agency trainer. In fact, some agencies require that candidates have a history of working as a decoy for the K9 teams over an extended period before applying for a position. This allows candidates to gain experience in manipulating canine behavior. It also gives other members of the unit and the unit trainer a chance to interact with and evaluate potential future handlers.

SO...YOU WANT TO BE A DOG HANDLER

It should be stressed to every candidate that they will be required to dedicate significant time to the care of the dog outside regular working hours, and that the assignment is a 24-hour responsibility. At times, potential handlers do not fully appreciate the amount of dedication involved in the care and maintenance of a working dog nor the amount of time away from family that this dedication implies.

In one program I implemented for my agency, I tried to give applicants a sense of the less-glamorous side of being a police dog handler. Applicants who weren't up to the task tended to eliminate themselves from the competition. The process involved posting an announcement titled "So...You Want to Be a Dog Handler," which invited all officers who were interested in applying for an upcoming position to go to an information session that would begin the application process. It was strongly recommended that attendees bring their spouse or significant other, if they had one, to participate in the session. The presentation was not on paid time and therefore required anyone interested in the posting to attend on their own time unless they were on assigned duty at the time.

The presentation was only an hour in duration and laid out basic qualifications for potential handlers. During the session, an experienced handler with long tenure in the unit provided a practical, real-world view of the time required to maintain a police dog, including common issues faced by handlers. While the information session was not a formal part of the selection process, it was designed to explain the application process and the rigorous life of a K9 officer.

The assignment of a police dog handler is challenging and demanding, and it requires a significant sacrifice of personal time from the handler. Time for personal and family activities will be impacted substantially, and extra time will be required, both on and off duty, for the care and training of the dog. The needs of the dog must be looked after even on days off. Moreover, additional training time over and above normal shift hours — a minimum of 16 hours monthly, or 4 hours a week — are required to keep the dog trained up to the minimum industry standard, and teams may be called out at any time on emergency calls.

The session also explained what handlers would be required to provide for the dog in terms of home preparation, care, and maintenance. For instance, they must be prepared to allow a kennel facility into the home environment to house the dog. If not already in place, they need to be willing and able to completely secure their yard with an enclosed fence.

The session stressed that families must understand the dog is a working dog and not a family pet. Furthermore, it was explained that there may be times when the dog will be injured or fall sick, and the handler will be required to tend to the animal.

All told, the training time, additional after-hours callouts, daily feeding and exercise regimen for the dog, and unforeseen events that require a visit to the department veterinarian, regardless of time of day, often add up to the position being hard on an officer's family and private life. It is well known in experienced circles that, at times, the handler will spend more time with the dog than with family.

Having the officer's spouse or significant other in attendance allowed both parties to ask questions of the presenters and better understand the full implication of how the assignment will affect their family life. The family needs to understand that caring for the dog is a 24/7 assignment and may impact their family time, including special family events such as Thanksgiving and Christmas should the team be called to an emergency. Often, K9 assignments take handlers away from home for extended periods of time; the handler and family need to understand and accept that this is part of the position.

A strong, productive team on the street will require the support of a strong team at home. It is important for the officer's household to be aware the assignment can create extra stress for the family and that family support is integral to the success of the team. Additional stress on an already-strained relationship or marriage benefits neither the agency nor the officer. The information session thus allowed for each family to do a self-evaluation of their situation and discuss the responsibilities before the officer continued further in the application process.

Hosting an information session like this one as a normal part of the selection process provides valuable insight into who is sincerely interested in the program. Officers who attend with their spouse or significant other are obviously interested and dedicated enough to attend on their own time and spend an hour watching the presentation and asking questions.

This type of session also tends to weed out a candidate or two who, after listening to the presentation and discussing it further with their family, decide it isn't a good fit for them. The decision to withdraw from the competition can be a difficult decision for a candidate to make. However, by taking what was learned from the presentation into consideration and discussing it with family, the decision to withdraw is one that is often in the best interest of the candidate officer, family, and department.

SUPERVISOR, PEER GROUP, AND BACKGROUND REVIEWS

A quick check of personnel records for each candidate will provide preliminary intelligence on their background, allowing for a review of any past egregious misconduct or citizens' complaints. Valuable insight can also be gleaned from the officer's current supervisor(s) and peer group. Interviewing a candidate's supervisors and fellow officers about the candidate's abilities and character is extremely beneficial to the handler selection process.

It should be noted that any officer that is actively doing their job is likely to have had some negative citizen contact, justified or not. Very few officers who are truly diligent in pursuing criminal actors will complete their careers without some form of complaint from a citizen who feels they have been wronged, or who simply attempts to use the system to cause problems for an officer who has acted against them. A few complaints lodged in an officer's personnel file should not automatically eliminate them from the competition. However, the information gleaned from the personnel files on such complaints can be a welcome resource for putting a candidate on the hot seat during the oral boards to see how they handle questions about past interactions.

ORAL BOARDS

Every selection process should require candidates to pass an oral board that involves the manager of the K9 program as well as the department trainer. A second oral board involving a peer group interview led by current members of the K9 program may also be held. A debriefing of all committee members from both oral boards is particularly beneficial in narrowing down the most qualified applicant or applicants.

Ultimately, the best dog handlers are those officers who are hardworking self-initiators with a passion for the "hunt." An officer who has a known propensity to be highly productive on the street, with good arrests backed up by good report writing abilities, and who exhibits good decision-making skills, will always be your best candidate.

Selecting Potential Police Dogs

The selection of potential police dogs is just as important to the success of your program as handler selection. Not every dog has the potential to become a police dog. In fact, quality dogs that have all the character traits needed to handle the stresses of police work are few and far between.

I have traveled to Europe — the Netherlands, Germany, Belgium, and the Czech Republic — numerous times to purchase dogs directly from European vendors. I have been to dog clubs that only had a few dogs available for sale and to European vendor kennel facilities that specialize in providing dogs for the North American law enforcement market. These latter facilities have the capacity to hold well over 100 dogs and are often filled to capacity. On each trip, I intended to bring back 10 to 12 dogs for our operations. On arrival, I would travel to different facilities, testing as many as 30 dogs a day in the hopes of finding the best potential candidates for the job, but only rarely did I ever fly back with more than six dogs. This speaks to the challenges of locating dogs that will meet the stringent requirements of law enforcement.

Some agencies, albeit rare, still depend on local, donated dogs from rescue organizations for their K9 units because they do not have the funding to properly commit to the program. This is a dangerous practice, as it often results in agencies relying on dogs that are less than adequate. Testing is an exhausting, but crucial process and involves much more than simply seeing the dog bite a sleeve. Investing adequate resources for testing and selection is vital to a strong K9 unit. If your agency cannot commit a proper budget to the program, not just for training and equipment but also for dog selection, consider postponing your program until proper funding and support can be provided and maintained.

GENETIC AND ENVIRONMENTAL ISSUES

Proper genetics and conscientious upbringing play an integral part in developing the proper traits required for a police service dog. It is paramount that a proper and exhaustive selection testing process be conducted by an experienced trainer. A good selection process will eliminate dogs that exhibit signs of weak genetics as well as determine problems with dogs that may have been created by a poor environment (i.e., upbringing or improper training).

A qualified trainer performing routine selection testing will understand the difference between genetic and environmental weakness and can quickly evaluate any dog for the presence and type of issues.

Genetic weakness cannot be changed. Any dog showing genetically linked unwanted behavior or poor performance must be rejected. While not ideal, a dog that exhibits minor weakness as a result of environmental issues can sometimes be improved through proper conditioning and training. If environmental issues are found, a qualified trainer can quickly determine whether these can be overcome, or if the problems are too severe to consider the dog as a potential police dog.

GENETIC STRENGTH VERSUS WEAKNESS

A common test to evaluate genetic strength or weakness of a dog is called a stake-out or courage test. The evaluator secures the dog to a fence and approaches it in a suspicious manner. They do not act aggressively toward the dog but exhibit body language that should make the dog wary. A strong dog will focus on and watch the evaluator, coming out to the end of the lead and showing body language that is confident: tail up, ears forward, erect posture, directly facing the challenger. As the evaluator approaches and begins to show body language that is more aggressive in nature, a strong dog will stand its ground and may begin to bark as the challenger gets closer. As the evaluator continues to approach in a threatening manner, a strong dog will show a strong intention to bite with no sign of backing down. If this dog also shows proficiency in the other evaluation tests, it will be capable of dealing with the stressors required to complete training and work the streets.

A genetically weak dog, when approached in the same manner, will often start barking long before the evaluator is within a threatening range. The dog's tail will be down, hackles up, and the pitch of the bark will be high. The dog's body will be at an angle to the evaluator, not face on. As the evaluator gets closer, the dog will begin to back away. Weak dogs will show different levels of weakness. A very weak dog may even try to escape, fighting to pull out of the collar to flee. This attempt at flight may occur at any point during the test, sometimes even when the evaluator is still acting only in a suspicious manner and not being directly threatening. It is clear that such a dog is genetically weak and unsound for police dog work. No further testing is necessary.

ENVIRONMENTAL CHALLENGES

Inexperienced trainers will sometimes mistake environmental issues for genetic issues, which may cause them to reject a potentially good dog. A simple example is a dog that shows an aversion to going up and down stairs. In these cases, it is important to know whether a dog has been raised in a kennel environment: these dogs may never have been exposed to something as simple as stairs. When attempting to run this type of dog up a set of stairs during testing, the dog may initially pull back and try to avoid going up the first steps. They may also go up a few steps, then turn around and jump off, becoming very resistant to the evaluator's attempts to encourage them to proceed.

I have seen trainers reject dogs like this outright and not test any further. An experienced and open-minded trainer understands, however, that this is not necessarily a symptom of genetic weakness but may simply be an indicator that stairs are a new challenge for the dog. If the dog shows hesitation but not fear or trepidation, it may be that it simply doesn't yet understand how to negotiate this new challenge.

A common and significant challenge for many dogs is that of slippery floor surfaces. Floors that are polished or feel slippery under the dogs' feet such as those commonly found in gymnasiums or school hallways can be insurmountable problems for some dogs. When required to step onto such a surface, the dog will become splay footed with extended claws, exacerbating the issue. Some dogs will even try to move towards the nearest wall to lean against it for support. The problem can be extreme in some dogs to the point of being a phobia. For these dogs, this issue is insurmountable, and they are unable to work in such environments. Even approaching a floor with a shiny surface may cause trepidation to the point of avoidance.

A good trainer will take a few extra minutes and work with the dog to determine if it has the fortitude to take on these challenges and the ability to recover. A dog that will continue to try until it succeeds and shows the ability to recover is one that is worth testing further. One that shows significant and ongoing issues should be avoided. This same philosophy will also hold true in other environmental testing.

HANDLER INVOLVEMENT IN K9 SELECTION

It goes without saying that the department trainer who will be responsible for overseeing the training of the dog should take the lead in evaluating new candidate dogs — but who else should be involved?

There are two schools of thought about who should take part in the selection of a law enforcement dog. Some agencies rely on the trainer to travel to local or international vendors to survey potential candidates and then advise their department's K9 supervisor on their recommended dog choices. The supervisor is ultimately responsible for the final decision. The trainer then teams the dog with the new handler.

Other agencies prefer to allow the new handler to participate in the selection process. Including the handler provides teaching opportunities and allows the trainer to see how the handler relates to the dogs being tested. There is value in this approach. While the final choice of dog still rests with the K9 supervisor and agency trainer, this method allows the handler to learn about the qualities of a strong dog and how to rigorously test and assess a dog for police work. It also gives the new handler a better understanding of K9 behavior and the extensive process involved in team development.

SOURCING POTENTIAL POLICE DOGS

Many agencies make a habit of going to the same vendor again and again to purchase dogs. However, it is always good to keep your options open, if you have multiple sources available to you, by looking into as many of them as you can. Tens of thousands of dogs are imported into North America annually because of the high demand of law enforcement, security, and military organizations. It is not unusual for a vendor to import a shipment of 10 or more dogs that have been preselected overseas, and to be out of stock at the end of the same day due to the high demand. If you have only one vendor to choose from, and the choice of dogs has been limited because other agencies have already completed their selection, your options are going to be that much more limited. Whenever possible, shop around before making a final decision on a dog.

BASIC TESTING OF POTENTIAL POLICE DOGS

It is always best practice to test candidate dogs away from the vendor's location in areas that are unfamiliar to them. A dog can be conditioned to perform very well on courage and environmental tests on a familiar training field yet may show signs of insecurity when in an unfamiliar environment.

Your trainer will know what tests to perform and what behaviors to look for during their survey of potential candidates. Test all of the dogs the vendor has available. If a strong candidate is found early on in the testing process, do not walk away without testing the rest of the dogs. Continue to test until you are satisfied you have selected the dog most suitable for your program.

Ensure that your trainer tests a complete regimen of requirements and looks for more than a dog that is strong in the courage testing phase and has a strong bite. A dog that is strong in the courage phase of testing but shows a lack of interest in other behaviors, such as the desire to hunt, will result in an unproductive dog on the street.

Figure 7.1. Surveying potential police dogs involves testing for environmental soundness as well as a wide spectrum of behaviors, including courage, sociability, and, most importantly, the desire to hunt.

An aspect that often is not considered in dog selection is the sociability of the animal: Is the dog social with people? Is the dog aggressive in social situations? Does it go out of its way to initiate a fight with other dogs on the field, or is it more interested in engaging and interacting with the trainer and others present?

Many dogs that are surveyed (tested) for police work by their very nature often have strong alpha characteristics and tend to be "dog aggressive." Although less common, dogs may also be antisocial toward people. Both characteristics can cause problems. Dogs that exhibit strong tendencies toward dog aggression will frequently become difficult to handle around other dogs, becoming distracted and confrontational both in training and when working. This can be a major problem during deployments, for instance if they initiate a fight with a citizen's family pet they happen across in the course of their duties. Given that thousands of searches result in entering homeowners' properties, this type of interaction is very likely. Antisocial dogs pose similar risks when officers interact with citizens on the street or when doing public demonstrations.

Antisocial and dog-aggressive dogs require the handler to constantly be on guard to prevent potential unintended consequences. While these dogs can certainly be trained and worked, it adds additional liability potential. Care must therefore be taken during the selection process to eliminate antisocial and dog-aggressive dogs from the process whenever possible.

If a choice is made to select a dog that is known to have one or both of these issues, great care must be taken to ensure the handler is well aware of the issues and willing to accept the added attentiveness required to keep the dog in check. Likewise, the agency must be willing to accept that they are potentially taking on greater liability.

RECONSIDERING SELECTION CRITERIA

One of the most difficult training issues we deal with today is the refusal of the dog to release a bite. This issue has been exacerbated by overseas trainers who condition the dogs, sometimes for months, to be intense fighters with a strong bite, but do not put any time into teaching the dog to release the bite. As such, when the dog is sold to a law enforcement agency via a local vendor, the agency inherits the lack of control issue related to the bite release. Depending on the level of conditioning for this behavior, the ability to manage the dog to a point where it will have a more controlled bite and will release on command becomes problematic.

This is a significant problem and can result in a handler having to deal with a dog that has control issues throughout its career. It can also raise potential liability concerns if it cannot be managed through training.

The toughest dog in the kennel is not always the appropriate dog for the job. A good trainer needs to be perceptive and discriminating in the selection process. Unfortunately, this issue has been created by an industry that has continued to demand stronger biting dogs from vendors rather than demanding that dogs show a good level of control with a bite release along with having a bite with a good grip. Until the industry puts pressure on the vendors who provide these dogs to do more than just push out strong biting dogs as the main criteria for selection, this will continue to be a problem for North American trainers (see also Chapter 4).

VETERINARY CLEARANCE

After a dog has passed all the testing requirements and before you agree to purchase the dog, you should have it examined by your agency-approved veterinarian. A complete physical exam should be conducted, and X-rays taken of the hips, elbows, and spine. These are all areas that are common points of disease and failure, even in young dogs and those that don't show any overt signs of pain. X-ray examinations will expose any underlying progressive disease that could potentially put the dog out of service in the future.

Always do an independent veterinary examination, and always do independent X-rays. Overseas vendors will often provide X-ray film for the dog to North American vendors, but the quality of X-ray may be such that it does not provide a true read of the areas of concern. More importantly, without having your own X-rays done, there is no guarantee that the film provided is a legitimate match to the dog you are purchasing. Go to a veterinarian you can depend on who has experience in assessing and caring for working dogs.

CANINE WARRANTY

Any vendor who runs a quality operation will provide some form of replacement warranty for dogs they sell. Most warranties revolve around medical issues that make the dog unsound for service. These warranties may extend for up to two years past the time the dog was purchased and provide a valuable safety net for your agency's investment.

Some vendors will also provide a limited warranty on the workability of the dog. Good vendors will have conducted enough testing on the dog prior to putting it on the market to know that it will meet all the criteria needed to make a good police dog for most agencies. The issue of workability, however, can be a gray area, as a quality dog put into the hands of a trainer who uses ineffectual or harsh methods can easily create issues for the dog and even make the dog unworkable. When an agency then attempts to return the dog, and it becomes apparent to the vendor that the dog has been pushed past its limits through improper training or even abuse, the vendor may not honor the limited warranty. In such situations, replacing the dog will not resolve the problems and consideration needs to be given to assessing the ability and methods of your trainer.

Teaming Dog and Handler

When selecting dogs and handlers, as is true of selecting a qualified candidate for any position we are trying to fill, we routinely look for traits that are easily quantifiable: traits we can test for, which will help us narrow down the best candidates for a given position. To most administrators, this is simply common sense. This sort of testing is objective and based on known standards. Many will make their selection of a dog handler based on quantifiable interviews, evaluations, physical testing, and written examinations.

Similarly, K9 trainers will test potential police dogs using stringent criteria. If the dog achieves success during each phase of testing, the trainer will accept the dog into the training program. Again, testing is based on established criteria that are known to produce strong police dogs.

It only makes sense that a candidate who has passed the required criteria and a dog that has met all the testing requirements will pair well together and ultimately produce your best potential for a productive team, right?

Not necessarily.

I have seen teams that have otherwise passed all testing requirements ultimately fail during their training. I have also seen teams get through their training but experience consistent training issues and challenges on the street. In some cases, despite the best attempts and intentions of the handler, the dog simply shuts down over time and must be removed from the unit because the team is no longer productive. In other cases, conflict develops between the dog and the handler to the point that the dog challenges the handler, sometimes attacking and even seriously injuring the handler. While extremely rare, it is not unheard of for a dog to turn on its handler with such severity that the handler subsequently shoots and kills the dog in order to protect themselves.

Why, when we have taken all the proper steps to ensure we have used quality criteria to test and select the best candidate dog and handler, do we run into training and street failures?

In most cases the problems can be traced back to inadequate or improper training. If you believe you have the right handlers and good quality dogs, and you still have problems, then consider auditing your current training program or even the trainer. Conflicts between dog and handler are often exacerbated by old-school trainers who push the philosophy that the handler must dominate the dog. Your training program may be lacking in some aspect and should be evaluated very closely. Trainers who are heavy handed, deal with behavior issues entirely through compulsive techniques, and choose not to follow the science of animal behavior should be replaced.

CASE STUDY OF A FAILED TEAM MATCH

As a young handler, I had an opportunity to spend seven weeks training with the Pierce County Sheriff's Department in Washington State under the guidance of Deputy Jack MacDonald. I had asked to participate in his program to learn about his unique style of teaching off-lead tracking techniques. It was here that I first began to understand the importance of the handler and dog selection and matching processes.

Jack's program was 14 weeks long, and I joined them in the seventh week. When I first arrived, Jack told me he was struggling with one of the student handlers in the class who had already gone through multiple dogs. He could not quite understand why each dog was shutting down and refusing to perform.

He told me that each dog that had been assigned to this particular handler had been carefully surveyed and tested for patrol work. They had all started out strong, but within a week of the pairing, each dog's performance would decline to the point where it became disinterested and aloof toward the handler. In fact, the handler's current dog at the time had its initial training started by an experienced handler — a sergeant in the unit. The decision was made to transfer the dog to this new handler to see if the dog's good start and foundation with the sergeant would help get the student handler over the plateau he seemed to keep reaching.

The handler appeared to be a good officer who worked hard. His handling skills were solid. He worked well with the dogs and followed direction well. Yet as the class was entering its seventh week, this officer was on his fourth dog. Jack asked me to observe the team and see if I had any ideas as to what might be causing the ongoing failures.

As I observed the team in their various exercises, I noted the handler was always upbeat and his timing was good when it came to commands, corrections, and directions. The team seemed to have a good bond, and the dog was initially responsive. As the week went on, however, the dog's performance began to decline just as Jack had described. If the student handler didn't put in extra effort, the dog became disinterested in the training. It was apparent there were issues.

The last two days of the week were set aside for a program run by the Pierce County K9 Unit called the Spouse Awareness Program. The spouses of the K9 handlers were invited to ride along and observe the training events for two days. The program was meant to help them understand the unique challenges K9 teams have and to create a supportive structure in which they could learn about the diverse responsibilities their significant other would have when assigned a dog.

When this student handler's wife attended, it became apparent why he was struggling with each dog.

We were training at the Fort Lewis military base doing tactical entries. During any down time, I noted the dog was very closely bonded with the officer's wife; when she was around, the dog showed little interest in or respect for the handler. In short, the dog preferred to associate with the wife. This observation alone started to tell me what might be occurring.

At one point, the wife took a break from observing the training, which gave me an opportunity to sit with her and ask a few questions to try to determine what the home life was like for the dog. At the time, I was simply searching for anything that might help us to understand what had been happening with the dogs assigned to this student handler. I asked her some general questions to determine if there were any problems with the dog at home. She advised me there were no issues at all and that she quite enjoyed having the dog at home. I asked if there were any behavioral issues, either in or out of the home, such as digging holes in the lawn or chewing.

Her answer was simple, but very telling: "He isn't allowed in the house, and I don't let him out of the kennel into the yard unless I am out working in the yard, so I don't have to worry about him digging in the garden." At this point, I was sure that we were dealing with a bonding issue that had its roots in the officer's home life, rather than in his individual ability and skill set. My thoughts were quickly confirmed. I asked the wife how she felt about her husband being a dog handler. Her reply was quick and to the point: "It's what I have wanted him to do his entire career."

An experienced trainer knows that there are certain feral or instinctive traits inherent in the canine species. Part of understanding canine behavior is knowing how they interact and relate to one another. This is important to understand because canines are very social animals. They are experts at reading body language, and experience has taught us that dogs, particularly working dogs, will fit themselves into a human social environment much in the same way they do within their own species. They are fully capable of understanding where every person is situated in the "family pack."

It became apparent to me — and to Jack, after I explained my observations to him — that the handler's wife was a strong alpha personality in the home environment. Although the husband was a good officer and was doing his best to work with each dog, it was apparent that he was subservient to his wife in the home environment. Every day after training and on weekends when they were off and at home, each of the dogs that had been assigned to the handler had learned that the wife was the dominant force in the family: she was in charge and should be respected. They thus quickly lost their connection to the K9 handler, began ignoring him, and no longer wanted to perform or obey his direction.

Unfortunately, this handler had to be removed from the program, not because he was a bad handler, but because his home situation would create problems for him regardless of the dog he was assigned. It is possible that a very independent dog that loved to work for the sake of the work without requiring much management by the handler may have been a good match for this handler. However, the dynamics of the home situation may still have created issues.

In this case, had the wife, and not the husband, been the assigned dog handler, there is no doubt she would have been able to work virtually any of the dogs Deputy MacDonald had previously assigned.

Home life is only one of so many variables at play when putting K9 teams together. This story also illustrates why it is imperative that you seek out trainers who have the experience needed to understand the many nuances and idiosyncrasies that can occur in K9 team dynamics. It is not always as simple as just selecting a good dog and handler. Sometimes, there are unique circumstances that can result in a team not working out. When it comes to trainers, those with years of experience — preferably decades — are your safest bet and your best insurance.

PERSONALITY: THE "INTANGIBLE" DIMENSION

While quantifiable criteria are very important — putting a team together based on these criteria will normally result in success and is the foundation from which thousands of K9 teams are created — in the world of police dogs, there is another dimension that I believe must be considered to assure success. This additional dimension involves the personality of both the handler and the dog. Put simply, certain personality types simply do not play well together; mismatched personality types on a team can result in conflict and/or failure after you have spent significant time and money in training.

Well-rounded trainers know this. They also know that there are no hard-and-fast rules for this process. Indeed, a common issue among some (often old-school) trainers is the impulse to match a strong alpha-type handler with a strong alpha-type dog. Their belief is that the handler is strong enough physically, emotionally, and mentally to handle a strong dog. If the dog challenges the handler, they instruct the handler to dominate the dog as needed to ensure that the dog understands its position in the team. This approach often fails. While the handler may win the fight from time to time, they rarely succeed in permanently changing the dog's behavior this way. In fact, this approach may even result in the dog attacking and seriously injuring the handler.

Even if the personalities of the dog and handler are in conflict, more forward-thinking trainers will help mitigate this situation by instructing the handler to take conflict out of the training rather than trying to dominate the dog. However, the best situation is one in which the personalities of the handler and dog are well matched from the start.

For decades, quality trainers have paired specific dogs with their handlers based on their understanding of the personality of the handler as well as the behavioral characteristics of the dog they are selecting for that handler. There has never been any formal name or explanation for pairing this dog with that handler. For seasoned trainers, the art of pairing a dog and handler becomes instinctual.

A good pairing starts with an understanding of the dog's and the handler's personalities. This, too, can feel rather instinctual. For instance, good police dog trainers can read and understand the type of dog they are working with. On top of assessing the usual stressors and tests for police dog work, they will also begin to see a certain personality in the dog during the assessment. Among other things, they will be able to tell if the dog has a strong "alpha-type" or more of a "beta-type" personality, whether the dog shows signs of "rank" behavior, and if the dog has a social character. If beta-type dogs are all there are to work with, the trainer will also be able to assess whether the dog still shows strong potential for street work.

The personalities of the handler and the dog play an integral role in the success of the team. While less quantifiable, there is a very real need to look beyond the basic testing procedures and recognize the value of personality assessment — and doing so is not as complicated as it may sound.

HANDLER PERSONALITY: THE SATIR MODEL

Back in the early 1990s, Dr. Stephen A. Mackenzie,[31] an animal behaviorist and friend, taught me the value of understanding the personalities of the people I train. Dr. Mackenzie taught a framework called the Satir model,[32] which categorizes people based on their personalities in situations of stress. I quickly found the concepts in this model to be invaluable. Not only can these concepts be applied to simply understanding how to deal with different people, but they are also useful for understanding the process of selecting police dog handlers and help explain the apparent "instinctive" abilities of some trainers to pair up handlers to the right dog.

Virginia Satir, after whom the model is named, was a family therapist and author who developed a way of assessing people's personalities with the specific intent of helping to improve relationships. Her methods are still used to this day, specifically regarding issues of relationships and communication within families. While this may seem like it has no relationship to police dog training, understanding Satir's personality types can significantly impact your decisions about dog handler selection and help administrators and trainers understand the need to be selective when teaming up dogs and handlers. As an added bonus, a solid understanding of the Satir model can help you understand the actions, emotions, and perceptions of others and deal with conflict in the workplace environment and even at home.

There are five personality or communication types that make up the Satir model:
1. The blamer
2. The placator
3. The computer

---

31 Mackenzie is the author of *Decoys and Aggression: A Manual for Training Police Dogs* (Dog Training Press, 2015), a resource I highly recommend. For more information, see the Resources section at the end of this volume.

32 See Virginia Satir, *The Satir Model: Family Therapy and Beyond* (Science and Behavior Books, 1991).

4. The distractor
5. The leveler

As you go through the following information, there is no doubt you will identify people within your family, friends, or work associates that fit into each one of these descriptors. This makes sense — Satir was focused on human behavior. However, you will soon see how the model can also be applied to handler and dog selection and teaming. Satir was, after all, extremely effective in understanding personality types and how to resolve communication conflicts, and dog training is all about communication.

THE BLAMER

A person falling into the "blamer" category is someone who has a strong personality and, in many cases, is not willing to take responsibility for their actions. They will blame others and will frequently initiate conflict. They often come across as alpha personality types and are aggressive in nature. They need to feel like they are in control. A blamer has a sense of insecurity and often feels alienated or lonely. Their defense is often a strong offense of being unwilling to admit to any mistake or weakness and passing the buck to others instead. Satir describes the blamer as overcompensating for their insecurity by being more aggressive. Police officers deal with blamers at virtually every domestic violence call they attend — in most cases, if there is a blamer, it is the husband.

In dog training, it is common for the handler to become frustrated if the dog is not performing to standard. A "blamer" handler may deal with this frustration by blaming the dog's inability to understand or to comply rather than realizing the dog is not capable of logically understanding what is desired. It is the responsibility of the handler to help the dog understand how to accomplish the task. From the K9 trainer's perspective, blamers tend to be difficult to work with as they do not easily admit mistakes or see the need to change. (If I had a nickel for every time I dealt with a handler that had a blamer type personality, I would be a rich man!)

THE PLACATOR

A placator is the opposite of a blamer. They are a beta-type personality: unassertive, submissive, and always willing to please. They will avoid conflict at all costs. They are also insecure and are always looking for approval. Like blamers, placators are also commonly found in domestic violence situations. They may even be willing to accept full responsibility for the actions of their partners to prevent any more trouble. In these situations, if there is a placator, it is often the wife.

In dog training, a placator handler is a problem, regardless of the dog to which they are assigned. A placator is hesitant to correct and take charge when needed. The dog, therefore, will control the relationship — and when the dog rules the relationship, there is no control. In effect, the dog will become a pet.

THE COMPUTER

A person with a computer personality type might be considered stiff-necked or uppity and have difficulty being expressive and animated. Their behavior is very proper but often lacks emotion. They will come across as calm and often appear cold and uncaring. They may feel angry or be in emotional turmoil on the inside, while on the outside they appear calm and rational. Computer personalities are judgmental. They make value judgments about others and assume that everyone will agree with their analysis. Often, they will have a difficult time expressing their love even for those within their family, which reveals some insecurity. Their sphere of friendship is generally small, with only a trusted few in their inner circle.

A good dog handler is someone who needs to be very expressive and outgoing. Dogs communicate through body language, and the way in which handlers express themselves is paramount to the dog's ability to understand what is desired of it. Good handlers are not afraid to have fun and express themselves; in fact, good handlers have no problem taking off that tough mask and being goofy and animated with the dog, without being concerned about embarrassing themselves. Sometimes this level of animation is necessary to get the point across to the dog. (From a trainer's perspective, this is sometimes why female handlers can be easier to train than male handlers. Most female handlers are naturally more animated and willing to act excitable and speak in excited tones to get the desired behavior from their dog, whereas male handlers are often less expressive and more reserved in their approach.) A computer personality type is not expressive in this way. In effect, this personality type is a poor communicator with dogs, making it difficult to find a dog that will understand and perform training routines with a computer-type handler.

THE DISTRACTOR

Distractors are attention-seekers and are very insecure. They tend to overcompensate to make up for their feelings of loneliness or perceived shortcomings. They will express a wide array of emotions to avoid a stressful situation or try to manipulate how others feel. Indeed, they are master manipulators: often their body language does not match what they are saying. They are difficult to work with and will use behaviors that include traits from previously mentioned personalities to achieve their goals. They frequently attempt to change the subject to avoid confrontation.

A person with a distractor personality is inconsistent. This is a K9 trainer's worst nightmare as it leads to inconsistent and unpredictable handling of the dog. The distractor gets frustrated easily and will blame the dog or the trainer for issues while at the same time looking for sympathy. Of all the personality traits in prospective K9 handlers, this is the most difficult type of person to deal with from a K9 trainer's perspective.

THE LEVELER

Levelers exhibit the appropriate behavior for any given situation and are problem solvers. They can be assertive and are emotionally balanced and secure. They have the ability to work and communicate with anyone. They do not make excuses for their behavior and approach situations with a focus on resolving issues. Making mistakes does not threaten their self-esteem. They are able to be accountable for their shortcomings and take the appropriate actions to resolve them.

When seeking to fill a position as a dog handler, it is imperative that we seek out officers who are levelers to fill the position whenever possible. They are productive, deal with training issues proactively, and are avid learners. They are not afraid to be animated and expressive when working with a dog and are patient when dealing with training issues. Levelers can be both patient and assertive without being aggressive and can modify their approach depending on the situation. They take direction well and understand the concept of communicating what is needed for the dog to accomplish the intended task. They can work with strong

Figure 7.2. Officers who fit into the leveler category are willing to interact with their dogs. They will do whatever it takes to motivate them and readily take guidance. Positive interaction between the handler and the dog is vital to success.

dogs and, when necessary, weak dogs too, making them easy to match. They think before deploying their dogs and make solid decisions for the right reasons. From a K9 trainer's perspective, a leveler-personality handler is easy to train and work with. All of these qualities make them the best choice for the job. These are the officers you want to have on your K9 team.

The Satir model provides us with an understanding of the "intangible" and "intuitive" side of trainer selection and handler-dog pairing that trainers have been practicing for decades. In fact, understanding the concepts in the Satir model has improved the intuitive ability of trainers in putting teams together. This underscores why, when selecting potential handlers for your agency, it is important that you consider the personality type of the applicants on top of the quantitative data from your standard testing models. By searching for handlers that exhibit a leveler-type personality, you offer your trainer the best opportunity to produce a successful team.

TEAM MATCHES THAT FAIL

Unfortunately, you won't find many agencies with a majority population of levelers. The personality types in police agencies are many and diverse. It is, therefore, likely that you will be matching dogs to handlers with other personality types. There is a multitude of possible dog and handler personality combinations. Let's look at some combinations to avoid when putting a K9 team together.

BLAMER AND STRONG ALPHA DOG

The blamer personality type is common, particularly in young K9 handlers. With age comes maturity and with life experience a person is more likely, if self-aware, to become more of a leveler. Often, strong alpha personalities with blamer characteristics are teamed with a strong alpha dog, as some trainers believe the handler is strong enough to handle a tough dog. This often results in conflicts between the dog and the handler, with the dog challenging the handler and the handler trying to control the dog.

The backlash by the dog in these situations is often severe; it is not uncommon to see handlers hospitalized by their own dogs with dog bites to the arms and wrists incurred during the handler's attempts to control the dog. Although the team may be able to certify and work the streets, conflict will continue to be an issue until it is dealt with proactively.

While this is not an ideal match, it is important to note that this type of conflict can be addressed and resolved with patience and proper training. Creative training techniques can be used to remove conflict from the relationship if the handler is able to be patient enough and accept that dominating the dog is not the solution. Most bites that occur on handlers by their own dogs are precipitated by a harsh correction by the handler, or the dog's perception that the correction was inappropriate. With strong dogs it is imperative that the training is adjusted to remove the conflict out of the training. Old school compulsive methods will only exacerbate the issue.

BLAMER WITH YOUNG OR MORE FORGIVING DOG

When paired with a young or more forgiving dog, a blamer handler runs the risk of being too heavy handed on the dog. Dogs assigned to blamer personality handlers may become "handler sensitive" and stressed during training, which may lead to training issues that ultimately result in failure. The dog may eventually shut down and be washed from the program. This is generally not because the dog is a poor choice as a police dog, but because the handler does not have the patience to build the dog. This type of dog may evolve into a very workable partner if it is allowed to mature and given the proper handler support.

PLACATOR WITH STRONG ALPHA DOG

This combination results in the dog controlling the situation. The placator is unable to manage and control the dog. I have seen teams of this type in which the dog simply ignores the handler. In the dog's mind, the handler is low in the pack structure. In other words, the dog does not respect the handler's authority. Even if this type of team manages to certify for the streets, they will achieve little if any productivity.

PLACATOR WITH YOUNG OR MORE FORGIVING DOG

This is a pairing of a weak handler with a weak dog. A young or weak dog will sometimes still dominate the relationship, but in most cases, this situation will result in the dog becoming more like a family pet to the handler. This is a team that may be able to function for public relations and demonstrations but likely will never be a strong working team on the streets.

COMPUTER WITH YOUNG DOG

Every dog needs strong communication from its handler, both in terms of vocal support and body language. A computer personality is naturally reserved and will have a difficult time communicating with their K9 partner. It is challenging to get the team through training, especially if the dog is green, with minimal or no previous training. A stronger, more independent dog that is self-motivated can sometimes work with a computer-type handler, but the success of the team will depend on the dog's degree of self-motivation and whether it is willing to work well without having a strong bond to the handler.

DISTRACTOR WITH ANY TYPE OF DOG

Consistency is paramount in developing working dogs, and this personality is very inconsistent. A handler with a distractor personality can be very destructive, regardless of the dog assigned to them. A distractor personality is a nonstarter in handler selection.

There are a few caveats to these examples. First, regardless of personality type, much depends, too, on the capabilities of your selected agency trainer and how receptive the trainee handler is to direction.

It should also be noted that even handlers with a leveler-type personality can experience conflict with a dog. The difference, however, is in the way the conflict is managed. A leveler will be much more capable of dealing with the conflict productively and coming to a positive resolution.

Finally, it is important to keep in mind that there is no such thing as a perfect dog. When you are dealing with a living, breathing animal, there are always unknowns. Proper handler and dog selection along with a forward-thinking, well-vetted trainer are your best options to mitigate training and deployment issues and potential liability.

8

Equipment

There is no question that police dog handlers dedicate more time, both on and off duty, to their assignment than any other position in the agency. It comes with the territory. Yet in some agencies, management teams fail to provide the support needed by K9 teams and also fail to show their appreciation for the work the K9 officers do.

K9 units are most likely to be productive and successful with limited liability when provided quality equipment, given the training required to maximize their capabilities, and supported by their management team. One of the most significant barriers to success is a lack of financial support, not least because this limits the amount and quality of necessary training and equipment a K9 unit can acquire. Management needs to have a realistic understanding of the significant resources required to maintain a quality K9 program.

This chapter lays out the basic equipment every K9 team should have in order to perform at their highest capacity. It also gives a few ideas and guidelines to assist management — and K9 supervisors in particular — in providing their officers with the equipment they need to do their jobs well. Further resources can be found at the back of this book. These ideas and resources are not exhaustive and are provided here as a starting point from which K9 supervisors should expand.

Vehicle Design and Build

One of the most demoralizing actions agency management can take toward the K9 unit is to assign the oldest cars in the fleet to the K9 teams (see Chapter 2). This is demoralizing because it makes K9 officers feel like they are not a valued part of the policing team or that management has little concern for their well-being. Too often, K9 officers have to deal with vehicles that frequently break down, are not dependable, and often simply look tired, offering no sense of pride to the officer.

Providing older cars that have been worn out by patrol is also dangerous. While efforts are made to ensure cars are kept in good operational condition, aged units have experienced stress and can be susceptible to failure under extreme running conditions. Police dog handlers respond primarily to in-progress crimes and emergency calls. If properly deployed, they will also become a primary player in every vehicle pursuit in case the suspect driver bails on foot. It is standard for a K9 vehicle to be driven hard multiple

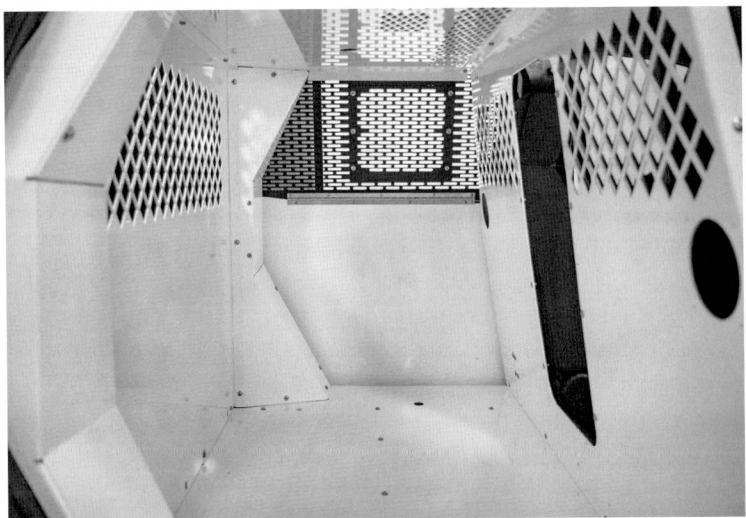

Figure 8.1. A kennel interior prior to installation of nonslip floor mats. The emergency access door can be opened and closed from the driver's compartment as needed. This unit is pre-fitted with a fan on the side windows and has an access for additional venting if required. These units are designed for easy cleaning.

Figure 8.2. The floor of the kennel is designed to extend to the edge of the door frame. It is sealed to facilitate cleaning the interior of the unit by allowing water to drain outside the vehicle.

times a day. An older vehicle is more susceptible to stress failures under extreme driving conditions: a potential invitation to disaster.

Individually assigned patrol cars that are new when assigned to handlers provide the best overall investment. When individually assigned as take-home cars, the officers are available for immediate emergency callout as needed. The officers are more likely to take pride in their vehicles and tend to take better care of them. When the time comes to trade in the vehicles, the seats that have been removed and stored to convert the car to K9 use can be reinstalled and the vehicle detailed. In some cases, individually assigned K9 cars attract better trade-in value than standard patrol cars.

Ask for input and involve your K9 teams when it comes to building your K9 cars. Handlers are always exchanging ideas and looking for ways to improve. In their travels, they will undoubtedly see well-equipped agencies with cars that are set up to maximize efficiency and performance. They know what they need and they will know what's available.

EQUIPMENT

The two most important factors that influence the acquisition and build of a K9 vehicle are the K9 compartment itself and the need to maintain ample space for equipment storage, though other factors should also be taken into account to ensure the safety and well-being of the dog. A quick survey of nearby agencies will give you a good idea of what the preferred K9 patrol cars are for your area, and also provide some good insight on vehicle builds.

K9 COMPARTMENTS

For both SUV and pickup installs, there are a number of rear-seat kennel installations available. K9 compartments or kennels designed for rear-seat installs should allow access to the dog via a sliding gate to the front compartment of the vehicle in addition to side- or rear-door access. This allows the handler to access the dog from the front of the vehicle when needed. It also provides an alternate emergency door for the dog should the unit be involved in an accident such as a rear-end collision that damages the rear door enough to jam it.

While transporting prisoners in K9 vehicles is not advised, small agencies and county sheriff departments are sometimes required to do so. Split-cage systems designed for this purpose allow the prisoner to be secured in the rear seat on one side and the dog to be kenneled on the other side with a solid barrier between them.

Some agencies prefer or need to install standard, box-style kennels in the rear bed of SUV or pickup units in order to reserve the rear seat for prisoner transport. While not preferred, there are a number of professional systems designed and available for these configurations as well.

Figure 8.3. A split kennel design allowing for simultaneous dog and prisoner transport.

EQUIPMENT STORAGE

The amount of equipment required to train and deploy police dogs can be significant and may influence the type of vehicle your department selects as a K9 unit. Due to the nature of the job, the equipment will often be dirty and difficult to store. For city agencies, an SUV with an equipment vault in the rear compartment is likely the most versatile choice. This type of vehicle allows significant space for specialized items and allows different types of equipment to be separated.

The trunk of a standard, four-door patrol car can also provide a unique set-up if carefully built and managed. For most K9 teams, however, it will not have adequate storage for the rest of the team's equipment. It will also be difficult to keep non-canine-related equipment clean.

Figure 8.4. A Havis-brand K9 set-up in a pickup truck. Good inserts provide ample ventilation and easy cleaning.

For some county and rural-based agencies, a pickup truck is often required due to the terrain. Covered equipment vaults can be obtained for these vehicles that are similar to those used in SUV set-ups.

AIR VENTS

Air flow is also an important issue. It is necessary for the safety and well-being of the dog to ensure that there is good, cool air flow to the rear compartment of the vehicle. Depending on the vehicle, air flowing through the vents in the driver's compartment is sometimes not enough to keep the rear compartment cool for the dog.

This problem can sometimes be solved with after-market products that funnel air from the front compartment vents through large hoses into the rear compartment. However, these products are bulky, inconvenient, inefficient, and can restrict the view of the driver. When acquiring a patrol car for a K9 team, it is best if the car is prebuilt with rear compartment air vents.

WINDOW TINT

Quality window tint should be an integral part of any K9 vehicle. Tint will significantly reduce the amount of heat the vehicle absorbs, adding additional safety for the dog. It also adds a privacy screen, so the dog is not as visible to the public. This may seem like a minor reason for window tint; however, it is more common than you might expect for certain people, when they see a dog in a parked law enforcement vehicle without the officer around, to walk over and start pounding on the windows to tease the dog. I experienced one occasion where this was done on a patrol car that had no window tint and no barrier between the kennel and the rear window. The dog in the car hit the window so hard that the rear glass shattered, giving the dog the opportunity to take care of business.

Regardless of the citizen actions that may create this type of issue, it is a potential liability that can be solved with a combination of window tint and a cage that offers 360-degree security.

HEAT ALARMS

Due to the nature of the work, dogs are often left in patrol cars. The cars must be left running for the air conditioning to flow and keep the compartment at a safe temperature for the dog. Good heat alarm equipment can contact the handler via cell phone should their car's engine or air conditioning fail. When such failures occur, electronics installed in the car can drop the windows to the K9 compartment and initiate auxiliary fans to facilitate air flow. The system also activates the emergency lights and horn on the car to bring added attention to the vehicle to anyone nearby should the officer be out of cell phone range.

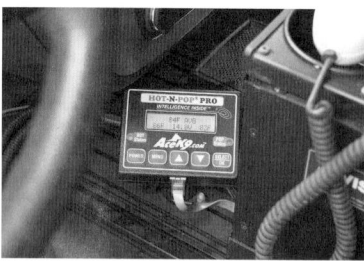 

Figure 8.5. Heat monitoring alarm systems are a necessity for any K9 transport unit. The Hot-N-Pop Pro system displays a vehicle's current settings and temperature. The control head is mounted where the handler can easily access it. The system is easy to use and vital to protecting your service dogs. If triggered, the system contacts the handler via cell phone to advise that the temperature has become dangerous for the dog, allowing the handler to respond to ensure the dog's safety. The system also provides an emergency remote release allowing the dog to be released from the car from a distance to assist the handler during an emergency.

Sadly, a significant number of police dogs experience a terrible death each year from heat stroke while in the back of patrol cars that are either not equipped with heat alarms or that have improperly installed or malfunctioning equipment. The public outcry is always significant and can have long-reaching negative public relations consequences for the agency involved.

I have been asked to investigate cases in which an agency is contemplating charges against an officer whose dog has died from heat stroke as a result of being left in a car. In every case, the death was accidental. In most cases, however, the death could have been prevented by ensuring the proper installation and operation of certain equipment. In some cases, a functioning heat alarm system would have prevented tragedy.

Every law enforcement agency that has a dog program should have a policy that requires a quality heat alarm system such as ACE K9's Hot-N-Pop Pro to be installed in every K9 unit. Your policy should require each handler to test the alarm system installed in their car weekly. It should also include maintenance guidelines that specify the action to be taken if a system is faulty.

When the installation of a heat alarm system is made a policy mandate, it becomes a requirement of the department to provide such equipment. This is particularly important for agencies that have a high turnover of K9 supervisors. One supervisor may actively support the success and safety of the K9 teams during their tenure and ensure the cars are properly equipped, while the next is less supportive or less willing to go to management for needed budgetary items. This may result in requests for such equipment being denied by a supervisor who is more willing to take risks than deal with the issue.

Figure 8.6. Should the heat alarm be triggered, the system automatically rolls down the rear windows of the unit and blows air through the rear compartment of the vehicle to keep the dog cool until the arrival of the handler.

Unfortunately, this is not an infrequent occurrence in some agencies. By embedding in agency policy the requirement that heat alarm systems be installed in every K9 car, it takes the choice away from the supervisor and places the responsibility squarely on management, ensuring the budget is in place to cover the cost involved.

Home Kennels

There are many home kennel configurations and ideas that can be implemented based on available space and climate. While size can vary, the kennel must be large enough for the dog to be able to move around freely and lie down without having to walk through or be affected by any waste deposit.

The kennel should be built in a location where the handler can observe the dog from inside the home and where the dog will have privacy from the street. The kennel foundation should be made of concrete that extends past the edge of the caged portion of the kennel. The foundation should be sloped to allow for water and liquid waste run off. A gutter should be built into the concrete just outside the cage that is at least as wide as a shovel. This way, any waste can be washed from the kennel floor into the gutter and easily scooped for disposal.

The kennel should also include a shelter that provides adequate protection from the local climate and privacy for the dog. Some officers place the shelter outside the kennel, giving the dog access by cutting an opening in the kennel wire and securing the shelter entrance to the opening. This saves space in the kennel and allows the dog more room.

A roof on the kennel is required to keep the dog comfortable, properly shaded on sunny days, and secure. The roof line should come into contact with the top of the cage portion of the kennel to ensure security and prevent any possibility of the dog escaping. If you live in a hot climate, you may also consider installing misters around the top of the kennel to keep the dog cool.

It is prudent to look for shelters with a removeable roof or a side door that allows for easy cleaning and access to the dog in an emergency. If you have a shelter with a side door or removable roof, ensure it can be securely locked to prevent unauthorized access.

Finally, be sure the kennel access gate has a secure latch that cannot easily be pushed open by the dog. If it is an easy-to-lift latch and the dog happens to accidentally nudge it up once, I guarantee you that he will soon be in and out of that kennel at his leisure. Most importantly, you must be able to lock the gate. Your agency policy should require the kennel shelter and kennel access gate to be securely locked any time the dog is left unattended at

Figure 8.7. This kennel allows plenty of room for the dog. It contains a sheltered dog house with a roof that can be removed to facilitate cleaning. The outside of the kennel is covered in material to help screen the dog from direct sunlight.

the home. This will ensure no accidents occur and reduce the possibility of undue harm or foul play by parties unknown when the family is away from the home.

Training Equipment

All K9 teams require basic equipment such as leather leads and collars. Beyond that, the type of equipment required by your teams will depend on the profiles in which your dogs are trained:

- Tracking dogs require items such as tracking lines and tracking harnesses.
- Patrol dogs require bite suits, agitation muzzles, and bite sleeves.
- Detection teams will benefit from training systems such as the Dogtra Ball Trainer and SciK9 Training Aid Delivery Device System.

The most efficient way to determine the needs of your teams is to meet with them as a group and to ask them what their needs are. Have them prioritize their absolute needs, and then determine other items that would be beneficial for them if budget allows.

Figure 8.8. A K9 Storm vest fitted with an Intruder camera system.

K9 BALLISTIC VESTS

K9 ballistic vests are an additional item that can be valuable for teams deploying on known high-risk operations. They are expensive, but if budget allows, it is prudent to have them available for each dog to be used at the discretion of the handler. This is not an item that is made to be shared from team to team. Just like body armor used by officers, K9 ballistic vests should be properly fitted to each dog. If your budget is tight, keep in mind that there are also organizations available that will donate K9 vests for agencies in need.

9

Fair Labor Standards and K9 Handler Compensation

The United States' Fair Labor Standards Act (FLSA) requires employers to compensate employees for any activities performed either before or after a regular work shift if those activities are an integral and indispensable part of the principal activities for which they are employed.

It is important that K9 supervisors in the United States have a solid understanding of the FLSA and how it applies to their K9 unit. After all, K9 handlers are expected to care for their assigned police service dog in their off-duty time, including regular days off and holidays. There is no respite from the responsibility.

Your agency needs to have a policy guideline or a memorandum of understanding (MOU) in place that mandates how and to what degree your K9 officers are compensated for the care and maintenance of their dogs. Failure to compensate a handler can and has resulted in litigation in which an agency has been found liable for years of back pay.

FLSA in Case Law

Truslow v. Spotsylvania County Sheriff[33] found that time spent in the care and maintenance of police dogs is compensable under the FLSA: "As an integral and indispensable part of the principal activities of a canine deputy, off-duty time spent caring for canine

---

33 *Truslow v. Spotsylvania County Sheriff,* 783 F. Supp. 274 (E.D. Va. 1992)

unit dogs must be compensated as hours worked in accordance with the FLSA."[34] This case was then cited in a second case, *Levering v. District of Columbia*,[35] where K9 officers of the Metropolitan Police Department of the District of Columbia brought action against their department pursuant to FLSA requirements. In their judgment, the court stated:

> Plaintiffs are entitled to compensation under the Fair Labor Standards Act for the actual time spent exercising, feeding, and otherwise caring for the canine detachment dogs. The evidence offered by plaintiffs demonstrates that care of these animals is plainly a part of the officers' duties. While the officers might at times be able to groom, exercise, and provide some care for the dogs while on regular work time, some of their duties clearly spill over into non-work hours. Moreover, on holidays and other days on which the officers are not assigned to work, all canine care necessarily takes place outside of regular working hours. Thus, the Court finds that feeding, exercising, and caring for the dogs by officers assigned to the canine detachment constitutes an "integral and indispensable part" of the officers' work activities, and, as such, time spent on those activities is compensable under the Fair Labor Standards Act.[36]

Although the handlers in *Levering v. District of Columbia* requested three years of back pay, they were awarded two years according to the statute of limitations for back pay claims. This decision was made because the handlers were unable to provide convincing evidence to show that the agency had *willfully* violated the FLSA. If the agency had, however, been found to have knowingly and intentionally failed to compensate the handlers, they would have received the full three years worth of back pay.

Both cases are lower federal court opinions that carry no binding or precedential weight. They are, however, persuasive opinions. The *Levering v. District of Columbia* decision, for example, resulted in what has become a standard base minimum compensable time: 30 minutes per day. It should be stressed that this is a minimum. Many departments also provide a variety of other types

---

34 *Truslow*, 783 F. Supp. at 278.
35 *Levering v. District of Columbia*, 869 F. Supp. 24 (D.D.C. 1994).
36 *Levering*, 869 F. Supp. at 26–27.

of meaningful compensation in support of their K9 teams, understanding that ongoing care of the dog is often more involved than basic feeding, exercise, and grooming.

Understanding Compensation

Agency management will sometimes question the need for any more than the required minimum compensation for their handlers, stating that daily compensation of 30 minutes is more than adequate.

From a budget perspective, particularly with large departments, agency management will often keep compensation limited strictly to the base FLSA requirements. They understand it is required by Department of Labor Standards yet consider it an unnecessary perk for K9 officers, not recognizing the extent of off-duty labor involved in the job. Understanding compensation for this off-duty labor begins with understanding the labor itself.

OFF-DUTY LABOR

Individual circumstances and responsibilities will vary from agency to agency. Some things, however, will be the same across agencies. Care and maintenance of a police dog, for example, requires more than just feeding and grooming. Daily kennel maintenance, disposing of the dog's waste, regular washing and sanitation of the kennel, and cleaning of food and watering bowls is all necessary work.

Police dogs also need regular training and exercise. While dogs do not need to be trained on every off day — indeed, it is important for the dog to have downtime to rest — they must be exercised daily and regularly involved in maintenance training. On schedules where a team works four days on and four days off, for example, a limited amount of training would be recommended on at least two of those days off. Such training helps to keep the dog proficient, sharp in all of its profiles, and fulfilling needed exercise regimens.

Holidays look different for K9 officers, too. When the family travels on vacation, the responsibility to care for the dog continues unless the dog is centrally kenneled or other arrangements are made to house the dog. There is no exemption for Thanksgiving, Christmas, or any other holiday. If the dog suddenly becomes sick in the middle of the night or needs urgent transport to a veterinarian on a day off, the handler has no choice but to take action to ensure the care and safety of his partner, regardless of family activities. Sickness is only one of many unforeseeable circumstances that every handler will experience and have to deal with on their own time during their career.

Some handlers are required to put in more off-duty time than others, dependent on work schedule rotation, training profiles, and agency. For example, some programs require handlers to work two dogs, one for patrol and a second for detection, in effect doubling not only the compensable time, but also the added responsibility these handlers assume.

COMPENSATION MOU

Agencies that appreciate the actual investment of personal time and sacrifice required in the ongoing care and maintenance of a police dog choose to provide more robust compensation packages through an MOU. A strong compensation MOU for K9 officers will adequately remunerate K9 officers for their labor, clearly lay out what the agency expects of its K9 officers, and provide a detailed explanation of what is included in the compensation package.

Every situation is different, and how an agency chooses to compensate its officers will impact the efficiency, productivity, and morale of each assigned officer. An MOU or policy that provides reasonable compensation for both regular care and emergent circumstances will go a long way toward positive productivity and program morale.

10

Certification Standards

While certifications have been used in support of K9 evidence in court, the reality is that there is no one standard that is considered *the* standard. There are many certification standards in the industry.

Most certification standards have been created over decades by experienced K9 handlers and trainers who have established K9 associations for the betterment of the police K9 industry. Some of these standards have been adopted by POST state boards and similar organizations. In times past, courts and law enforcement agencies alike relied heavily on certifications as a way of validating the quality of police dog performance. These certifications are normally done annually with the intent of ensuring K9 teams can meet minimum standards of performance for their assigned tasks and responsibilities.

Certifications from credible organizations with independent, objective evaluators will always provide an extra layer of integrity for your K9 teams, but it is unwise to rely on certification alone. Without further supporting documentation, certification can be disputed by a good expert in any case. Put another way, courts have recognized that while certifications provide a minimum standard for performance quality, they are not a true reflection of the day-to-day performance of the dog. They are merely a snapshot of a team's performance at the time of testing.

Certification Is No Substitute for Training Records

Annual certifications are no substitute for a strong training regimen with good documentation. Current court decisions indicate that strong training records alongside certification carry more weight than certification alone. Courts want evidence that a dog can perform proficiently in a controlled training environment under circumstances similar to those at play in the case at hand.

More importantly, training records provide a tool for analysis. Documentation of a well-thought-out training plan that includes your training objectives and actions taken during each exercise are necessary and are the industry standard. Log all training via an electronic K9 records management system and ensure that all dogs can pass your chosen standards at any given time (see Chapter 11). Ongoing logs that show training objectives being met successfully provide accurate patterns of capability for each team. This is what the courts look for when determining the veracity of the capabilities of the dog. It is essential to include any shortcomings and the actions taken to resolve those issues in this documentation as well.

SATURATION TRAINING

It is common knowledge in the industry that as annual certifications come due, vast numbers of teams begin to prepare for accreditation by doing saturation training to resolve issues that would otherwise prevent them from passing annual certification. Once annual certifications are achieved and the pressure is off, however, many handlers fall back into their regular routines and their training ethic declines. These practices create a false sense of security about the capability of your K9 program.

Among patrol dog teams, this is a serious problem, particularly in the criminal apprehension profile or bite work. Every certification I am aware of requires the dog to release its bite on a suspect on verbal command of the handler. Failure to do so results in the dog failing certification. Yet vendor preconditioning of dogs for law enforcement and misplaced training and handling priorities have placed emphasis on working the intensity and depth of the bite to the detriment of maintaining the dog's ability to reliably release the bite (see Chapters 4 and 5). This has contributed to significant failures in modern-day deployments of police dogs to reliably respond to and obey verbal handler commands to release the bite on a suspect.

In order to certify these unreliable dogs, handlers engage in intensive, short-term training. Two weeks prior to any certification, they begin to work their dogs on verbal call-offs from a bite or on the certification tracking standard so that on certification day the dog is able to perform up to the required standard. I have also witnessed dogs at different accreditation workshops fail their verbal bite release testing multiple times. Such teams are then sent to an instructor to work on the issue and a short time later on the same day, return to testing and manage to certify the dog.

Any qualified trainer or handler knows this quick fix is not going to last past the time it takes to test the dog. It is not a true indication of how the dog normally performs. A true picture of the dog's level of performance consistency comes from regular training, with the results documented immediately after every training regimen. Good agency trainers will develop a routine of pulling teams in for testing at random intervals without warning and performing a mini certification in all their assigned profiles to ensure they always meet expectations. Any teams not meeting the standard are provided remedial training until they meet the standard before returning to the street.

If you as a supervisor believe that your teams are up to standard simply because they pass annual certification — if, that is, you depend on certification as evidence that your teams are street ready — you leave yourself and your agency open to unnecessary liability.

Selecting K9 Certification Standards

Law enforcement K9 certification has become big business in the United States and has significant influence within law enforcement itself. High-quality certifications conducted by K9 evaluators with law enforcement experience are offered through professional associations such as the North America Police Work Dog Association (NAPWDA) and the United States Police Canine Association (USPCA), amongst others. However, there are also "certifications" and standards that have been created by vendors and trainers who are in business to provide certified police dogs. This raises concerns regarding the legitimacy of these certifications.

Selecting a minimum training accreditation standard to certify your police dogs can be difficult. With a multitude of K9 associations having different standards and many vendors having created their own standards, the information available is convoluted and confusing at best and it's hard to get a straight answer about where that minimum should be set. K9 accreditation choices can be especially challenging for agencies, particularly small ones, that depend on vendor-based training and on the advice of their chosen trainer. This lack of consistency in certification standards and advice creates no end of complications for good law enforcement agencies that are doing their best to maintain the highest standard of ethics for their unit.

Any good trainer with law enforcement experience can tell you that any reasonably trained dog can be conditioned to meet most minimum standards, but the dog itself or the K9 team will not be ready to work the streets. The purpose of a K9 certification is to ensure your teams are meeting a *minimum* performance criterion for the standards your department has chosen to use. They are not a checklist of the only things a street-ready K9 team must be capable of doing. Understand that just because your teams pass a certification standard does not mean they are prepared for street deployment. While it is true that the more challenging the certification, the more prepared the team will be when deployed, most K9 teams that are genuinely street ready will exceed all the basic requirements of the various certification standards currently in the industry.

Remember, too, that current certifications are primarily a test of the dog's basic ability to perform certain skill sets: Can the dog perform efficiently in detecting contraband odor and pinpoint its location to the handler? Will the dog terminate a fight with a decoy, release the bite, and enthusiastically return to the handler's side on a verbal command? A significant factor missing in all certifications, however, is an evaluation of the dog handler's own performance in tactics and decision-making.

WHO SHOULD CERTIFY YOUR TEAMS?

Certifications are an important component of the overall management of your teams. There are different philosophies as to who should examine the skills of the teams and sign off on their certification. In the past, K9 qualification standards were managed by law enforcement agencies. Agencies trained in-house using similar methods and had similar testing criteria. After a 12-week basic training program, each team was required to be evaluated in-house prior to being authorized to work the street. This was efficient and no different than in-house firearms or emergency vehicle operation accreditation.

There are still agencies that do in-house certification by experts in the K9 field. Those agencies that still have in-house training programs with their own K9 instructors may have those instructors certify the dogs. Others prefer to have a K9 instructor from another agency provide certification to add a layer of objectivity to the process. Still other agencies will entrust the process to one of the bonified K9 associations whose standard they have chosen to adhere to. The examiner will be provided by the association to test the teams to the certification standards required by the association. This also provides a layer of objectivity to the process. All of these certification options — whether done in-house or by a recognized K9 association — have been accepted by the courts.

Under no circumstances, however, should any agency accept a certification provided solely by an organization or vendor that is in the for-profit business of selling police dogs or providing training for the agency. Unlike law enforcement agency trainers and K9 associations, allowing vendors to validate dogs in which they already have a financial interest opens the door for abuse of certification and can raise questions about the veracity of the certification.

It should also be front of mind that there is no national or state body that qualifies vendors to certify police dogs. The courts do not recognize vendors as certification bodies. If your agency is dependent on vendor training, ensure you have your teams independently evaluated and certified to a court-recognized standard by a trainer with a K9 association, a state certification board, or an independent law enforcement agency that has no relationship to the vendor. No credible vendor will have any issue with ensuring your dogs are trained to your selected certification standards, nor with you mandating that your service dogs be certified by an independent party recognized by the courts.

EVALUATING FOR STREET CAPABILITY

Be mindful that even when done by a qualified examiner using standards created by a legitimate organization, certification is a validation that the team meets that basic minimum standard. It provides a "measuring stick" against which teams can assess their skill levels but does not on its own guarantee that your dogs are street capable.

Certification aside, the final word on whether your teams are ready for street deployments should come from the person responsible for their training. Your team's regular trainer, whether they are a trusted vendor or an in-house trainer, sees your teams perform on a daily basis and can assess more than just the basics that are tested on a certification exam.

The trainer's decision should not be based on opinion alone but backed up by strong training records that reflect the team's consistent performance and readiness for their intended assignment. In the end, it is the documented daily regimen of scenario-based training, including decision-making challenges for the handler and the reliable performance of the dog, that are the truest measure of street readiness.

Train for the street, document everything, and certification will fall into place. When your teams are truly well trained, they will *easily* meet and surpass the requirements of any certification standard and be capable of doing the job well in the streets.

A Closer Look at Vendors and Certification

The advent of various K9 associations and vendors who imported European dogs combined with a push on sport training methods resulted in a wide spectrum of training standards and philosophies and opened the door for corporate influence. Business interests and politics began to influence and fracture the industry. Vendors, many without any law enforcement background and experience, began to influence how dogs were trained and evaluated for law enforcement street readiness.

Through the years, these vendors have had significant impact in the industry, eroding the practice of in-house certifications by law enforcement agency trainers. Most certifications are now being done by either independent evaluators from K9 associations or, in many cases, by the vendors themselves. Some K9 associations even allow vendors on their board of directors. This has been beneficial in some respects, introducing new and forward-thinking ideas; however, it has also meant that those in the business of selling and training police dogs for profit were given significant political influence within police K9 organizations and associations. At the end of the day, commercialism should have no place influencing professional police dog operations and standards in any organization.

VENDOR CERTIFICATION STANDARDS

Many vendors have created their own certification standards, including those that offer three-week "police dog training schools" that sell dogs with training programs that are, from a professional standards perspective, entirely insufficient. At the completion of whatever course they have provided for their trainees, the vendor puts the teams through their own standard certification, rewards teams with a certificate of proficiency, and advises the agency that their teams are ready for the street.

These vendors stay in business because agencies continue to buy into their concepts and believe that the vendor certification is adequate. Agency administrators feel these programs are beneficial because the trainer is always close at hand or simply because the course is short and their officers are offline for only a few weeks.

This, however, is a dangerous practice. When it comes to certification and street readiness, at issue is that each vendor can create whatever requirements *they* feel are suitable for their certification. When a vendor is certifying dogs that they are also selling and training, credibility and conflict of interest concerns, justified or not, can arise.

Vendors design their certification programs to match their training programs, meaning that a team trained and certified in a short-term school may very well pass that school's certification test, whether or not that certification is actually meaningful from a law enforcement perspective.

While there are some very high-quality vendors in the K9 industry who can provide superior training and guidance, there are also those who simply are not qualified or do not have the integrity to be in the business. It bears repeating that schools that are only a few weeks long cannot provide the knowledge and skills necessary for a K9 team to be safe and effective on the street. If you cannot afford to send your officers to a recognized law enforcement agency or minimum 8- to 10-week (preferably longer) vetted vendor school for training, *you should probably reconsider the viability of your program.*

Any vendor your agency considers hiring to provide police dogs and/or basic and maintenance training needs to be thoroughly scrutinized. Regardless of their quality, you should not rely on vendors to certify their own dogs. Even if your dogs are certified by the vendor, this certification should always be followed by a further certification by a bonified and independent organization.

VENDOR CERTIFICATION IS NOT ENOUGH

In my capacity as a trainer, I have been hands-on with thousands of dog teams over my decades of experience. In numerous training programs, I have seen teams that are clearly incapable of meeting any normal minimum standard — yet these teams had been "certified" by their vendors annually and working on the streets. In almost every case, the handler knew they had major problems but were helpless to effect any change.

One example clearly demonstrates the point. For over two decades, I operated the International Police K9 Conference, a well-known and well-respected hands-on police dog training conference. During that time, I had a team of instructors who were second to none in the industry. These included both active and retired law enforcement officers who had years of experience in real-world training and deployment.

One year, I had 18 instructors working the conference. Virtually every dog team that went to the conference had the opportunity to train with each instructor during the week. One officer in attendance was working a weak dog and several of the instructors were concerned about the team. When the team attended the exercise at my station, it became clear to me that the handler had been teamed with a dog that had none of the basic qualities that would enable it to be a police dog. The dog exhibited clear signs of low confidence and was afraid to leave the handler's side. In discussions with the handler, I learned that the vendor had selected and assigned the dog to her. She knew from the beginning the dog was a problem, but the vendor was insistent on her continuing to work the dog and even "certified" the dog for the street.

The handler had attempted to convince her management that there were issues. Her supervisor followed up with the vendor/trainer, who told him that

Figure 10.1. Tactical shield drill training at the International Police K9 Conference, Alameda, California, 2009. This training combined K9 teams with patrol teams to prepare for exigent circumstances.

the dog was not a problem. The K9 supervisor for the agency up to this point had trusted the vendor's advice over the obvious and justified concerns of the handler. After all, the dog had been "certified."

Concerned for the safety of the dog's handler, I invited the K9 supervisor and management team for this agency to attend the conference to meet with me and another trainer and to observe a basic selection testing of the dog. The dog was posted and set up for a basic courage test — a fundamental for every police dog (see Chapter 7). The decoy attempted to approach the dog twice. Both times, the dog began barking with hackles up while the decoy was still at least 30 feet away. Both its behavior and body language showed a lack of confidence. On one occasion the dog attempted to bolt and was stopped only by its being tethered to the fence line. Clearly, the vendor had been able to condition this dog to appear competent on familiar training grounds; in these circumstances, however, it was apparent he was not genetically sound.

This same scenario played out again two years later at another K9 conference we held in the same state. Another agency and handler attended the program with a dog from the same vendor as the one noted above. The story was almost identical, and again we went through the same process.

There is no way this vendor could have mistakenly believed these dogs were sound. To provide these dogs to any agency or K9 handler as any type of working dog was unethical at its core. As a result of the demonstration, the K9 supervisors washed these "certified" dogs from their respective programs, confronted the vendor, and acquired new dogs for their handlers.

These incidents took place more than 10 years before this writing. Since then, I have seen other dogs from this same vendor. While most have been better quality dogs, they have remained weak performers. As of today, this vendor is still in operation selling and "certifying" police dogs.

Police Dog Competitions: Training to Excel

There are many benefits to sending your teams to compete in police dog competitions and in hosting these events. As we saw in Chapter 1, police dog demonstrations can be a powerful public relations tool. This includes police dog competitions. They're fun to participate in and to attend and have the potential to create strong community bonds.

Police dog competitions can be an important resource in another regard, as well. As a supervisor, you should not accept your K9 teams training to meet only the minimum requirements of any standard. Expect more and help your teams meet those expectations. Sending K9 teams to competitions can facilitate this goal.

Competitions encourage handlers to train not just to meet minimum certification requirements but to excel in their field. In competition, handlers are able to see each other perform. Most importantly, they are able to see how their performance compares to officers from other agencies. In effect, these K9 competitions often cause K9 officers to challenge themselves to be better.

It's impressive to see a handler able to easily recall their dog off strong bite work. The crowd always cheers when a dog instantly drops to a down when called off the pursuit of a decoy. The obvious control of the dog is impressive even to fellow handlers. When they see more-experienced teams performing at a high level, they return to their agencies with a renewed sense of what can be accomplished, and some with the intent of matching or surpassing their stronger competitors in subsequent years.

For all the positive aspects of police dog competitions, it is important to only send teams to compete if you know they are ready

Figure 10.2. The ability to recall the dog off an intense fight is a challenge in which every K9 team should strive to excel. Impressive control work speaks to the quality of your unit and your trainer.

to perform. The optics of a dog that does not respond to the handler's command to recall from a pursuit or to release a bite will not look good in public, and any failures will be visible and easily videotaped by observers. Any professionally trained and qualified dog should not have an issue with these skills. In fact, if an officer wishes to compete in these events, it will be an incentive for them to ensure their dog exceeds the competition requirements.

11

Records Management

The purpose of maintaining a well-designed K9 records management system (RMS) is to protect yourself, your officers, and your agency from civil liability and to provide court-ready documentation to assist in convicting suspects whose arrests involved K9 applications.

Whatever record-keeping system you have in place for your agency, it must be designed to avoid scrutiny due to poorly prepared reports or the unnecessary capturing of potentially damaging data. This does not mean that you should capture data selectively. On the contrary, it is essential that you capture your information thoroughly and honestly. However, it is unwise to capture extraneous information that is unnecessary for reporting purposes and that risks being misinterpreted.

From Paper Trails to the Computer Age

HANDWRITTEN K9 RECORDS MANAGEMENT

Handwritten reports are essentially a thing of the past. In modern policing, having an electronic RMS in place is essential — yet there are still K9 units that maintain basic, handwritten training notes. By relying on handwritten notes, K9 units risk losing or failing to document critical statistical information that may be needed in court.

RECORDS MANAGEMENT

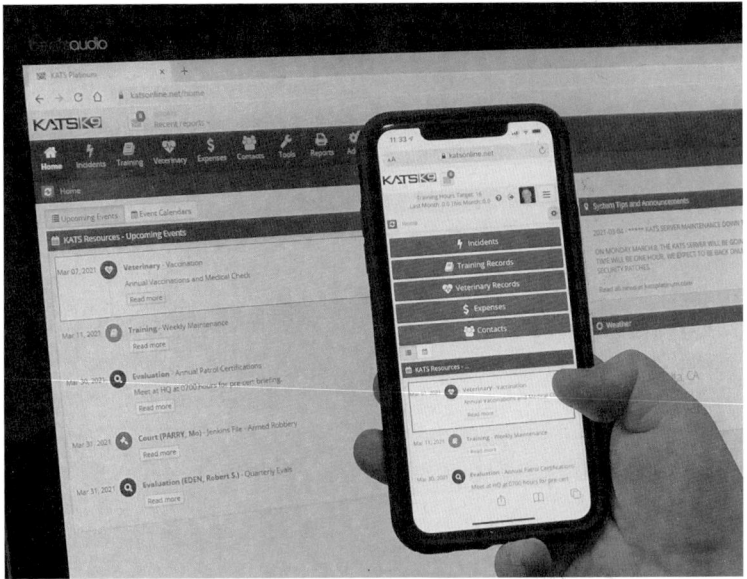

Figure 11.1. Electronic K9 RMSs are your first line of defense against lawsuits. Look for systems that are easy to use and versatile enough to be used in the field during active training and on deployments.

When proper records management is not in place, the handler may be open to direct liability and the supervisor(s) and agency may be open to vicarious liability, if not more. Agencies that require their K9 teams to use handwritten notes normally do not have procedures in place for supervisors to scrutinize the handlers' notes for thoroughness, to determine if the unit is maintaining the minimum number of hours recommended to meet industry standards, or to assess whether K9 team training is balanced.

Moreover, when a subpoena hits the desk of a K9 supervisor whose agency does not use a computerized K9 RMS to collect its data, hundreds of hours can be spent retrieving the information the courts have directed the agency to produce. Courts frequently subpoena years of K9 training and deployment records and require specific statistical breakdowns — for instance, bite demographics that detail how many times a dog or an entire agency's dog unit has arrested suspects of every race and detailing the numbers and bite ratios for each demographic. Statistics detailing K9 teams' training hours and content along with proof of recent certifications are also common court requests. Compiling written data and statistics in a format that is acceptable for submission to the court, even when the proper handwritten records have been maintained by every K9 officer, is a daunting task. In one case, an agency that relied on handwritten records needed three weeks for two clerks, with the assistance of the K9 unit supervisor and the officer involved in the case, to produce and prepare the subpoenaed information.

Beyond the sheer number of resources required to produce court-requested records, supervisors should consider that, in a court subpoena situation, you may not always have much time to produce the required information. For instance, one agency was given just 72 hours to produce a year's worth of records by a district judge. Had they relied on handwritten records, it would have been impossible to meet this deadline. Because the agency used a digital K9 RMS, however, the supervisor was able to provide that information within an hour.

DIGITAL K9 RECORDS MANAGEMENT

The first computerized records management program specific to law enforcement K9 needs was developed in 1992. The K9 Activity Tracking System, commonly referred to as KATS and known by the trade name of KATS Platinum, was initially developed using records management paperwork collected from both Canadian and American police agencies.

Up to that point in time, every agency maintained their records with handwritten or typed reports. As the use of dogs in law enforcement became more prevalent, so did liability risk. Predictably, training documentation and histories of specific dog teams in both criminal and civil court became more common as well. Every request for this information made it apparent that typical paperwork was a cumbersome and inefficient way of maintaining records.

Advances in technology have helped address this problem. We have gained the ability to easily quantify and disseminate the information we collect via computerized RMSs that are specific to police K9 operations.

NOT ALL SYSTEMS ARE CREATED EQUAL

K9 records management is complex and requires a significant amount of detail. A K9 RMS must be capable of accurately

Incident Summary
ALLEN POLICE DEPARTMENT

Incident Date	Incident #	Incident Type
Stryker/Eden		
2018/05/24 11:45	2021-00011	Burglary - Commercial
B&E to Industrial Complex. 2 Suspects arrested on site subsequent to building search.		
2020/04/21 16:31	2021-13056	Carjacking
Seizure of 2 kilos of cocaine as a result of roadside sniff. Street value $27,000.00. Two suspects arrested.		
2021/05/16 15:15	2021-6475	Attempt Murder
Area search in bush for two suspects wanted for attempt murder. Both subjects located by K9 Stryker within 150 feet of one another. Both suspects surrendered without incident.		
2021/05/27 8:35	2021-7021	Drug Search
Executed a drug sniff on parked 53' refrigerated trailer in J&M Roadside Stop. No tractor attached. Positive indication by K9 near the front of trailer. Search warrant obtained. Insulated wall removed from inside front wall of trailer revealed 40 packages of kilo size cocaine. Approx. value $720,000.00. SUI by Drug Task Force. See narrative for details.		
2021/06/01 10:30	2021-7635	Burglary - Residential
Intruder alarm at residence. Confirmed burglary. Suspect vehicle on site. Suspects fled on arrival of patrol. Containment set and PSD Stryker deployed. Three suspects apprehended. Property recovered.		
2021/06/03 15:22	2021-7778	Drug Warrant
Executed a warrant to search for narcotics aboard the fishing vessel Starling III in Ladner Harbour. Positive indication by K9 below deck on the port side of the engine room. Insulated wall removed to reveal 170 packages of kilo size cocaine.		
Jula/Parry		
2021/05/24 13:21	2021-6735	Alarm
Intruder alarm confirmed false by attendance.		

Figure 11.2. The focus of good records is to cushion against liability and assist in obtaining convictions, but they also provide valuable insight for trainers to analyze training issues and provide the management team with updated information on what the K9 unit is doing. This report shows a summary of each call these teams attended. Quick pull reports such as this can keep team leaders appraised of all their teams' activities for any period of time. In the author's department, the chief held daily management meetings where this information was shared. This is quickly accomplished with computerized RMS systems.

recording all necessary information. However, some systems, in attempts to be creative and more competitive, have created unnecessary procedures that have been detrimental to the industry and have created problems for agencies in the courts.

For example, one record system actively prompted officers to record alerts on detection deployments where no subsequent contraband was found, scoring and valuating K9 reliability on live deployment alerts. This type of system produces extensive reports based on the number of alerts a dog has on live deployments where no substance was found compared to the number of alerts the dog has where the product being searched for was found. Attorneys have used this information to bring the reliability of the dog into question by inferring that alerts where no contraband was found are "false" indications or errors by the dog.

This is not the only way in which an RMS can cause confusion. For instance, there have been digital RMSs that included formulas designed to produce reports on the "scent threshold" of a dog. In reality, "scent threshold" can only be properly determined by quantifying studies in scientifically controlled environments. You cannot determine a "scent threshold" on a dog through general K9 training or deployment. This type of report is, thus, false. When such reports become part of the training records released to a defense attorney or introduced into court, they create unnecessary confusion. They serve no legitimate purpose and create complications for agencies that must then explain to the courts how this information is related to the reliability of the dog, when in fact it has no scientific foundation in real-world deployments.

Scrutinize your K9 RMS and record-keeping procedures carefully to ensure your officers are not logging unnecessary and possibly damaging procedures. There is no reason to track and quantify information that scores hits and misses on live deployments when it is not required by the courts. In fact, reporting extraneous information can cause confusion in a case and can open you and your agency to undue scrutiny. This can easily be avoided by recording and quantifying only that which is required by case law. If you are currently using a system that tracks and quantifies K9 reliability on live deployments, consider implementing a policy to prevent officers from using that part of the program.

Records Management and the Courts

FLORIDA V. HARRIS: REPORTING THE RIGHT INFORMATION

The 2013 US Supreme Court decision in *Florida v. Harris*[37] demonstrated that improperly reported information can be deceptive.

Florida v. Harris addressed both false alerts and K9 reliability, noting that reliability can only come from training and certification. In its conclusion, the US Supreme Court stated:

> If a bona fide organization has certified a dog after testing his reliability in a controlled setting, a court can presume (subject to any conflicting evidence offered) that the dog's alert provides probable cause to search. The same is true, even in the absence of formal certification, if the dog has recently and successfully completed a training program that evaluated his proficiency in locating drugs.[38]

It is important to note that to prove the dog has completed a training program, accurate and detailed records are required to back up the training. Without training records, there is nothing to support the proficiency level of the dog.

The US Supreme Court unanimously held that Florida's highest court erred when it "created a strict evidentiary checklist"[39] that must be satisfied to establish that an alert by a drug-detection dog provided probable cause to, for example, search a car. The Court specifically found fault in the Florida court's treatment of field performances as a "gold standard in evidence, when in most cases they have relatively limited import," noting that "errors may abound in such records."[40] For instance:

> If a dog on patrol fails to alert to a car containing drugs, the mistake usually will go undetected because the officer will not initiate a search. Field data thus may not capture a dog's false negatives. Conversely (and more relevant here), if the dog alerts to a car in which the officer finds no narcotics, the dog may not have made a mistake at all. The dog may have detected substances that were too well hidden or present in

---

37 *Florida v. Harris*, 133 S. Ct. 1050 (2013).
38 *Florida*, 133 S. Ct. at 1057.
39 *Florida*, 133 S. Ct. at 1056.
40 *Florida*, 133 S. Ct. at 1056.

quantities too small for the officer to locate. Or the dog may have smelled the residual odor of drugs previously in the vehicle or on the driver's person.[41]

Indeed, it is precisely this kind of situation we see in *Florida v. Harris*. As the Court notes, Harris regularly cooked and used methamphetamine. As a result, there were likely trace amounts of the substance on Harris's truck door handle on the driver's side. Although Wheetley, the handler at the center of this trial, did not find any drugs in Harris's truck, he conjectured that his K9 Aldo likely responded to the trace amounts of methamphetamine on the truck door handle. As the case decision notes, "a well-trained drug-detection dog should alert to such odors; his response to them might appear a mistake, but in fact is not":[42]

> *Field data thus may markedly overstate a dog's real false positives.* By contrast, those inaccuracies — in either direction — do not taint records of a dog's performance in standard training and certification settings. There, the designers of an assessment know where drugs are hidden and where they are not — and so where a dog should alert and where he should not. *The better measure of a dog's reliability thus comes away from the field, in controlled testing [and training] environments.*[43]

In its decision, the Court reiterated previous decisions that had concluded that probable cause to search is based on facts available at the time of a search that would "warrant a [person] of reasonable caution in the belief" that contraband or evidence of a crime is present. The previous decision also said that the test for probable cause must be based on "fair probability" because it is not reducible to "precise definition or quantification," nor to "finely tuned standards such as proof beyond reasonable doubt."[44]

Florida v. Harris further established that detailed logs of a dogs' field performance should not be automatically required in establishing the reliability of drug-detection dogs as such an inflexible requirement would not be consistent with the more flexible concept of fair probability that underlies probable cause. Using this

---

41 *Florida*, 133 S. Ct. at 1056.
42 *Florida*, 133 S. Ct. at 1059.
43 *Florida*, 133 S. Ct. at 1056–57.
44 *Florida*, 133 S. Ct. at 1055.

standard, the Court noted that the performance of a dog in training scenarios would be at play in the officer's decision-making and relevant to the determination of probable cause for a drug search "if the dog has recently and successfully completed a training program that evaluated his proficiency in locating drugs."[45] It concluded that evidence of training, even without certification, can be sufficient to establish reliability.

The Court also emphasized that the defendant must have the opportunity to challenge the dog's reliability by cross-examining the handler and presenting expert evidence. The initial arguments that questioned the K9's reliability in this case were the result of documentation from a system that had created a "K9 reliability" report on live deployments. This was a flaw in the reporting system that gave the impression that the dog involved was unreliable, not because it failed in training and certification standards but because of the way the computer system scored live deployments — that is, the way it assessed field data.

By arguing the case up to the Supreme Court, the issue created by the computer system was challenged and rectified. The Court was able to discern the truth of the situation despite the system's flawed reports. However, this outcome was far from guaranteed. These types of issues have the potential not only to discredit the officer and the agency but also to set bad precedent, which is something the K9 industry can ill afford. *Should bad case law ever evolve from flawed reporting such as this, even by a single agency, it can affect the entire industry.*

Records management needs to be efficient, provide appropriate and accurate information, and only deal with known and quantifiable information. Whether you are using paper trail records management or electronic records management, ensure you thoroughly understand the implications of what you choose to track and how you track it.

CONSEQUENCES OF POOR RECORDS AND POOR TESTIMONY

A more recent case from a lower court in Utah demonstrates the weight and value that courts place on the training notes provided by handlers during training events and how the officer presents

---

45 *Florida*, 133 S. Ct. at 1057.

in court. *United States of America v. Jordan*[46] involved a motion to suppress all evidence obtained during a traffic stop that occurred in Utah in 2019. The request to suppress was subsequently granted by the District of Utah court, and the indictment against the accused was overturned. This case is significant in that it exemplifies the importance of a strong training ethic, well-kept records, and the ability to provide credible testimony.

In the judge's analysis of the case, the court had serious concerns about the dog's training and reliability as follows:

> In allowing a K9's indication, or even its alert, to serve as a basis for finding probable cause to search an individual's personal property, we, as a society, are placing an enormous amount of trust, and indeed our very civil liberties, in the responses of creatures that have limited ability to communicate with us. It is therefore imperative that a K9 be meticulously trained so that we can be assured that its signals are clear and direct and that we, as a community, can be confident in the reliability of the message that the K9 is communicating.[47]

The court noted that the Tenth Circuit uses K9 certification in its assessments of K9 reliability in court:

> The courts have consistently recognized that that the training necessary to support certification must be completed successfully, that the certification must be current and updated through ongoing training, *and that both must be supported by accurate and timely kept records.* Here, the manner by which [K9] Tank was trained and certified, together with the supporting records, does not warrant such confidence.[48]

The judge then became critical of the Utah POST certification process under which the team had been certified (which he described as "deficient") and the amount of training the dog had received since the certification. The judge noted that K9 Tank's training was infrequent and insufficiently challenging, consisting of "scenarios that made it impossible for Tank to make a false-identification of narcotics." He further found, based on the testimony of the officer at the center of this case, that Tank's training

---

46 *United States of America v. Jordan*, D. Utah 2:19-cr-125 (2020).
47 *United States of America*, D. Utah 2:19-cr-125 at 13A.
48 *United States of America*, D. Utah 2:19-cr-125 at 13A.

records were unreliable: "he filled in reports from 'muscle memory' and on occasion simply disregarded filling in boxes or providing information."[49]

The decision in this case reflects the important role documentation plays in supporting the claim that the dog's trained response satisfies the requirement for probable cause: "To meet the requirement to allow a K9's responses to satisfy the Constitutional requirement for probable cause, there must be a record supporting both the reliability of the K9 and the handler. There are lapses in this case as to both."[50] Ultimately, the court rejected K9 Tank's Utah POST certification as evidence that he was a reliable source of information for the officer in this case.

While this case is a drug case, the exact same obligations for accurate record keeping in every aspect of training apply. Just as a forensic lab expert meticulously documents everything they do, so must a K9 handler document every action and nuance of training in every profile in which the dog is trained.

Take the training and documentation circumstances of the above case, and apply them to a case in which a dog has tracked a robbery suspect. Without training records that show in detail that the dog is trained to track human odor and has a proven record of finding hidden decoys under similar weather conditions and time delay parameters, the results of the case would likely be the same, and the tracking evidence would not stand.

Apply the same supposition to a lawsuit based on the apprehension of a suspect by the dog. The agency, officer, and K9 supervisor are being sued. If such a case were met with inadequate records as in the above case, the outcome would no doubt be in favor of the plaintiff.

TOO GOOD TO BE TRUE

Training records that show a dog is successful 100 percent of the time are another area of concern. This type of record keeping was common in the 1990s, and some trainers still believe in this training philosophy. This belief stems from trainers who instructed handlers in ways that always ensured the success of the dog in every training profile. Every track, every search, virtually every

---

49 *United States of America*, D. Utah 2:19-cr-125 at 15.
50 *United States of America*, D. Utah 2:19-cr-125 at 15.

exercise was set up in such a way that the dog always succeeded, even if that success had to be accomplished through the support of the handler. In doing so, the handlers recorded a 100 percent efficiency rate no matter what exercise or training profile was being performed or how much support the dog needed to accomplish the goal.

However, there is no such thing as a perfect dog. It did not take long before training records that showed dogs performing with 100 percent efficiency were being questioned by the courts, raising doubts about the value of the training records and subsequently the reality of the true abilities of the dogs.

Challenges to the credibility of records showing 100 percent proficiency levels have taught agencies to change their documentation approach to include both successes and failures. Whether you are using in-house records software, handwritten documentation, or commercial RMS products to track your training, ensure your officers record their training events clearly and honestly. Documentation should include clear training objectives, any training issues that occur, the steps taken to resolve those issues, and the results of those corrections. This approach produces records that provide credibility and demonstrate that the agency is transparent and taking appropriate steps to address training deficits quickly and efficiently to maintain high standards of performance.

If your K9 unit has a record-keeping system that shows 100 percent performance in any given training profile, you need to seriously consider making changes to how you record your training performance. Failing to do so may put your unit credibility at risk and could have a ripple effect throughout the industry.

BE OBJECTIVE

Ensure that your officers, when tracking actual deployments, are not documenting unnecessary, subjective information. Subjective input has the potential to open a Pandora's box you will not want to deal with.

All records need to be clear, objective, and unbiased. As already mentioned, there is no purpose in collecting data that uses a handler's subjective reports in an uncontrolled environment to develop a report on the dog's scent threshold. It serves no purpose and can only create confusion in a courtroom.

Accurate, appropriate, and objective record keeping ensures you have the best protections in place to prevent officer, agency, and industry liability. It will provide documents that show your unit's professionalism and intent to provide the facts of, not the

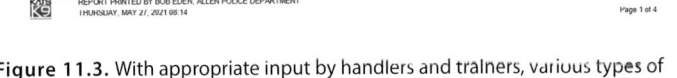

Figure 11.3. With appropriate input by handlers and trainers, various types of training reports provide an accurate picture of training plans and training outcomes that are scrutinized by the courts. Proper documentation provides you with the ammunition you need to show that proper training and corrective measures have been taken when necessary to ensure the highest levels of performance.

opinions on, any given case. In the end, that is our purpose: to present the facts that will allow the courts to do their job. Doing so will have significant positive impact on the courts.

RECORD KEEPING TO MITIGATE RISK AND IMPROVE CONVICTION RATES

In my early career, I got into the habit of preparing strong documentation for every training event. When I was directed to provide training records that would end up in the hands of an opposing attorney, I took pride in what I was able to produce. Along with my training records and any other requested information about a case, I attached my CV. As my expertise and CV grew and my training record documentation continued to improve, I eventually found that my time on the witness stand was significantly reduced. Attorneys in my jurisdiction knew who I was. Knowing the level of preparation I put into my records, they inevitably agreed to a plea deal for their clients when I showed up to testify. I learned then that solid records management can be a powerful tool.

When an officer walks into court with a cornerstone of well-kept records that they know are well written and complete, they go in confident and comfortable knowing full well they have left nothing to chance. The confidence and strong testimony that ensues as a result have a significant impact on a judge or jury.

In *United States of America v. Jordan*, had the training involved higher standards and a consistent training regimen backed by strong documentation, the search may very well have stood up to the constitutional requirements for probable cause. As in *Florida v. Harris*, the Utah court put significantly more weight on the training records of the dog than on certification. In both cases, the courts leaned on record keeping even more than certification as proof of a K9's reliability.

Comprehensive records are the key to reducing liability, ensuring convictions, and demonstrating the professionalism of your teams. Success in K9 record keeping comes down to deploying a quality K9 RMS and policy that requires officers to enter detailed and accurate training and deployment notes. K9 teams must be backed up by a supervisor who supports them by scrutinizing the records for accuracy and ensuring that teams have everything they need to do their jobs safely and efficiently.

Selecting a K9 RMS

When a subpoena hits the desk of the K9 Unit supervisor demanding specific training record details, you need to be able to pull that information efficiently and know that it's strong enough to protect you and your agency from liability. Rudimentary paperwork that provides limited information is no longer acceptable or wise when it comes to documenting K9 training or deployments in any aspect of the K9 profession.

Make it a priority to research and implement a quality computerized K9 RMS. Before deciding on a K9 RMS, consider your teams' training regimens and other needs and ensure the system can handle them. Most importantly, once implemented, ensure your K9 handlers are using the system to its full capability.

STANDARD AGENCY RMS VERSUS K9-SPECIFIC RMS

Standard police reports are critical to any criminal case. These reports are just as critical, if not more so, in the context of K9 teams. In most criminal cases, standard police records requested for evidence pertain only to the details of the case in question; in cases where an officer is required to provide expert witness testimony based on a specialized field, their background and training certifications can come into question. However, only in K9 cases is there an expectation by the courts to produce daily training logs that can be scrutinized.

Some standard law enforcement RMSs will offer rudimentary K9 supplements with their packages. Needed K9 training records are nonexistent in most of these applications. When they do exist, they tend not to meet the needs of K9 training and deployment records. RMSs built specifically for K9 operations are the most thorough and efficient and provide the best protection to your teams when K9-specific information is required in court.

Consider, for example, how an RMS deals with bite ratios. Well-designed, K9-specific RMSs will provide you with bite ratios for any of your teams at the touch of a button. You will further be able to pull specific numbers on these ratios based on

Bite Ratio
ALLEN POLICE DEPARTMENT

Stryker/Eden

Subject Name	Status	Offence	Incident	Arrest	Bite
Black					
SLACK, Jonathan	Charged	Assault - Domestic	2019-79515	Yes	No
JEFFERSON, Kyle	Charged	Vehicle Pursuit	2019-79603	Yes	No
JEFFERSON, Lloyd	Charged	Assault	2020-11511	Yes	No
BITE COUNT BY RACE:					0
East Indian					
DHALIWAL, Rhapinder	Charged	Burglary - Commercial	2021-00011	Yes	No
SINGH, Jaswinder	Charged	Burglary - Commercial	2021-00011	Yes	No
BITE COUNT BY RACE:					0
Hispanic					
HERNANDEZ, Pablo	Charged	Assault	2019-42134	Yes	Yes
GARCIA, Romeo	Charged	Disturbance	2018-1011	Yes	No
MARTINEZ, Santiago	Charged	Carjacking	2021-13056	Yes	No
MERCED, Brandon	Charged	Assault With A Weapon	2020-5682	Yes	No
BITE COUNT BY RACE:					1
White					
HELLER, Ricky Nelson	Charged	Burglary - Residential	2021-7635	Yes	Yes
JOHNSON, Steve	Charged	Burglary - Residential	2021-7635	Yes	No
FRIESEN, Taylor	Charged	Attempt Murder	2021-6475	Yes	No
JESPERSON, Brett Robert	Charged	Attempt Murder	2021-6475	Yes	No
SULLIVAN, Randy	Charged	Burglary - Commercial	2018-0002	Yes	No
VAN TOL, Neil	Charged	Burglary - Commercial	2018-0002	Yes	No
THIBEAULT, Chris	Suspect	Arson	2019-000002	Yes	No
RATHMUSSEN, Bobby	Charged	Arson	2019-000002	Yes	No
MCDONALD, Raphael	Charged	Homicide	2019-79877	Yes	No
RATHBURN, Jesse	Charged	Carjacking	2021-13056	Yes	No
ROTHBERGER, Kelly	Charged	Assault	2020-11511	Yes	No
SHANNON, Randall	Charged	Burglary - Residential	2020-24529	Yes	No
BITE COUNT BY RACE:					1
TEAM BITE TOTAL:					**2**
BITE RATIO:					**9.52 %**

REPORT PRINTED BY BOB EDEN, ALLEN POLICE DEPARTMENT
THURSDAY, MAY 27, 2021 12:43

Figure 11.4a. Bite ratio reports that include demographic information provide agencies with insight into potential issues. They collect factual statistical data that can be referred to at the touch of a button to address any accusations of abuse against a particular demographic, thus protecting the agency. In this fictional example, the team had an overall bite ratio of 18.75 percent involving all demographics.

AGENCY BITE RATIO: 9.52 %

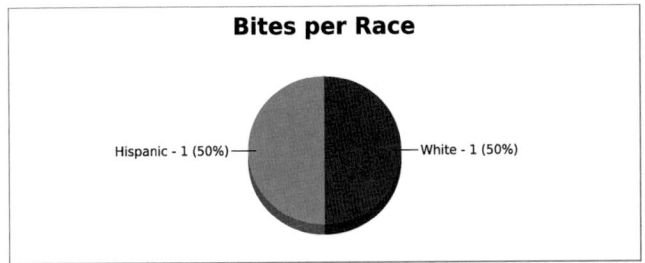

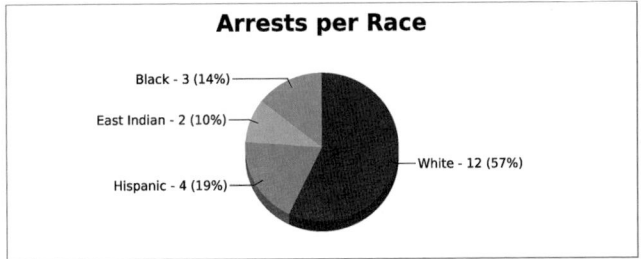

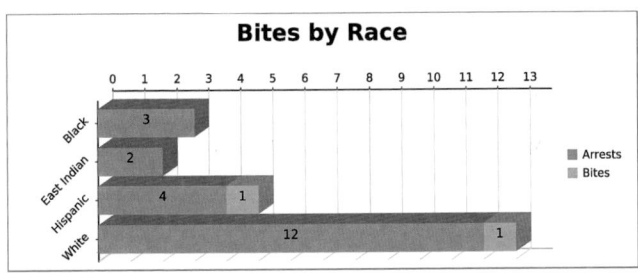

Figure 11.4b. *Continued from Figure 11.4a.*

demographics, which can be key to defending your teams against accusations of, for example, racial profiling. Importantly, algorithms in a K9 RMS should discern between K9 deployments where physical apprehension of a suspect is not a possibility (for instance, in detection operations) and those where a deployment can lead to a physical apprehension. This is necessary to keep bite ratios accurate.

BASIC RECOMMENDED FEATURES

TRAINING AND MAINTENANCE PLANS, REPORTS, AND DEVELOPMENT
At minimum, your K9 RMS should allow you to create and record a regular training maintenance plan that includes training objectives and expectations. Regular maintenance training usually involves the team and assigned agency trainer or a contracted vendor getting together once a week for a 4- to 6-hour training session. During each training session, the trainer analyzes both dog and handler performance and provides real-time instruction to the handler, including explanations on the many behaviors exhibited by the dog and suggestions on how to deal with the nuances of the dog's performance. K9 RMSs that do not allow for customized entries and comment insertion, relying instead on default settings alone, are inadequate.

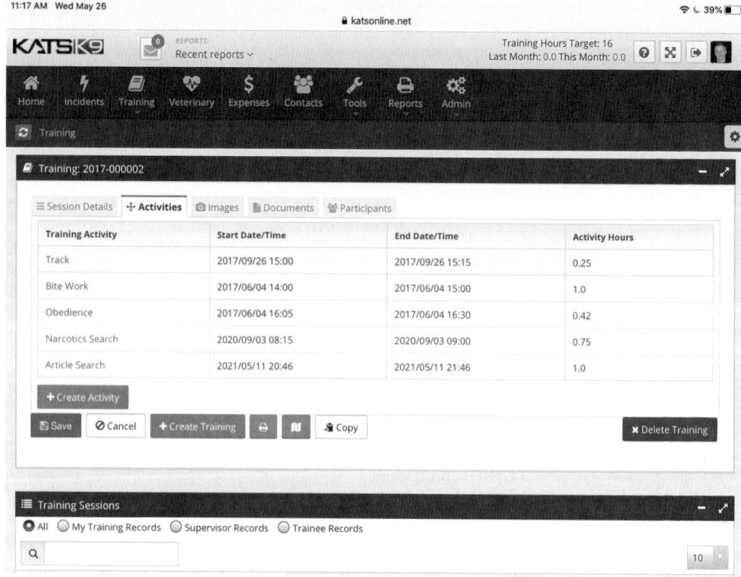

Figure 11.5. Every training activity performed by a team needs to be documented, including training objectives, training outcomes, and trainer notes. If a training deficiency is noted, it should be documented along with recommendations for corrective action. See Figures 11.6, 11.7, and 11.8A.

RECORDS MANAGEMENT 197

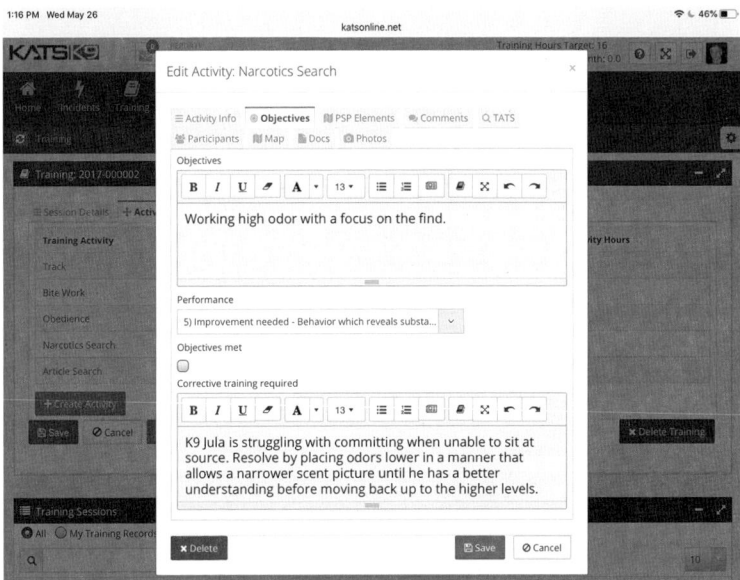

Figure 11.6. Recommendations for correcting deficiencies form part of both short- and long-term training plans for remedial training. Subsequent training documentation will demonstrate due diligence in resolving the issue to expected working standards.

Training reports should provide details of each training activity, including any required corrective action, any corrective action taken, and the results of those actions, as well as any recommendations provided by the trainer. They should also include important time frames, environmental conditions, and distances for exercises as these become important factors in cases involving tracking or trailing events. The reports should gather statistics that prove the performance capability of the dog in all of its training profiles under controlled conditions. This is particularly important in detection and tracking/trailing applications.

In addition, a well-designed system will have reports that will assist in the development of your training routines. Look for reports that assess the balance of detection training regimens or that can assist in pinpointing sudden drops in performance. These can be very useful in helping both trainers and handlers monitor performance and develop their training goals.

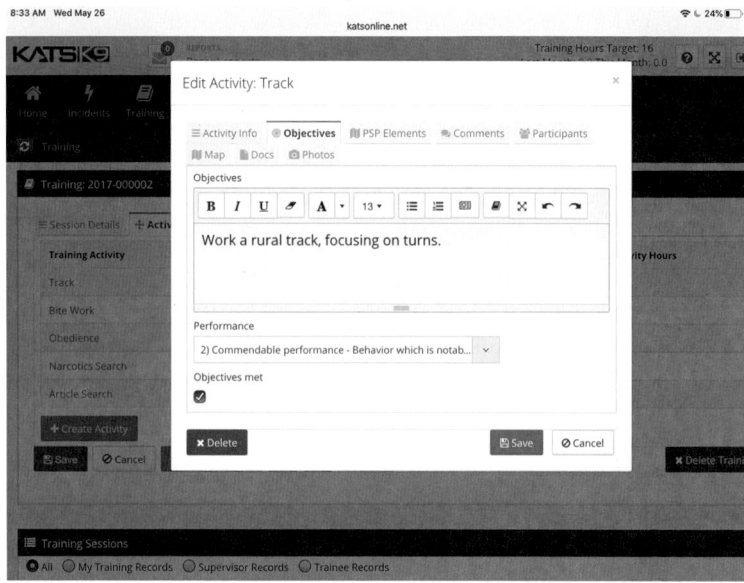

Figure 11.7. Each training activity must have a clear training objective as part of the training plan.

UNIT MANAGEMENT

Quality RMSs provide additional benefits that can assist in managing your K9 unit. Look for a package that can assist in tracking veterinary appointments and maintaining medical records for each dog and that will notify you when annual medical checks or vaccinations are due. The system should also maintain a record of annual certifications and other evaluations for each team.

Some agencies will benefit from a system that can further assist in tracking the unit's annual expenses and assist in developing the K9 budget. Agencies may also find value in systems with features that help you schedule K9 teams for demonstrations, training, or other assignments and send these schedules to the assigned officers.

EFFICIENT REPORTING

Finally, a well-designed K9 RMS will make all of the recorded data quickly and easily accessible. When you are served with a subpoena by the court to provide this information, responding to freedom-of-information (FOI) requests, or simply replying to news reporters' questions pertaining to the use of dogs, a good system will put the facts at your fingertips. Some K9 RMSs make this type of information retrieval easier than others, which is why it is important to research the capabilities and design of any systems you consider and critically examine them against your needs. Facts matter, and being able to respond to allegations in times of heightened tensions is invaluable.

SIDE-BY-SIDE, TRAINER-SUPPORTED COMMENTS

A good, K9-specific RMS should also allow the unit trainer to write on a handler's training record entry in order to comment on and evaluate the training. The purpose of having side-by-side K9 trainer and handler notes is to encourage interaction and discussion about training events.

This idea evolved from handwritten RCMP service dog training records extending back into the 1980s. At the end of each training session, the handler would enter their comments followed by the trainer, who would enter comments and recommendations on how to improve the training. This method ensures that the handler and the trainer are aware of each other's feedback and helps avoid misunderstandings.

Many trainers, particularly private vendors, are hesitant to maintain training logs. This is an unwise practice in today's environment, and consideration should be given to encouraging your K9 unit trainers to establish a secure connection with your K9 RMS to enter their assessments of training activities. At the very least, trainers should maintain an activity log of each training event they are involved in.

Documentation entered by agency trainers protects the trainers and offers supervisors an opportunity to review training events from the trainer's perspective, keeping them current on the training status of each team. Trainer records are also advantageous should the trainer be summoned to court, either for litigation or to provide supportive testimony about the capability of a handler they have trained. If the K9 instructor has made notes, those notes can be referred to in order to refresh their memory of training events. Finally, record keeping that involves the trainer's input can protect the trainer from accusations of vicarious liability.

A

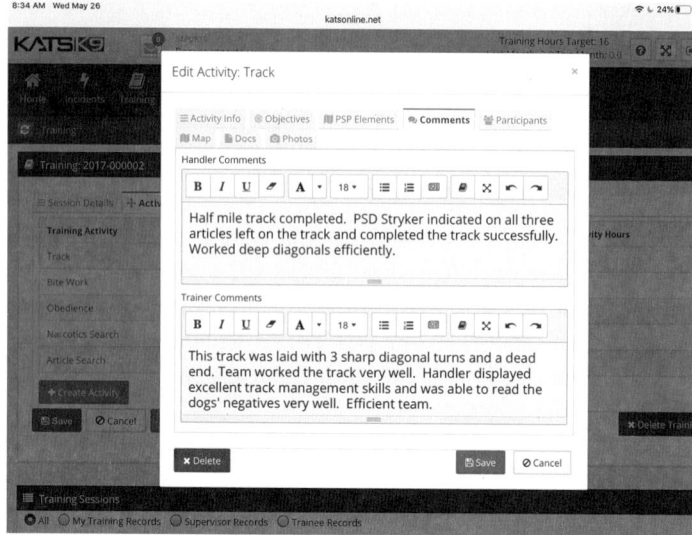

B

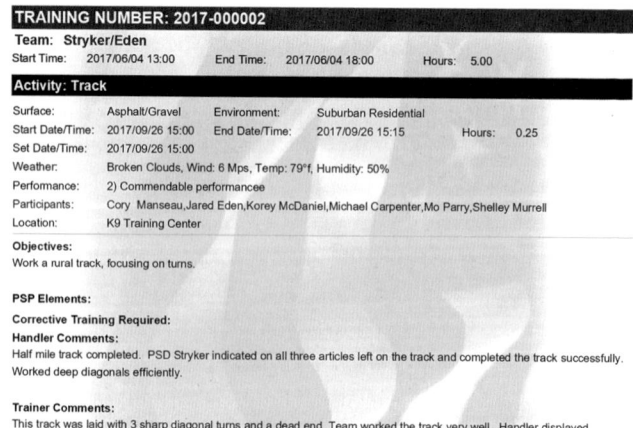

Figure 11.8. A: An example of a KATS Platinum RMS training report showing side-by-side comments from the handler and trainer. Notes are succinct and provide all necessary details to satisfy court requirements. B: A sample of a four-page training detail report.

TRAINER COMMENTS: A CASE STUDY

As the K9 trainer for my agency in the late 1980s, I was periodically assigned to assist in developing and training K9 teams for other police agencies. At the time, all training logs were handwritten. Our agency used a side-by-side training entry log divided into multiple sections. The design allowed for three training activities to be recorded on each sheet, with space for a short paragraph from both the handler and the trainer for each activity.

A K9 team from another agency that I had been assigned to train alongside our own teams included a neutered Belgian Tervuren. The department had limited funding to purchase a dog, and it was all they were able to provide. An intake assessment quickly exposed weaknesses in the dog; under normal circumstances, this would not have been a dog I would have attempted to train. At that time in my career, however, I was a regular patrol officer with no authority and was directed to get the job done.

The dog was adequate in most training profiles. He was a good tracking dog and showed some potential but at times lacked motivation and was inconsistent. He was a weak performer in aggression profiles and was overall challenging to work with.

After consulting with a vet, we attempted to bring his behaviors up with a regimen of testosterone injections designed to overcome issues caused by the lack of hormones resulting from the dog's neutering at an early age. Initially we saw a bit of improvement in performance, but ultimately it was apparent that the dog was not capable of doing the job and it was unwise to move forward.

Every training event and all veterinary intervention was documented, and the handler and I discussed the need to replace the dog. As it happened, our agency had an excellent dog available. Our agency made an offer to provide that dog as a replacement, but the handler was not open to doing so. It was apparent that his decision was not based on objective consideration but on his attachment to the dog; however, he had total autonomy from his department to make the decisions regarding their K9 program.

I documented my impressions and concerns in detail during each of the numerous discussions I had with the handler about replacing the dog. I specifically documented that the dog did not have the drive or appropriate behaviors to work as a police dog. I included my recommendation to replace the dog in my documentation and noted that the handler had rejected an offer to replace the dog. As was the process with every entry, the handler and I both initialed the entries.

The dog continued to perform at mediocre levels. He could go through the motions of bite work if he was worked in a manner that did not put too much pressure on him, and by the end of the program, his tracking was relatively good. When the handler left our training to return to his agency, I again advised him of my concerns, and he assured me he understood.

Eighteen months afterwards, I was approached by a senior officer from our department. I was advised that a formal written complaint had been lodged against me by the chief of this handler's agency. The dog had failed during a deployment on a major incident and was known during his short tenure to be inconsistent on deployments. When discussing the failure of the dog's performance with his chief, the handler said I had failed to teach him about K9 behavior and that I had allowed the dog to proceed through the training. He advised that if he had known there were so many issues, he would not have continued training with that dog.

The issue was quickly resolved when I produced the side-by-side training notes. It was evident that I had spoken to the officer on numerous occasions explaining K9 behavior and the lack of drive in the dog. I had clearly stated my recommendations to remove the dog from the program and replace him with another dog that we knew was of high caliber. Both of our signatures appeared on each entry.

Without this documentation, I would have had nothing to contradict the handler's accusations, short of an extensive internal investigation. It speaks to the value of side-by-side documentation and is an excellent example of the benefit of records input from a trainer's perspective.

While this incident is not court related, it can be extrapolated to a court scenario. Had someone been injured because of the dog's failure, it is possible that I and my agency would have been named in a lawsuit because we were responsible for the training of the team. Without the protection of strong documentation, it would be more difficult to mount a strong defense.

SUPERVISORY OVERSIGHT AND AUDIT TRAILS

Supervisory oversight in K9 operations is a priority. It is essential not only to provide your K9 handlers with a quality K9 RMS, but also to scrutinize the quality of the records kept. Choose a K9 RMS that allows for and facilitates thorough supervisory oversight.

K9 supervisors will often leave the decision up to the handlers as to what RMS they prefer, and it is indeed important to allow the handlers significant input in this decision. However, while they are willing to put effort into training and deployments of their K9 partners, many handlers are resistant to comprehensive training and deployment report writing. Some handlers thus prefer certain systems simply for their ease of use. Handlers that lean toward this type of RMS may fail to consider the consequences of weak report writing. This is the Achilles' heel of K9 programs and a major weakness when it comes to litigation in criminal cases and civil lawsuits.

Some easy-to-use systems are rudimentary, involving quick, uncustomizable drop-down menu selections and few options for handler and trainer input. Many such systems come without any supervisory management ability. The resulting reports are only marginally more helpful in court than simple pass/fail or checkmark paperwork and offer little to no protection from lawsuits. When asked for details about months' worth of training events prior to a specific court appearance, handlers have no notes to refer to. The officer is just as much in the dark as the opposing counsel. At best, the officer and agency appear to be unprofessional.

Even the best K9 RMS available will not be effective if handlers don't make use of the features in it that are designed to protect them and their agency. To that end, it is essential that supervisors regularly read both training and live deployment reports for clarity and accuracy, ensuring adequate and appropriate information has been recorded. RMS design should allow K9 handlers to send their completed deployment reports to a supervisor for approval, and supervisors should be able to easily return the reports to handlers to clarify any discrepancies or complete any missing information. The RMS should allow the reports to be locked once they have been approved by the supervisor. The system you choose should make this process smooth and simple.

Systems that offer keystroke logging provide further valuable audit trails. These systems show who is or was logged in, what was done by the user, and any changes the user made to the documents in the system. For example, in KATS Platinum RMS, keystroke logging shows how entries looked before and after any changes are made, noting both who made the changes and the date and time of all entries. These logs are secure and cannot be altered, providing an added level of integrity.

From a supervisory perspective, the audit trail provides the agency with an extra line of defense should the integrity of recorded entries ever be questioned. This can prove invaluable should any internal reviews be initiated.

AUDIT TRAILS: A CASE STUDY

A dog working in a major metropolitan agency was suffering from significant medical issues and was under the care of the department veterinarian. The assigned handler was provided with prescription medications and given specific instructions on when and how to administer the medication. The unit supervisor directed the handler to create an entry in the K9 RMS every time the prescription was administered. As time progressed, the dog's health continued to decline and he eventually died.

After the dog's passing, an internal affairs investigation was initiated into the handler. The supervisor checked the K9 RMS and found the officer had logged each time he administered the medication as directed by the veterinarian. It appeared the dates and times were appropriately logged along with pertinent notations. However, there had been ongoing tensions between the supervisor and handler even before this event, and the supervisor mistrusted the findings and suspected the handler of doctoring the records after the dog's death.

The K9 RMS audit trail of the K9 officer's activity in the system was pulled, and a quick review of the logs proved the medications had been given as directed: the entries were complete and entered at the appropriate times without any subsequent changes.

In this instance, the audit trail protected the K9 handler from being inappropriately accused and potentially disciplined. This example demonstrates the value of having a system that provides unalterable logging of reporting activity.

Best Practices in Records Management

A few common issues get in the way of agencies maintaining quality training and deployment records that will stand up in today's courts.

SCRUTINIZING RECORDS

Checks and balances need to be in place for officer reports to ensure compliance with agency policy and expectations. It is the supervisor's responsibility to scrutinize training and deployment records thoroughly and regularly, and to take action when records are insufficient or incomplete.

Management of your K9 RMS should be no different than how you deal with regular police reports. As a supervisor, you should

Table 11.1. Common Issues in Records Management

ISSUE	DETAILS
Management employs a K9 RMS with minimalist pass/fail or checkbox documentation. *"Minimal information provides less ammunition for attorneys to work against you."*	• Marking an exercise as a "pass" or "fail," or simply as "complete," provides no information about K9 training and performance. • Limited information restricts you from having documents that support the team in court. • No documentation = no proof of training standard = no credibility.
Handlers encourage management to employ a K9 RMS that requires minimal input and allows minimal supervisory oversight. *"It is excessively time consuming to document activity. This system is quick and easy."*	• Little input is required and there is little to no supervisory management capability. • Information is inadequate when subpoenaed. • Default entries with minimal supportive documentation are minimally effective in court and have resulted in lost cases.
Management employs a quality K9 RMS, but handlers fail to use it to its full capacity. *"My handlers input minimal information and miss basics that are often easy to complete. They use the drop-down boxes to quick fill, but resist detailing the training."*	• The K9 RMS is well designed, but when records are subpoenaed, vital information is missing, leaving records incomplete. • Incomplete records are not only inadequate but work against the handler in court. • Supervisory oversight is imperative to ensure K9 officers are providing written documentation on training activities.

expect and insist on detailed documentation from your officers as it relates to any K9 training or deployment. Monitor the records and peruse them regularly. Watch for discrepancies, check for accuracy, and be aware of common errors. Ensure the officers input their records immediately after training or deployment rather than trying to catch up later. This helps to safeguard against skepticism about officer credibility.

Mismanagement can cause issues for both your handlers and you as a supervisor. Consider the example of a unit supervisor who was served a subpoena requesting a year of training records for one of his K9 handlers. The case involved litigation for a dog bite that occurred during a criminal apprehension. When reports were run, all entries about specific training activities were blank. Investigation revealed that the K9 officer had only been creating training entries to note the dates and times of his training and to tally total training hours. No effort had been put into creating training objectives, what training routines were done, the amount of time conducted on each exercise, or the results of the training exercises. Because the supervisor had not been prudent in regularly examining the reports for substance and accuracy, he was unfortunately put in an exceedingly difficult position when served with the lawsuit.

MONITORING TRAINING AND DEPLOYMENT REPORTS

Always have your officers input their involvement at the completion of every event. Most K9 RMSs not only have the option to be run on vehicle mobile data terminals, but also from handlers' smartphones, making it easy and efficient to keep records up to date immediately following K9 training or deployment.

Supervisors should pull handler training statistics weekly or biweekly and ensure the recommended minimum industry standards of 4 hours a week and 16 hours a month are being met. Ensure all documentation is complete and any training problems documented have been resolved with remedial training. Recommendations for corrective training should be noted for any issues that appear to require long-term remediation.

Monitor all use of force reports carefully and pull your bite ratios by demographics reports monthly to ensure that bite ratios are within normal limits. Normal limits will differ from agency to agency depending on population and crime rate demographics. If all officers in your unit serve a population of generally equal demographics, any teams that have disproportionately high bite ratios, or high bite ratios in a certain demographic, will be immediately visible.

If checked regularly, these reports will assist you in staying ahead of any potential issues. As a supervisor, it is important to note that every case involving physical apprehension of a suspect must be judged on its own merits. Statistical analysis of bite ratios and bite ratio demographics are only a guide to assist you in identifying potential issues. When a team has a bite ratio higher in one demographic, this does not necessarily indicate that there is an issue. Take into account other factors, as well, such as the demographics of the zones the team is working and the amount of criminal activity in those zones.

ENCOURAGING OFFICER COMPLIANCE

Inadequate training and deployment documentation occurs for many reasons, but most issues are related to lack of K9 handler initiative in producing needed reports and failure of the supervisor to maintain proper oversight of submitted records. In some cases, it is the result of a dependency on paper documentation that is cumbersome. Whatever your K9 RMS, you must ensure each deployment is within your agency policy and meets the requirements of *Graham v. Connor* (see Chapter 3).

Records management issues can be avoided upfront by encouraging officers to provide complete and accurate documentation in the first place. This can be done in part by educating them on why it's important. Ensure your K9 handlers understand that what they record and how they record it is as integral to their job as the training and deployment of their dog. The same is true of how they present their evidence in court.

Courts expect professional officers to properly document the training regimens that support the work they do on the street, and to be able to clearly and confidently present that information. As stated earlier, United States Supreme Court case law does not simply accept K9 certification. They rely heavily on the training records that back up that certification. More recently, courts have been comparing specific information documented in the training records to the testimony provided by the officers in court as to how their dog performed during the case in question.

Think back, too, to the *United States of America v. Jordan* case from the District of Utah. In that case, the officer testified that he sometimes completed his documentation from "muscle memory" and sometimes would neglect to fill in all pertinent information. Unfortunately, this type of documentation corner-cutting is not uncommon. As mentioned above, one of the common issues in K9 record management is insufficient information input on the part of handlers using purpose-built, quality K9 RMSs. However, these systems offer the robust database structures that, when used correctly, provide the detailed information now expected in today's courtroom environment.

Particularly for supervisors without extensive K9 experience, it is not always easy to identify missing information in reports. If your agency has in-house trainers, it is recommended that supervisors share the responsibility of scrutinizing training and deployment reports with the unit trainer. The unit trainer can provide expert input analyzing information specific to canine behavior and will be able to identify important gaps in reports, places where the handler should be providing additional or more-detailed information, and instances where training entries have been improperly entered.

Common Requests for K9 Records

The following are the most common requests from the courts or public FOI requests. As a K9 supervisor, you need to be ready to supply this information when it is requested. Your K9 RMS, combined with thorough record-keeping habits and quality management, should be able to quickly and easily deliver the reports and documentation to meet these requests for each dog:

- Full incident reports and all material information related to K9 deployments
- Full training history of a dog within a specific time frame, or for the lifetime of the dog
  - › These requests may be specific to a particular profile (e.g., narcotics training: hits/misses/false alerts and any corrective action taken to bring the dog up to a specific standard) or related to general training.
  - › Full history requests are common in litigation requests.
- A record of the bite history of the dog on deployments
- A record of the dog's bite ratio
  - › The bite ratio is the number of bites compared to the number of arrests attributed to the deployment of the dog in a patrol application.
  - › Bite ratio may also be requested by racial demographic. The same qualifications as a standard bite ratio report, but the statistics are broken down further to determine if there is any indication of one race being targeted over another.

- A bite training report
  - What were the training objectives?
  - Were the training objectives and performance standard achieved?
  - Were there any deficiencies and, if so, were the deficiencies noted and subsequently rectified to acceptable standards?

See Figure 11.9 (p. 210) for an example of the variety of reports you may find useful.

Take a look at your K9 unit, and ask yourself seriously: Can you provide this information with all the required elements without manually pulling every training record? Are you satisfied that every record is accurate and that each record provides the information required to protect your K9 officers from direct civil liability and you from vicarious liability or accusations of failure to supervise? If you got hit with a subpoena today, would you be able to provide the above information with all pertinent details and feel comfortable the records are a true and accurate representation of your teams?

Would you bet your career on it?

This is the standard you want to achieve. In doing so, you are operating liability aware, prepared for any contingency, and a practicing example of professional standards in K9 operations.

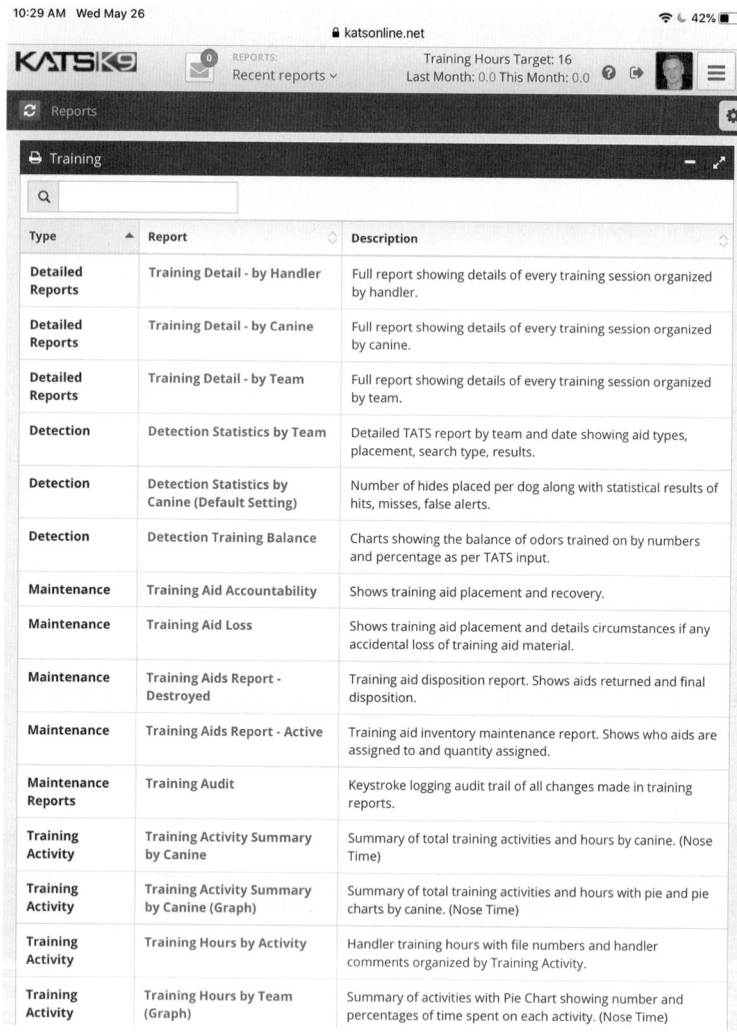

Figure 11.9a. Demands for training and incident records can be extensive, and electronic RMSs are a must in modern policing. Manually compiling paper records is tedious and can be extremely time consuming. Computerized records management allows you to pull pre-developed reports to fulfill any request at the touch of a button. Reports like the examples here can assist in fulfilling FOI requests and court demands. Reports on bites by demographics and bite ratios can be invaluable in fighting false accusations of race baiting and can be pulled in real time if data has been properly entered.

RECORDS MANAGEMENT

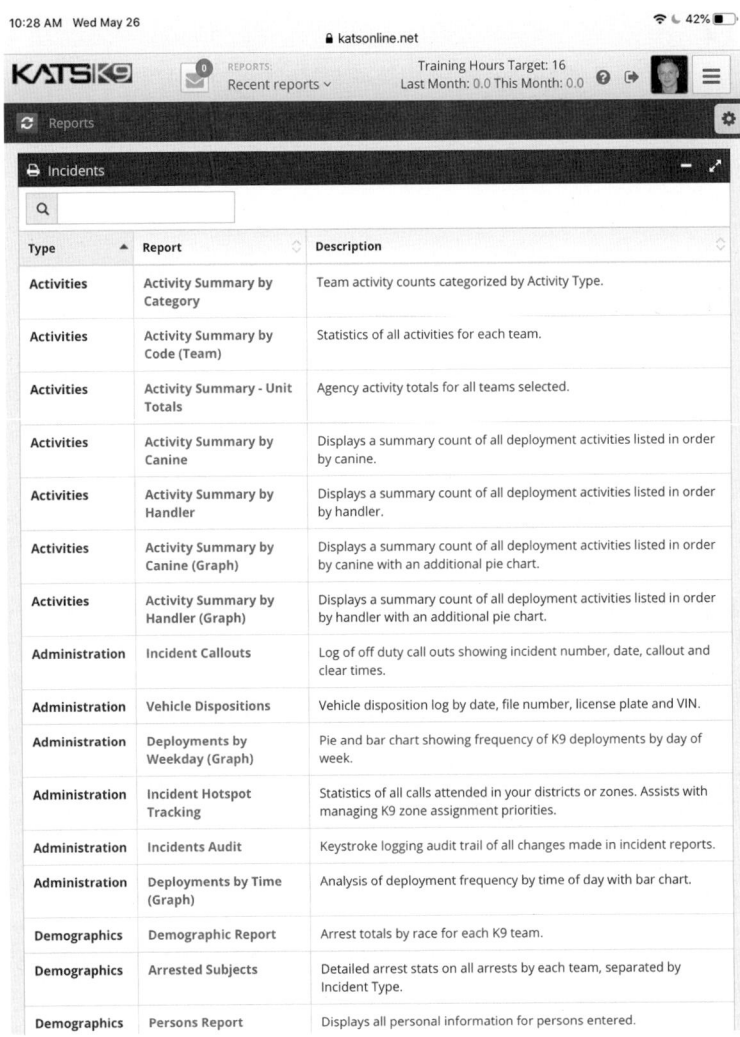

Figure 11.9b. *Continued from Figure 11.9a.*

12

K9 Policy

Agency police dog policies should be comprehensive. K9 policy should address, at minimum, apprehension use, non-apprehension use (e.g., on-lead searches for children or other non-criminal suspects), training, on- and off-duty care. They should also cover aspects such as control of the dog, labor standards issues, reporting, handler and dog selection, as well as issues indicated by professional organizations such as Lexipol, which provides policy and training for public safety departments.

Many policies related to these issues have already been mentioned in the relevant chapters of this book. This chapter expands on the importance of K9-specific policies and issues related to them. The chapter also details several administrative policies related to handlers, dogs, and supervisors in K9 units in particular.

The Importance of K9-Specific Policy

Some agencies make the mistake of placing their police K9 policy under the umbrella of their use-of-force policy instead of adopting a stand-alone K9 policy. For comparison's sake, think about your agency's police vehicle policy. Agencies don't list police vehicles in their use-of-force policy because this is not the vehicle's primary function. Even so, a situation could potentially arise in which an officer has little choice but to use his unit to eliminate the threat — for instance, if an armed suspect were shooting into the front of the police car. In other words, the police vehicle may be appropriately applied as an improvised weapon, but this does not warrant placing it in a use-of-force policy. Its primary function is transportation.

The same is true for police dogs. While it is true that a police dog might occasionally be deployed in a force situation, the primary value and function of the dog is not as a force option. The primary value and function of a police dog is its olfactory capability. It is this sensory advantage that makes police dog programs invaluable tools for applications such as efficiently and safely locating lost children, evidence, and suspects at a tremendous savings of resources to the agency and the public.

DEVELOPING AGENCY POLICY

At some point, every agency will create a policy that is unique to the area they serve. Such policies are based on local, state, and federal laws as well as the demographics of and issues specific to the community. Like any policy, K9 policy must be carefully developed and maintained. Adopting or developing any policies without professional guidance and legal counsel will ultimately prove to be penny wise and pound foolish.

When developing any law enforcement policy, including police K9 policy, agencies should avoid "borrowing" policies from neighboring agencies without vetting them against your own agency's needs and current policy. Agencies should never blindly adopt boilerplate policies offered by free, online sources. Such policies are rarely maintained to current legal standards and thus raise the question as to whether they reflect best practices. Moreover, agencies that adopt such policies will inevitably find themselves bound to requirements that they cannot follow due to lack of resources or to language that is inconsistent with the agency's philosophy or training.

Beyond seeking professional and legal counsel when developing agency policy, you may also consider subscribing to a service such as Lexipol. The system stays current on case law issues in every aspect of law enforcement operations and is the leading provider of customizable, state-of-the-art policies for public safety organizations.

BALANCED POLICY IS GOOD POLICY

Policies must carefully balance the need to give officers sufficient guidance on agency and legal standards with allowing well-trained officers enough discretion to properly apply policy to the endless variety of situations encountered in the real world. In other words, the policy must be enforceable, but not overly restrictive. This, for example, is why the concept of a "use of force continuum" has been long since rejected as unrealistic and impractical. There is nothing in police work that is black and white (except, perhaps, the car you drive), and decisions rarely, if ever, fit starkly defined models. Thus, while a K9 policy must give the handler guidelines for the application of the canine, it cannot dictate that the dog must only (or never) be deployed in X situation, since it is highly unlikely that X will ever precisely occur.

To illustrate this point, some agencies have unwisely restricted the deployment of a police dog to "felony" suspects only. While police dogs should, of course, never be deployed on very minor offenses such as traffic infractions, the question becomes: Would you authorize the deployment of a dog on a "felony" fraud suspect, but not a misdemeanor suspect resisting arrest? It is important that policies not get locked into statutory definitions of offenses, but instead take the serious nature of the suspected offense as a further consideration among many others.

Similarly, some agencies have made the mistake of only permitting the deployment of the dog on "adult" suspects. Once again, while no handler should be deploying a dog off-lead when searching for suspects described as, for example, 8 to 10 years of age, there are plenty of 17-year-old suspects (i.e., minors) who are quite capable of very violent acts. As such, it is important to include suspect age in your policy as one factor for handlers to consider, but policy should never impose unrealistic limitations that do not take into account real-world variables.

SHALL VERSUS *SHOULD*

The need to provide flexible considerations in any K9 policy is why most well-written policies avoid absolute language such as *shall* and *shall not*. While some absolutes might be dictated by statute or other local considerations, the better approach when possible is to preface various provisions with qualifying language such as *should* or *should not*. According to Lexipol,[51] *should* communicates expected conduct that allows for exceptions if the officer is able to articulate sufficient justification for having deviated from the expected standard. Such language still allows the agency to enforce the policy but is flexible enough to account for the inevitable exceptions that are encountered in the field.

A good example of this is the issue of an officer providing warnings before deploying their dog. While a clear verbal warning is expected whenever feasible (i.e., "a verbal warning should be given"), there are situations in which such a warning is unwise. Consider, for instance, a handler in a situation where a potentially armed suspect is confronting several officers at the front of a location. The handler is able to tactically position the dog to the rear of the suspect to attempt to apprehend them. In such a situation, if the suspect turns out to be armed, it would be unrealistic, if not suicidal, to make a verbal announcement before deploying the dog. By deploying the dog in a stealth mode, however, the handler may be able to apprehend the suspect and save lives in the process. Had agency policy dictated that a verbal warning "shall" always be given before deploying the dog, this handler would be in violation of policy despite having chosen the life-saving option.

Handler, Dog, and Supervisor Policies

COMMUNICATION OF POLICY

In many agencies, the supervisor assigned to the K9 unit will have a number of other assignments, as well; the K9 unit is not their sole responsibility. They often work a standard five-day work week, while the K9 teams for whom they are ultimately responsible work staggered hours and, in many cases, predominantly night shifts. Because of this, the assigned K9 unit supervisor will not always be available in real time to the K9 teams. In these situations, road supervisors become the first line of supervision for the K9 teams.

For this reason, all road supervisors need to be aware of police K9 policies. The K9 unit supervisor should facilitate familiarization meetings to ensure road supervisors are well informed of

---

51 Bruce Praet (cofounder of Lexipol and partner in the law firm Ferguson, Praet & Sherman), personal communication, 2020.

K9 team expectations and must update road supervisors about all policy changes.

K9 HANDLER TENURE

Handler tenure is an issue that will vary from agency to agency. When developing policy about handler tenure, you should keep in mind the amount of time and resources that go into training a new handler to have the knowledge and skills necessary to be capable of their job.

All dog handlers require an understanding and ability to work the dog in diverse profiles. The foundational training includes profiles such as contraband detection, tracking, area search, building search, article search, criminal apprehension, and obedience. To facilitate these skill sets, handlers must have knowledge of K9 behavior, behavior modification, line handling (which includes track management skills), care and maintenance of the dog, and rudimentary trauma care skills. Every handler must understand scent and scent characteristics and be able to explain how the dog detects different odors in order to clearly articulate the evidence to a judge and/or jury in layman's terms. To efficiently work a dog and interpret the dog's body language, the handler must understand canine behavior as well as the unique nuances of their dog's individual behavior. A handler must also understand how air flow conditions in different environments affect odor, both inside buildings and outdoors, and how these conditions may affect the dog's behavior. The time, energy, and resources put into initially developing these basic skills are significant, not to mention the innumerable hours teams put in on the street, further honing those skills.

Some agencies apply a policy that allows handlers only one cycle with a dog. These agencies tend to see the K9 assignment as a way of offering diverse work opportunities. Once a team has served and the dog comes up for retirement, the hander is reassigned, the position is posted, and a new handler is selected. Giving officers the opportunity to work in this desired assignment is commendable but should be balanced against other considerations. From an efficiency perspective, for instance, this may not be the best policy (though much will depend on agency size and needs as well as the quality of applicants to the position).

Consider that a rookie dog handler with no previous experience takes roughly one and a half to two years after the initial training to start feeling comfortable enough to be significantly productive on the street. Much of this is related to the time it takes for the dog and handler to fully connect with each other and meld together as a team as they gain experience through real-world deployments. That time is significantly reduced when an experienced handler who has already spent eight or more years working a dog is given a new assignment. A new team with an experienced handler at the helm becomes productive much more quickly than a rookie team simply because of the skills the officer developed with their previous dog.

Efficiency aside, giving officers with a genuine desire to work a K9 assignment may be seen as a way to increase morale. However, attempts to satisfy these desires tend to actually work against this goal. Some agencies have taken short-tenure policies to extreme levels, reassigning a dog to a new handler every two years. As ludicrous as this sounds, some large agencies still turn to this type of policy in the interest of "creating opportunities." Agencies that apply such policies are not productive on the street and often struggle with poor cohesion and low morale within the unit.

Your policy should recognize the valuable resource that is a qualified, well-trained, and productive dog handler. Just as most well-run agencies provide for and encourage long-term assignments for specialists in other fields, such as crime scene investigators and homicide detectives, wisdom dictates that, given the extensive knowledge and expertise K9 officers bring to the table, it is good policy to allow the officer to work another rotation with a new dog.

The decision to design policy that allows for long-term K9 assignments comes with a few caveats: the assigned officer must be a positive influence on the unit, be productive on the street, be physically capable, and still have that desire for the hunt that makes most K9 teams successful. If a handler has become unproductive or is having trouble keeping up with the significant physical demands of K9 deployment, the best time to rotate a new handler into the position is when the current handler's dog retires.

PROMOTION POLICIES

Many officers with K9 experience apply for promotion as they near the end of their tenure as dog handlers. There are different philosophies when it comes to promoting out of the unit, particularly when there is an opening for a new K9 unit manager. The best leader any police dog program can hope for is someone who has previous experience working a dog on the street.

Some management teams will promote experienced K9 handlers within the unit, allowing them to take the next natural step of overseeing the teams or becoming the department K9 trainer. In some respects, this can provide significant benefits and set the stage for strong and positive productivity.

Other agencies prefer not to promote within the unit and require any handler that is up for promotion to take a patrol assignment if successful in the promotional process. The officer is then allowed to reapply for the K9 supervisor position after having served a certain tenure as a supervisor in patrol.

Many K9 handlers who are required to leave the K9 program to promote have little or no desire to go back to a patrol function. However, resistance to this sort of promotion is shortsighted: if the officer's sole assignment for a significant number of years has been restricted to the K9 program, it can limit their future career opportunities. The opportunity to work other assignments before moving back into the K9 program as a supervisor gives the officer much broader experience and a wider perspective to draw from. They will have the knowledge they gleaned when working a dog and the experience of working in a supervisory capacity in other duties. The experience allows them to look at the bigger picture of operations and how the K9 program can better meet the needs of the department as a whole. Further, if later in their career they wish to promote again to another assignment, the diversity of experience provides a better background for their future endeavors.

UNIT SUPERVISORS AS HANDLERS

Any handler of worth does not work a dog simply because it is an assignment. Great handlers will be those who are passionate about the hunt. They will do whatever it takes to achieve their goals, whether it be locating a missing person, searching for contraband, or finding and taking into custody those who are often the most dangerous members of society. It only makes sense that when an officer who has previously worked a dog becomes the K9 program manager, they may have a strong desire to work a dog.

Most agencies find that a supervisor dedicated to the K9 program is more efficient when not working a dog. Supervisors that do not have the added responsibility of training, maintaining, and deploying their own dog can be better focused on working to improve the K9 teams in the unit. That being said, a dedicated K9 supervisor who has come from a background of working a dog on the street in the past, if they have had enough training and experience to meet the necessary requirements, may also perform as the agency's lead K9 trainer.

Agencies that have supervisors who also work a dog on the street have varying degrees of success. A supervisor who works a dog can still be effective with strong time management in a K9 program that can afford a supervisor who is dedicated exclusively to a K9 unit and has a small number of teams to manage. However, when such a supervisor is responsible for more than two or three teams, that efficiency tends to diminish.

Effective supervisors need to be equally available to all teams. In today's policing environment, supervisors have a myriad of time-consuming responsibilities. They must ensure their officers have what they need to do their job, pursue continuing education and training opportunities for the teams, scrutinize records and deployments, ensure the proper implementation of training, answer public demonstrations requests, and respond to information requests about K9 operations from both inside and outside the department, all while monitoring K9 team activity. If served with a subpoena demanding information for legal proceedings, significant time may be required to locate, research, and vet the requested documentation, depending on how efficient the agency K9 RMS is.

K9 RETIREMENT POLICY

When a dog is retired from the program due to illness or injury, or is rotated out due to age, decisions must be made as to the disposition of the dog and any support the agency is willing to provide. Every agency should have a policy concerning K9 disposition upon retirement.

Most commonly, agencies gift the dog to the handler. In some cases, guided by the agency legal department, agencies will sell the dog to the handler in fee simple for $1. These are the wisest disposition options as the handler and dog have had, from the dog's perspective, a life-long connection and the handler is the person most qualified to continue the care and maintenance of the dog.

This type of disposition also takes into consideration the fact that the family of the K9 officer has also already been in the life of the dog. Allowing the dog to retire to a familiar family unit is a humane disposition that benefits both the dog and the family, who have undoubtedly also become attached to the dog and see it as a family member.

When the dog is transferred to the handler, a waiver is negotiated and signed by both parties. Usually, the handler becomes solely responsible for the dog, with most agencies ceasing all responsibility at that point. Knowing the handler and the handler's family will not abandon the dog at any cost, some departments simply abandon any further responsibility, including those related to feeding, ongoing vet care, and accidents. For the agency, it is just a part of doing business. For the handler and their family, however, it is an added monthly cost to the family budget. Any additional veterinary bills provide even more financial stress. Most handlers have young families, and the added financial strain can make matters difficult.

An annual budget for the care and feeding of retired police dogs is something to be considered for inclusion in department policy. Departments should consider the significant positive impact of caring for retired police dogs that have served the community. An agency that looks after its employees, regardless of position, will always reap the benefits of high-quality employees with better morale and higher productivity. Providing basic care for retired dogs such as a monthly supply of dog food, covering annual veterinary checks, vaccinations, minor appointments, and prescriptions has small impact on a department budget but a big impact on the unit's morale and the officer's family budget.

K9 HANDLERS AS AGENCY TRAINERS

Management teams often assign the most experienced dog handler as the department's K9 program trainer. The selected officer may have extensive experience in training and working dogs on the street and may even have been sent to a K9 trainer certification program.

Unfortunately, this seemingly straightforward assignment can create conflict when the assigned trainer lacks any formal rank or position of authority. Conflict is frequent when a training officer who has no authority finds themselves training handlers who are senior to them or who do not respect the trainer's position. In almost all cases, these conflicts would not occur if the K9 handler assigned as the trainer had been given the authority to make decisions and give direction related to all training and handler development.

Consider, therefore, initiating policy that mandates that any K9 handlers assigned the task of being the department trainer will be given some form of rank authority. When a policy is written providing a mandate to the K9 program trainer to make decisions and give direction that must be adhered to by trainees assigned to them, operations run more efficiently and conflict is considerably reduced. Such policy recognizes the talent of the trainer and infers that the decisions made are supported by agency management. The trainer will further benefit from policy that allows them to actively participate in the interviewing and selection of potential trainees, not least because being involved in this process helps establish their credibility in the eyes of new handlers.

A TRAINER WITHOUT MANDATED AUTHORITY

In the decades I have traveled and instructed throughout North America, I have met several K9 trainers who have described facing serious challenges that stemmed from lacking a mandate to have a supervisory role over the officers they trained. For one trainer, these challenges were severe.

The selection of the new candidates for this trainer's K9 program was done by the management team without input from anyone experienced in K9. One of the officers selected had much more seniority than the trainer at the time. He had also purchased his own dog and joined a Schutzhund club to show his interest. Two other officers — one senior to the trainer in agency tenure and one junior — were also assigned as new handlers.

From the first day of training, the officer who had purchased his own dog defied the trainer at every opportunity. He refused to cooperate with any direction given and was insistent on attending his Schutzhund programs and implementing Schutzhund routines in ways that were inappropriate for law enforcement applications. His attitude had a significant negative impact on the cohesion of the unit, influencing the attitudes of the younger handlers and making training tedious and challenging for everyone.

More than once, the officer was seen to be physically abusive to his dog. After attempting to speak with him about it, the trainer found himself in the untenable situation of going to his direct supervisor to report the ongoing issues and asking for intervention with what had become ongoing violent abuse of the dog. Unfortunately, the handler-in-training was close friends with the unit supervisor; they had spent years on the job together even before the trainer had been hired. The supervisor did not intervene, and the trainer's attempts to have the issue rectified only made the situation more difficult for him and the other officers in the training group.

Upon completion of training and certification, the handler in question and his dog worked the street for two years without any significant success despite being strong in local Schutzhund competitions. During the weekly maintenance training sessions, the trainer continued to observe intermittent outbursts of severe abuse of the dog. The team's success in dog sports competitions earned them media exposure, which agency management welcomed. This made it even more difficult for the trainer to obtain intervention, and any attempts made to bring the issue to the attention of upper management were intercepted by the K9 supervisor.

It was only after a citizen observed the officer violently assaulting the dog during Schutzhund club training and reported it directly to the agency's chief of police that any action was taken. Ultimately, the handler was removed from the program. It is clear, however, that these long-standing issues could have been dealt with immediately had the trainer been supported by the K9 unit supervisor and given the proper authority.

K9 SUPERVISOR TENURE

Agencies should consider policies that allow for longer supervisor tenures. Longer supervisory tenures allow the supervisor the time necessary to become truly effective in their position and are more conducive to creating positive working conditions for handlers. Supervisory stability is key to a successful program.

Managing any police dog program, like becoming a K9 handler, involves many unique aspects and responsibilities that are unlike any other law enforcement assignment. The supervisor is dealing with specialists who are on the front lines every day working with a live animal that takes significant training to manage. The need to understand dog selection and behavior, police dog selection and purchasing issues, veterinary screening, and training options creates complex challenges for a K9 supervisor. Add to this the need to become familiar with specialized equipment for training, patrol cars designed for the transport and safety of the dog, and the usual knowledge required to manage a patrol squad, it becomes apparent that running a police K9 program is challenging.

It can take up to a year or more for a supervisor to feel confident managing a K9 unit. For any K9 program to be productive, the handlers need to have confidence in the supervisor. They need to be able to trust that their supervisor understands the teams' unique expertise and is responsive to the specific issues that can arise when working with dogs in law enforcement.

Beyond the time it takes to actually learn the job, short-term tenures for K9 supervisors can create undue tension within the unit. Some handlers may see a new supervisor three or four times during their tenure with one dog. When program managers are rotated out to a different assignment every two years, handlers are left feeling like they are constantly starting from scratch. Usually, the senior handler keeps the unit together while the new supervisor is initiated into the program. Then, when the supervisor starts to really get up to speed and the program is functioning well, they are rotated out and the cycle starts again. This can be demoralizing to team members.

Not all supervisors assigned to K9 programs have requested the position. In fact, some take the assignment begrudgingly. They know nothing about police dogs and do not want to accept the potential vicarious liability related to police dog operations. It is simply one of several sectors within the department they have been directed to manage. A supervisor who doesn't want to be over the K9 unit quickly creates negativity within the organization, demoralizes the officers in the program, and creates the potential for conflict.

Programs have been lost because of lack of support from the program supervisor and conflicts between handlers and supervisors. Handler frustration can become so high that the management team disbands the unit, not realizing or being willing to accept that the supervisor assigned to the unit was the real catalyst of the discord.

K9 handlers are extremely committed individuals. On top of their on-duty time, they dedicate hundreds of hours of off-duty time to care for and maintain their dogs. While labor standards in the United States ensure that they are compensated for this time, full-time care of a law enforcement dog goes far beyond the compensated hours. If supported by their supervisor and management team, these dedicated officers will make any supervisor look good. All they ask in return is for active involvement and support.

It is difficult for that to happen if the tenure for program managers is so short the handlers continually feel like they are starting from the beginning again, or that the department does not care enough to provide a supervisor who is dedicated to their efforts. To that end, consideration should be given to consulting with members of your K9 program and the department management team to discuss the potential of developing a system that would allow for more consistency of supervision. Developing a policy that supports longer supervisor tenure while also meeting the department's other needs, will bring long-term success to your program.

Resources

There is a lot to take in when learning to manage a K9 program. You'll spend many hours researching products needed to support your organization. I hope this list helps kick-start that process. While this is far from an exhaustive list of K9-related resources and suppliers, each is a proven entity and will give you a basic starting point from which to begin your research.

Books

There are several excellent publications available for police dog operations, but very few that specifically support K9 management. The difference between a K9 unit supervisor that helps their program flourish and be productive and one who is simply there on assignment is how well they understand the nuances of police dog training and deployment. Below are a few books that will help you, as a K9 program supervisor, become more well-rounded and better educated in your position by giving you a better understanding of the diverse training your handlers require. These books are also excellent reads for every K9 officer and would be a good addition to any police dog program library.

K9 Officer's Legal Handbook, 3rd ed. by Ken Wallentine (Blue360° Media, 2013)
- Now in its third edition, *K9 Officer's Legal Handbook* contains the most complete and detailed case reports

related to law enforcement K9 operations. It discusses constitutional search, seizure, and use of force principles and goes into detail on patrol dogs, detection dogs, and a multitude of other K9 profiles. Wallentine deals with labor law issues specific to service dog handlers and gives invaluable information on court testimony for both patrol and detection dog handlers. This is an excellent resource for K9 supervisors as well as K9 officers.

K9 Officer's Manual, 2nd ed. by R.S. Eden (Dog Training Press, forthcoming)
- This book provides a broad spectrum of information on police dog operations and has chapters that deal with operational deployment, apprehension techniques, and K9 officer safety issues during building searches, tracking, and vehicle stops. Other topics include K9 administration, preparing for courtroom testimony, and police dog protection and safety. This book is currently being refreshed and will be published with updates in the near future.

K9 Decoys and Aggression: A Manual for Training Police Dogs, 2nd ed. by Stephen A. Mackenzie (Dog Training Press, 2015)
- *K9 Decoys and Aggression* provides the best fundamental understanding of training issues related to aggression training in police dogs and how to manage the inherent problems related to bite training. Most importantly, it teaches the reader to understand what is going on in the head of a dog who refuses to release a bite and why there is so much conflict in training. This book challenges decades of traditional training methods that have continuously failed to provide solutions for trainers. It will give a supervisor an understanding of the complexities of dog training and the vital role of the K9 decoy. It will also open the eyes of any K9 trainer or handler who takes the time to read the concepts and has the patience to use the book's training sequences.

Consulting, Training, Unit Audits, and Best Practices

The following organizations offer a variety of services to support the development of your K9 unit at every level.

EDEN CONSULTING GROUP

Eden Consulting Group has been training law enforcement K9 teams since 1991. Based in Canada, team members provide K9 handlers and supervisors with the guidance and training they need to optimize their unit performance on the street. They also provide consulting and unit audit services to management teams, and specialized workshops and schools for urban tracking and K9 problem-solving.

Website: www.policek9.com

PROACTIVE K9

Based in the United States, ProActive K9 provides quality training, consultation, and audit services to the law enforcement K9 and working dog communities. Traveling and teaching worldwide, ProActive K9's principal, Steve White, has focused his 45-year law enforcement career on innovation and excellence in police K9.

Website: www.proactivek9.com

TACTICAL K9

Tactical K9 is operated by team of active and retired Los Angeles police officers and was started with the sole purpose of offering the police and military K9 community advanced tactical K9 training. Each member of Tactical K9 is or was a certified K9 handler and/or supervisor in the law enforcement community. Tactical K9 also provides a highly recommended e-collar program.

Website: www.tacticalk-9.com

TOP DOG POLICE K9

Top Dog Police K9 is operated by Ron Cloward, a retired lieutenant of the Modesto Police Department in California. Top Dog Police K9 offers a dynamic, scenario-based training experience for senior K9 handlers, K9 supervisors, and agency managers. The classes provide knowledge and insight into the supervision of K9 teams in both large and small agencies based primarily from hands-on experience. Highly interactive, the program challenges the participants with new ideas through group exercises that draw on the mixed expertise of the students in attendance and the diverse knowledge of the instructional team. This program is taught annually, is POST certified in the state of California, and can be delivered anywhere in the United States on request.

Top Dog is also a vendor of quality police dogs, provides basic and specialized patrol and detection dog programs, and offers handler problem-solving and e-collar classes from its home base in California.

Website: www.topdogpolicek9.com

K9 Tracking

Tracking is the most valuable tool when it comes to locating suspects who have fled crime scenes. Evidence attributed to tracking dogs is accepted throughout Canada and in most of the United States with limited exceptions. Locating suspects or lost persons is the primary purpose of a good police dog.

The school below is a solid option for K9 tracking training. For other options, see Eden Consulting Group and Top Dog Police K9 (above).

GAK9

Operated by retired police officer and author Jeff Schettler, GAK9 offers schools in a wide variety of K9 disciplines, including obedience training, service dog training, dog tracking and trailing, and narcotics detection. In particular, their tracking and trailing programs are world renowned and set a strong foundation for law enforcement tracking programs.

Website: www.tttk9.com

Detection Training

FORD K9

Based out of Henderson, Nevada, Cameron Ford has worked with and trained dogs as the senior trainer for a US Navy SEAL dog program. He was also a police/SWAT K9 handler and a national-level police K9 evaluator. While not limited in his scope of training, he specializes in detection dog training.

Website: www.fordk9.com

ALPHA K-9

Alpha K-9 is a training center with schools in Nashville, Tennessee, and Jackson, Mississippi. Owner Randy Hare is an internationally recognized trainer in the field of detection work with more than 40 years of experience, award-winning expertise, and innovative proprietary methods. He has an unsurpassed and proven track record in teaching police and military trainers and handlers and offers a full schedule of courses designed to make K9 teams and trainers more effective in law enforcement.

Website: www.alphak9.com

Detection Training Aids

Detection dog training is being scrutinized more carefully by the courts. This increased scrutiny makes it all the more important to implement the best in training and training gear. Precision timing is paramount when shaping canine behavior and the storage, handling, and deployment of odors must be almost clinical in nature. These resources can assist in accomplishing your target goals.

DOGTRA BALL TRAINER

The Dogtra Ball Trainer is ideal for remote behavior marking and detection training. The device allows the officer to reward a detection dog from a distance, marking the correct behavior at the appropriate time. This is the best quality and most versatile device of its type on the market (and at the time of writing is significantly cheaper than some of its competitors). The dual-function trainer is controlled remotely and can launch and drop balls from up to a 100-yard distance — ideal for training detection dogs. It is expandable up to eight devices, with each device holding up to three balls and able to launch balls up to five feet.

Website: www.dogtra.com

SCIK9 TRAINING AID DELIVERY DEVICE SYSTEM (TADDS)

TADDS is a new and innovative system of packaging training aids for detection dogs. Simply put, it's a container, impermeable by moisture, that lets the odor of your training aid out, but not the training aid itself. The system was initially created for the US Army and designed by canine trainers and scientists. The containers are designed using extremely low-odor NASA outgassing-compliant materials, so the scent you place in the containers is the only scent the dog focuses on. With limited exceptions, these units can be used with most training aids and are rugged enough for daily use and training. The membrane used on these containers is not permeable by water. The membrane allows the odor to escape but keeps the aid safe from moisture, making these ideal training containers for cadaver detection work.

Website: www.scik9.com

K9 Body Armor Suppliers

If budgets allow, custom-made body armor for use on high-risk calls is a valuable addition to any kit. Body armor has saved the lives of a number of dogs. Some vests can double as a tracking harness, making them ideal when a team is deploying on a known high-risk track. For SWAT operators, vests are available with rappelling gear hookups as well. When considering the purchase of a vest, custom-fit vests are always the most practical option. For another option, see Vested Interest in K9s ("Non-Profit Support," below).

K9 STORM INC.

K9 Storm is the industry leader in custom-fit vests. Located in Winnipeg, Manitoba, K9 Storm was the first K9 vest manufacturer to provide custom-fitted vests for police dog operations. They have expanded into a full spectrum of options and equipment for high-risk K9 operations, including a variety of K9 vest options and a remote camera system known as the K9 Storm Intruder.

Website: www.k9storm.com

LOF DEFENCE SYSTEMS

LOF Defence provides a wide variety of law enforcement gear, including armored options. They develop handcrafted tactical gear, lightweight body armor systems for officers, and K9 gear.

Website: www.lofdefence.ca

K9 Equipment Suppliers

There are a number of high-quality manufacturers of police dog equipment in the United States and Canada. Good suppliers are key to keeping your teams properly equipped with quality gear.

RAY ALLEN MANUFACTURING
Ray Allen Manufacturing has been developing training gear for law enforcement and military working dogs since 1948. They are known for developing new and innovative equipment and answering the specific tactical needs of police and military operators, as well as the unique sporting needs of Schutzhund professionals.
Website: www.rayallen.com

K9 TACTICAL GEAR
K9 Tactical Gear is a family-owned, California-based business run by Bill and Susan Forbes. It has been building custom K9 equipment since 1986. All their products are designed and manufactured in the United States. They stand behind what they make.
Website: www.k9tacticalgear.com

Non-Profit Support

K9S4COPS (POLICE DOG PROVIDER)
The Texas-based K9s4COPs foundation was formed to address law enforcement agencies' need for funding to purchase police dogs. Most departments can budget for the required care, training, and transportation of the dog, but many agencies struggle when budgeting for the purchase of a dog. K9s4COPs was founded to bridge this gap and ensure that the cost of purchasing a police dog does not prevent a police agency in need from implementing a K9 program.
Website: www.k9s4cops.org

VESTED INTEREST IN K9S
Vested Interest in K9s is a Massachusetts-based 501c(3) nonprofit whose mission is to provide bullet- and stab-protective vests and other assistance to law enforcement dogs and related agencies throughout the United States.

From 2009 to the time of writing, Vested Interest has donated more than 4101 K9 ballistic vests, 1300 K9 opioid reversal NARCAN kits, and more than US $152,000 of K9 medical insurance premiums through their Healthcare for K9 Heroes program. They have also distributed over US $62,000 in K9 medical first aid kits and three custom-fitted Chevy Tahoe SUVs valued at over US $50,000 each.
Website: vik9s.org

Online Legal Repositories, K9 Case Law Updates, and Policy Guidance

LEXIPOL
Lexipol is a risk management solution for public safety and local government that provides continuously updated policies for public safety agencies and an ideal solution for building K9 policies. It was cofounded by Bruce Praet, who provided guidance on this book. Bruce Praet is a partner with Ferguson, Praet & Sherman, a law firm that has specialized in defending police in civil matters such as shootings, dog bites, and pursuits for over 30 years. The firm also represents management in personnel matters.
   Website: www.lexipol.com

SHEEPDOG GUARDIAN
Sheepdog Guardian provides an online resource and classes designed to improve K9 risk and liability through canine legal updates and jurisdiction-specific law resource courses on police service and working dogs.
   Website: www.sheepdogguardian.com

Promotional Gear

RENAISSANCE ARTS & DESIGN
Renaissance Arts & Design has provided custom art, graphic design, and screen printing since 1992. The owner, Mike Spivey, has designed generations of law enforcement K9 team shirts and is actively engaged in law enforcement K9 circles as a decoy.
   Website: www.renarts-design.com

DELTA CHALLENGE COINS
Delta Challenge Coins is a family-owned business run by father-and-son team Michael and Tyson Wright. Michael worked in the law enforcement profession for 28 years and has supervised tactical and police canine units as well as the Northern Nevada interdiction unit. Tyson is pursuing a career in firefighting. The team is well versed in the promotional needs of emergency services. The business has been serving the law enforcement community for more than 25 years and is a leader in challenge coin production.
   Website: www.deltachallengecoins.com

SIGNATURE COINS
Signature Promotional Group, LLC is based out of central Florida and was founded in 2000. They provide a variety of promotional products, along with an exemplary line of challenge coins and custom patches.
Website: www.signaturecoins.com

Records Management
Research and implement a K9 RMS if your agency does not already have one in place. Computerized record systems allow you to retrieve information quickly when, for example, you are suddenly confronted with a subpoena for records by the courts.

KATS PLATINUM K9 RMS
The K9 Activity Tracking System (KATS) is a dynamic record-keeping program specifically for police K9 operations, training, and deployments. It is designed to protect officers and agencies from potential liability and is unique in the industry in being fully customizable to the end user. KATS provides for supervisory oversight and has been protecting law enforcement since it premiered in 1992. At time of this writing, this RMS can produce over 60 report types that span everything from court-ready documentation for training and incidents to reports that assist in managing your unit. It was the first software ever developed for law enforcement K9 operations and can be used from virtually any computer platform or smart phone without needing to download additional software.
Website: www.katsplatinum.com

K9 Heat Stroke Prevention
There are many more police dogs lost each year as a result of heat stroke than felonious assault, yet the focus of budgets and volunteer organizations is on the purchase of ballistic vests for canine use rather than on the more formidable and prolific danger of heat stroke. The installation of K9 heat alarms should be embedded in the policy of every K9 unit.

ACE K9
The ACE product line was first introduced as Radiotronics in 1986 and has consistently been the industry leader in protecting

dogs from heat stroke. During my career, I had the Hot-N-Pop unit installed in my patrol car. The system saved two of my dogs during the hot summer months. On the first occasion, the system notified me when my unit stalled while parked in a courthouse parking lot. In the second instance, the system notified me of a broken fan belt that had caused the air conditioning to fail while I was writing reports in the office. In both cases, the outside temperatures were high, and my dogs would have suffered heat stroke and likely died had the system not notified me of the failures.

ACE K9 provides several variations on their system, including the ability to remotely open the K9 compartment to call the dog out of the car should the handler require the dog's assistance in an emergency. In my opinion, this equipment should be standard in every patrol car.

Website: www.acek9.com

K9 Vehicle Inserts (Kennels)

SETINA K-9 SYSTEMS

Setina provides a wide range of custom vehicle inserts for transporting the dog, including a split K9/prisoner transport option. Their systems include a K9 containment area with a rear cargo storage management system. These units are meticulously designed, made of powder-coated aluminum alloy, and come in multiple configurations.

Website: www.setina.com/k-9-systems/

HAVIS INDUSTRIES

Havis Industries K9 inserts are custom designed for every individual vehicle they serve. In addition to rounded corners and heavy-duty white powder coating, they feature large side openings for improved canine entry and exit as well as easy access for cleaning. Available for sedans and SUVs, Havis has 30 different models of K9 inserts, including a combination prisoner/K9 transport option for SUVs.

Website: www.havis.com

Image Credits

1.1 Bill Sawyer, Longmont Police Department
1.2 Bill Sawyer, Longmont Police Department
1.3 Bill Sawyer, Longmont Police Department
1.4 Eden K9 Conference
1.5 Eden K9 Conference (left); Eden K9 Consulting & Training (right)
1.6 Eden K9 Consulting & Training
1.7 Eden K9 Conference
1.8 Courtney Spiess, St. Charles County
1.9 KATS Platinum K9 RMS (left and right)
1.10 Jack Kuhl, New Braunfels Police Department
1.11 Nate Beckstrand, Allied Universal K9
1.12 Todd Kobitz, Valparaiso Police Department
2.1 Jake Simmons, White County Sheriff
2.2 Andrea Micheli
3.1 Eden K9 Conference
3.2 Eden K9 Conference
3.3 Eden K9 Conference
4.1 Jerry Kitchens, Fresno County Sheriff
4.2 Eden K9 Conference
4.3 Eden K9 Conference
4.4 Eden K9 Conference
4.5 Jared Eden
4.6 Eden K9 Conference
5.1 Malin Reisinger
5.2 Shaun Gray
5.3 Bob Eden (left); Mike Spivey (center); Delta Challenge Coins (right)
5.4 Mike Spivey (top left); Vacaville Police Department (top center); (top right); (bottom left); Signature Coin (bottom center and right)
7.1 Howard Young, White Beard Inc.
7.2 Jeff Schettler
8.1 Havis Industries
8.2 Havis Industries
8.3 Havis Industries (left and right)
8.4 Havis Industries
8.5 Ace K9 (left and right)
8.6 Ace K9
8.7 Tyler Houldsworth, Kennel Seabrook
8.8 K9 Storm (left and right)
10.1 Eden K9 Conference
10.2 Billy Sawyer, Longmont Police Department
11.1 KATS Platinum K9 RMS
11.2 KATS Platinum K9 RMS
11.3 KATS Platinum K9 RMS
11.4 KATS Platinum K9 RMS (left and right)
11.5 KATS Platinum K9 RMS
11.6 KATS Platinum K9 RMS
11.7 KATS Platinum K9 RMS
11.8 KATS Platinum K9 RMS (top and bottom)
11.9 KATS Platinum K9 RMS (left and right)

About the Author

R.S. Eden has been training police dogs for 40 years and is a retired police veteran, having served 28 years with the Delta Police Department in British Columbia. In 1982, he submitted the initial proposal to start a K9 unit to Inspector Gale Parker, who subsequently received approval from city council to initiate a four-dog program with an annual budget of $13,500. During his tenure, he served 16 years as a dog handler and was the department-assigned agency K9 trainer. In 1991, he created the International Police K9 Conference, a hands-on training program for law enforcement K9 teams throughout North America, ultimately working with over 3500 K9 teams over the course of its 20-year tenure. In 2003, he was contracted to coordinate the redevelopment and retraining of the Phoenix police K9 unit and, in 2005, traveled to Brazil on contract to establish and train the country's first explosives dog program in preparation for the 2007 Pan American Games. Eden has testified as an expert witness on police K9 cases in both Canada and the United States and is the creator of the K9 Activity Tracking System (KATS), a K9 records management system designed to protect agencies and officers from K9-related liability. Most recently, he has worked as a consultant to the Department of Foreign Affairs, Canada, in developing explosives detection dog requirements for Canadian embassies. He is the author of two previous books, *Dog Training for Law Enforcement* and *K9 Officer's Manual*. Currently, he operates Eden K9 Consulting & Training Corporation, and resides with his wife Natasha in Calgary, Alberta, Canada.